Human Resource Management

Human Resource Management: Concepts and Perspectives

Edited by

V. ANANTARAMAN
CHONG LI-CHOY
STANLEY RICHARDSON
TAN CHWEE HUAT

Singapore University Press,
National University of Singapore.

© 1984 Singapore University Press
National University of Singapore
Kent Ridge
Singapore 0511.

ISBN 9971-69-090-X (case)
ISBN 9971-69-091-8 (paper)

Typeset by International Typesetters

Contents

List of Contributors
List of Abbreviations
Foreword
Preface

Part One: Overall Perspective

1. Human Resource Management: An Overall Perspective
   Tan Chwee Huat   1

2. The Individual, Organisations and Society
   S. Richardson   9

Part Two: Societal Perspective

3. A Societal Perspective
   Chong Li Choy   21

4. The Singapore Context
   Tan Chwee Huat   26

5. Productivity and National Development
   Chong Li Choy   35

6. The Significance of Non-adversative Union-management Relationship in Singapore
   V. Anantaraman   43

7. Organizational Structure and Human Resource Development
   Edith C. Yuen   61

8. Human Resource Management in Singapore: Some Current Issues
   Tan Chwee Huat   75

9. How Singapore may Learn from other Countries
   Chong Li Choy   86

10. Increasing Productivity
    S. Richardson   95

Part Three: Interpersonal Perspective

11. An Interpersonal Perspective
    V. Anantaraman   104

12. Developing People-centred Management Systems
    V. Anantaraman   112

13. Group Dynamics and the Human Relations
    Organisational Model
    V. Anantaraman   143

14. Leadership
    S. Richardson   164

15. Leadership Effectiveness
    V. Anantaraman   175

16. Managerial Effectiveness
    V. Anantaraman   194

17. Communication
    S. Richardson   208

18. Team-Building
    V. Anantaraman   217

19. Conflict Management
    Edith C. Yuen   237

20. The Management of Change: Overcoming Resistance
    Chong Li Choy   250

21. The Process of Changing Value Orientation
    V. Anantaraman   261

22. Training: A Tool for Human Resource Development
    Anthony T. Tseng   271

Part Four: Individual Perspective

23. An Individual Perspective
    S. Richardson   289

24. Perception
    S. Richardson   296

25. Personality
    S. Richardson   307

26. Singapore Managers: Some Aspects of Personality
    Dolores Thomson   316

27. Motivation and Behavioural Change
    Chong Li Choy   328

Index   341

List of Contributors

Anantaraman Venkatraman graduated in 1950 with a first class honours degree in economics of the University of Madras. He obtained his Ph. D. in Industrial Relations in 1960 from the Industrial Relations Research Institute, University of Wisconsin, and specialized in Organizational Behaviour during 1968-69 in the International Teachers' Programme at the Graduate School of Business, Harvard University.

Beginning his teaching career as a lecturer in economics in 1951 at the Annamalai University in South India, he joined the Faculty of Humanities and Social Science in the Indian Institute of Technology, Madras as an assistant professor in 1961. He became a professor of Management in 1970, and was head of the department during 1973-76. Between 1976 and 1978 he was visiting professor to the Faculty of Commerce and Administration at the Concordia University, Montreal. Currently he is an associate professor in the School of Management, National University of Singapore.

Besides his rich experience in conducting management development programmes he has published a number of articles in professional journals and authorised a book on human relations in industry.

Anthony T. Tseng is an industrial/organizational psychologist and a member of the Society for Industrial and Organizational Psychology (Division 14 of American Psychological Association). He is a lecturer in the School of Management, National University of Singapore and an associate professor of organizational psychology at Christopher Newport College, Virginia, U.S.A. (on leave). He has also taught at the University of Utah and at State University of New York at Geneseo. He teaches courses in organizational behaviour, human resource management and organizational development. Dr. Tseng has extensive experience as an organizational psychologist for numerous organizations in U.S.A. in the areas of programme evaluation, performance evaluation, and consumer behaviour. He has had specialized training at the NTL Institute for Applied Behavioural Science in designing and conducting experiential training programmes and in organization development and change. He has conducted executive development seminars for various organizations in U.S.A., Singapore, and Malaysia.

Chong Li Choy, B.A., B. Soc. Sc. Hons., M. Soc. Sc., Dr. Soz. Wiss., is currently lecturer at the School of Management, National University of Singapore. He was a DAAD (German Academic Exchange Service) Fellow at the University of Bielefield in the Federal Republic of Germany where he obtained his Dr. Soz. Wiss. (Doctor of Social Sciences) degree in 1977. He was also a ISEAS Research Fellow as well as a Stiftung Volkswagenwerk research fellow in Southeast Asian Studies at the Institute of Southeast Asian Studies in Singapore. He has consulted for business and has published several academic papers, including the books, *Open-Self Reliant Regionalism*, and *Multinational Business and National Development*.

Dolores Yong Thomas has a B.A. Hons. in Social Psychology, (University of Western Australia), and a M.A. in Occupational Psychology (University of London). Her work experiences include supervisory research at the London School of Economics, U.K. and management consultancy at the Anglian Regional Management Centre, U.K. Her current research interests focus on psychological measurements of executives in the Southeast Asian environment.

Stanley Richardson, B. Sc. (Eng), M. Sc., Ph. D., C. Eng., is a senior lecturer in the School of Management, National University of Singapore. From 1974-82 he was Head of the Production and Industrial Engineering Department, Hong Kong Polytechnic. Prior to that he taught in the Faculty of Engineering, University of Singapore. He has been a consultant in several countries for UNESCO and has published research and other papers on management, ergonomics, and engineering.

Tan Chwee Huat, Ph. D., MBA (Management) Ms (Industrial) Relations), B. Acc. (Hons) is an associate professor and Head of the School of Management, National University of Singapore.

LIST OF CONTRIBUTORS

He was also Head of the Human Resource Management Unit in 1983 and Vice Dean of the Faculty of Accountancy and Business Administration 1981-1982. He has published numerous articles on industrial relations and management topics.

Edith C. Yuen, Ph. D. (Sydney), is a lecturer in the School of Management, National University of Singapore. She previously taught at the University of Tasmania and Canberra College of Advanced Education in Australia. Before coming to Singapore she was co-director of two post-graduate diploma programmes at the University of Hong Kong: the Diploma in Management Studies and the Diploma in Arts Administration.

List of Abbreviations

BEST	Basic Education for Skills Training
COWEC	Company Welfarism Through Employers' Contribution
CPF	Central Provident Fund
EDB	Economic Development Board
HRD	Human Resource Development
HRM	Human Resource Management
MINDEF	Ministry of Defence
NPB	National Productivity Board
NPC	National Productivity Council
NTS	Non-traditional Sources
NTUC	National Trades Union Congress
NWC	National Wages Council
PAP	People's Action Party
PIEU	Pioneer Industries Employees' Union
PSLE	Primary School Leaving Examination
QCC	Quality Control Circles
SDF	Skills Development Fund
SILO	Singapore Industrial Labour Organization
VITB	Vocational and Industrial Training Board
WIT	Work Improvement Team

Foreword

Singapore has precious few natural resources and even its human resource is small in size. Just as Singapore must maximize the use of its land resource by turning swamps into solid ground, extending its coastline wherever possible and ensuring intensive use of its limited commodity of land and space, Singapore must also make the fullest use of its small human resource by encouraging and exhorting each individual to contribute his utmost for the well-being of Singapore.

The young graduate who enters the world of employment is soon made aware that no matter how excellent his academic performance might have been, he cannot achieve the desired results without being able to relate to his fellow workers in the working environment. And sooner or later he may acquire a management function that relate to staff; in other words, he has a human resource management function.

Human resource management seeks as high a level of performance as is possible from every person. In the context of Singapore, this is essential if we are to survive and prosper.

Realising the importance of human resource management to university graduates, the University introduced a human resource management course for its students in 1982, initially for students in the Faculties of Arts and Social Sciences and Science. It has since covered all faculties. Of course, students in the Faculty of Accountancy and Business Administration have been taught the course all along.

The Human Resource Management Unit which was established in May 1983 has encouraged its staff to put together their teaching materials into a book. The 27 chapters written by seven staff members contain basic material on the subject. It is hoped that this book will enable the student and the public to understand the concepts and practice of human resource management.

Professor Lim Pin
Vice-Chancellor

Preface

Human Resource Management: Concepts and Perspectives by V. Anantaraman, Chong Li Choy, S. Richardson and Tan Chwee Huat is brought out at a time when the need for Human Resource Development is greatly felt in the Singapore context.

The contents of the text are well laid out with introduction of an overall perspective on Human Resource Development, followed by the focus of Human Resource Development at the individual, organisational and societal levels. Issues related to Singapore are discussed. Theoretical background on topics such as, perception, personality, motivation, leadership, communication and conflict is provided.

The readings present Human Resource Management concepts, techniques and issues at three levels, namely, individual, organisational and societal. While the various theories on Human Resource Management are stressed in some chapters, current issues and practical illustrations are discussed in other chapters thus maintaining a balance between theory and application.

Those who are interested in acquainting themselves with Human Resource Management would benefit from the material presented in this book.

Associate Professor Joseph M. Putti
Head, Human Resource Management Unit

PART ONE

OVERALL PERSPECTIVE

1
Human Resource Management: An Overall Perspective

TAN CHWEE HUAT

In simple terms, human resource management means the management of people. This simplistic statement does not explain much if the reader is looking for a comprehensive definition of human resource management. There are two reasons why such a definition will not be attempted. First, the term "management" has been defined in so many ways that one can easily fill pages simply by listing the more widely used definitions. Secondly, the term "human resource" is used in many disciplines and the same difficulty will be encountered if one tries to define it without relating to the context in which it is used.

Human resource management is not a new field of study or a new academic discipline. Rather, it is a broadly defined concept which has been popularly used in recent years to accommodate ideas from various disciplines such as demography, development planning, manpower economics, industrial sociology, personnel management, social work, industrial psychology, ergonomics and education administration.

As long as the subject matter is people, each discipline can claim its contribution in the study of human resource management. Terms such as manpower planning and human resource development are often used to connote similar meanings. Due to its inter-disciplinary nature, the study of human resource management has stimulated diverse views among scholars, researchers and practitioners alike.

Keeping in mind the multi-disciplinary nature of the scope of human resource management, we may view its related issues at three different levels, namely, (1) societal; (2) organizational and interpersonal; and (3) individual.

Societal Perspective

Human resource management may be viewed from a socio-politico-economic perspective. From this viewpoint, discussion can range from the objectives of national development, economic growth, social well-being to industrial productivity. These objectives can be achieved through proper management of the nation's human assetts. At one end of the spectrum, one may begin with a systematic view of the nation's socio-political ideals — its population trends and related issues such as family planning, housing, public health and education. The essence of a society is its people. The well-being of a society is the well-being of its people. In the broad socio-political context, discussion can be extended to focus on the building of a new nation whose ideals are happiness, prosperity and progress for its people. These ideals can be achieved through social and economic development planning centering around the involvement and commitment of its human resources.

In the pursuit of peace and prosperity in a new nation comprising groups of different ethnic descent, it is essential that the groups pledge to live in harmony and view diversity as a cohesive force for nation-building. History has shown that many new nations lack this commonality in social value. As a result, economic achievement by one ethnic group has often been mistakenly perceived as the outcome of depriving or exploiting another group. Social peace or economic prosperity in a nation cannot be sustained without ethnic harmony.

Social harmony cannot be taken for granted especially in a new nation. Integration efforts must be continually sustained to foster a new identity. Traditional community organization by clan, communal, or ethnic affiliation must gradually make way for new organizations to facilitate integration and to inculcate a new sense of belonging. In the context of Singapore's development as a new nation over the last decades, we have witnessed the emergence of community centres, citizens' consultative committees and residents' committees — all examples of a newly integrated organization — one which reflects a new identity.

The basic pool of the human resource of a nation is its population. During the early years in the history of any migrant nation, population growth was always affected by immigration patterns. The rate of natural increase was affected by the level of fertility and by the infant mortality rate.

To improve the economic well-being of its people, every government recognizes the need to include family planning as an integral part of its social and economic development plans. Failure to contain rapid population increase will magnify problems down the development chain in terms of the need for more facilities in education, housing, public health, employment and other social services. The acceptance of family planning necessitates a change in attitude towards the concept of the small family as a social norm; the use of birth control devices; abortion; sterilization; and related incentives and disincentives.

The outcome of the family planning effort and the resultant change in population composition have long-term social and economic implications for human resource planning for a nation. In the case of Singapore, the demographic objective is to achieve zero population growth and to stabilize population size by the turn of the century. With declining births and a higher life expectancy, the emerging phenomenon is that of an aging population in the years ahead. This necessitates a closer look at the present employment policy on retirement age and its related social and financial implications for senior citizens. In some Western countries, the retirement age has been extended to retain senior citizens in the labour force. In an economy with a shortage of labour, an extension of the retirement age would be an attractive solution to increase the supply of labour. This thus leads us to examine human resource management in the context of the labour market.

The term "labour market" describes the many factors influencing the supply and demand of labour in the economy. Labour is needed in the various sectors of commerce and industry. These include the manufacturing, finance, construction and services sectors. Economic growth which is not supported by proper manpower planning will result in a shortage of labour in some sectors and high unemployment in others.

To ensure optimal use of the human resource in a nation, close coordination is needed among the various bodies involved in economic planning. Most planners rely on economic statistics compiled by government agencies and information provided by the various sectors in commerce and industry.

In Singapore, the Department of Statistics and the Ministry of Labour are the two primary collectors and publishers of labour market information. The Ministry collects, compiles, analyzes, and disseminates statistics on the labour force, earnings, and on other related data. Analysis of such information helps the human resource planner identify trends and patterns in the supply and demand of labour.

One key indicator is the labour force participation rate. Historical patterns tell policymakers that the participation rate for men is higher than that of women, and that people of a specific age group are more active in the economy. There have also been some changes in the labour force participation rate of women. To encourage more working mothers to remain in the labour market there has been a need to provide adequate child-care services, either through day-care centres or family day-care arrangements.

In the context of Singapore, over the past decades, the employment growth has matched the supply of labour, resulting in full employment by the 1970s. Labour force participation rates have also increased, due mainly to more female workers entering the labour market.

Statistics on the educational qualifications of the working population show that young workers are better educated today. This implies that their aspirations and job expectations would be different from those of their older colleagues. With better education and improved skills, they would prefer jobs which suit their qualifications and training.

Furthermore, the changing requirements of employers have had an impact on the demand for workers in terms of location, industry and occupation. In Singapore, the major demand sectors are in manufacturing, commerce, finance and services. There has been however, for many years, a shortage of labour in industries such as construction and shipbuilding. To alleviate this problem, employers have to rely on foreign workers.

Organizational and Interpersonal Perspective

Part III of this book examines human resource management from an organizational perspective. To ensure success, all organizations in society must naturally respond positively and move in harmony towards the goal of national well-being.

Within each organization, ethnic, cultural or religious differences must be accepted by all its members. Different backgrounds must be viewed as added strength rather than a deterrent in forging unity of purpose in the organization.

The term "organizations", would include all economic, social and educational institutions, such as, companies, trade unions, community groups, government agencies, training institutes and professional bodies. In this book, the term refers to organisations of an economic nature, such as companies and trade unions, it should however be noted that the concepts of human resource management are applicable also to other organizations.

Historical confrontation or traditional competition between organizations must give away to cooperation to reflect new political or economic realities. For example, the confrontative union-management relations inherited from the colonial past must be transformed into a new collaborative relationship for the mutual benefit of employers and workers. In the case of competing firms, it may be better for them to pool resources to take advantage of economies of scale for their long-term growth and economic viability. The latter is particularly relevant in a world of rapid change in production technology and a scarcity of high-level expertise. Furthermore, as an economy moves into its maturity stage, world competition necessitates an upward move along the technological ladder. Outdated managerial thinking must give way to reflect new realities. Corporate decision-makers must take into consideration external factors such as technological innovation and inter-national competition. Employees can be convinced of wanting to move into a high-technology society through persuasion, education and training. Proper planning and development of human resource in organizations thus remain the key to solving problems.

In seeking solutions, the economic performance of Japan has attracted the attention of many nations. The centre of attention has been the high productivity, motivation and morale of the Japanese workforce. The organizational climate and harmonious labour management relations in the Japanese companies have become a point of envy for governments which are often troubled with industrial conflicts.

Furthermore, in a competitive industrial world where free market forces operate, productivity holds the key to success in the international race. Productivity must however be a national effort, with contribution from all organizations involved either directly or indirectly in the production process. Thus, it is necessary for all involved to work towards this end. One is reminded that such success will ultimately result in one's own well-being.

At the organizational level, productivity can be translated into objectives, such as, better performance at the workplace, higher job satisfaction for the workers, and overall managerial effectiveness. These objectives can be achieved if management pays special attention to skills needed to enhance better interpersonal understanding. These include an appreciation of how human beings are motivated, and how the various styles of leadership and patterns of communication can have an impact on group effectiveness. Proper training in human relations skills will foster the building of a cohesive team with minimal conflict problems.

At the interpersonal level, many of the human resource management concepts are drawn from research studies on the behavioural sciences. Topics include motivation, leadership, communications, team-building and conflict resolution. In the organizational context, implementation of these concepts affect job performance, job statisfaction and managerial effectiveness.

In organizations, motivation is the key to many human problems. Behavioural scientists have many suggestions to give regarding absenteeism, carelessness, tardiness, sabotage, low productivity and poor performance. Such suggestions include active involvement or participation by the employees in making decisions affecting their work. Other ideas include job redesign, job rotation and job enrichment. The enhancement of employee motivation through participation in Quality Control (QC) circles in Japan and other East Asian countries has drawn world attention. This participative method of human resource management seems to be a promising solution in improving productivity in organizations.

Leadership is another major determinant in increasing effectiveness and efficiency. Many theories on leadership styles and effectiveness have been postulated by researchers who have spent much time searching for the ultimate solution. It is recognized that one of the qualities of an effective leader is his ability to communicate and to build a team. He should be able to resolve conflict among his subordinates and lead them towards the common organizational goal despite individual differences. Over the years, researchers have developed many models and techniques in communication skills, team-building and conflict management. The need for leadership training and the acquiring of these interpersonal skills have become the prerequisites of a good human resource manager.

A commonsense solution to people-related problems is the adoption of a people-centred approach. Regardless of the label one may give to this management philosophy, in the context of an organization, this philosophy must be translated into real terms, such as, its recruitment and selection practices; working conditions; compensation and benefit schemes; the performance appraisal system; employee development; promotion opportunities; and career planning. It is only within these organizational realities that interpersonal skills can be effectively exercised.

Individual Perspective

The individual is the basic unit in any organization or group. A study of the individual encompasses the study of psychology and human behaviour. Each person is a different being as explained by his physical, mental and emotional make-up. Here, personality, that is, the totality of the individual comes in. Tests have been designed by psychologists to measure the different types of personalities. Individuals are different in their perception of things. These differences are further complicated by the various learning processes experienced. Such learning includes both the formal and informal processes. Knowing what makes an individual tick creates both self-awareness and a better understanding of other people.

The effectiveness of an organization depends on its members. The organization should therefore provide opportunities for personal growth and development. As each individual is different in terms of personality, perception and learning experience, the organization should acknowledge these differences in the management of its human resource.

An effective human resource manager matches the ability of the individual employee with the job he is assigned to. In order to do this, the manager must understand the ability of the worker and what is involved that motivates him to work. Ability refers to the capabilities the individual has acquired through training or through previous experience. Motivation refers to the worker's willingness to perform the task. The manager matches the ability of the employee with the job requirements and skills necessary for the job. He provides the necessary rewards (both tangible and intangible) to motivate the employee into doing his best.

Effective job performance depends on whether the ability of the individual matches the requirements of the job. It also depends on how the reward system motivates the individual's work behaviour. The basic concern in managerial effectiveness is to ensure that employees can perform their assigned tasks. The ideal situation is to match the individual's ability and the work involved. There are two ways of achieving this. Firstly, by selection of the right person. One may also modify the worker's abilities through training. Secondly, the job may be redesigned to fit the individual. However, if he is not motivated to perform, his ability will not be put to use. Hence, a person's motivation is an important driving force in job performance. This explains why so much research has been done to understand employee motivation.

Motivation can thus be enhanced through better management of this man-job matching process, by providing challenging job opportunities and by assisting the individual in his career development. The individual on the other hand, ought to know his own needs, skills, interests and potential. He should seek a job which will give him the opportunity to fulfil these needs and one that would make use of his skills and potential. If necessary, with the support of his organization, he should seek additional training that will help him in his career.

REFERENCES

Heneman, H. G. III., Schwab, D. P. Fossum, J. A. and Dyer, L. D. *Managing Personnel and Human Resources: Strategies and Programs.* Illinois: Dow Jones Irwin, 1981.

London, M., and Stumpf, S.A. *Managing Careers.* Addison-Wesley, 1982.

Pang Eng Fong. *Education, Manpower and Development in Singapore.* Singapore: Singapore University Press, 1982.

Shantakumar, G. "Human Resource Management in Singapore", in You Poh Seng and Lim Chong Yah (eds.), *Singapore: Twenty-five Years of Development.* Singapore: Nan Yang Xing Zhou Lianhe Zaobao, 1984.

2
The Individual, Organizations, and Society

S. RICHARDSON

Summary

An organization is defined and contrasted with the family. The nature of the individual is examined and related to the concepts of formal and informal organization. Interactions between individuals and the enterprise are related to the various roles one plays in life. The need to recognize human resistance to change and how to overcome it is stressed. The dynamic nature of the inter-relationships is emphasized throughout.

Introduction

The aim of this paper is to define and explain "organization", to examine the functions and importance of organizations; and to discuss the impact of internal and external forces on organizations. The dynamic nature of organizations (especially in Singapore) will be considered, together with the need for individual and group adaptation to change.

The Nature of Organizations

An organization may be defined as a group of people created and maintained for the purpose of achieving an aim (or aims). An organization is the result of organizing (i.e., the grouping of activities and the defining of relationships, responsibilities and functions). These definitions distinguish organizations from other groups such as the family. Since organization and organising are sometimes used as synonyms, some people prefer to use "enterprise" instead of organization. One way of countrasting an organization with a family is to note that people in an organization are either appointed (e.g., a manager), elected (e.g., a political representative) or they inherit a post (e.g., a sovereign). In a family, roles are assumed (e.g., mother) or one is born into them (e.g., son) and these are roles for life, unlike roles in organizations which can be given up at any time (although such action may carry penalties). The foregoing discussion epitomizes the semantic problems that all human resource management students face and which, for instance, engineers and scientists usually escape. Because universally accepted (and sufficiently precise) definitions of management terms rarely exist, particular attention needs to be paid to the meanings of words, otherwise efficient communication and clear thinking will be hampered. Clearly, human resource management is concerned with human beings so some consideration of the individual is necessary.

The Nature of the Individual

The outstanding characteristics of people are their differences (one from the other), and their differing behaviour, from time to time. When discussing or thinking about people most of us generalize (e.g., "I like people", or "Those people are lazy"). Sometimes generalizations cannot be avoided but we need to remember the necessity to analyze individuals (including ourselves) rationally. This is difficult because people are a mixture of many different types of behaviour. For example, sometimes an individual is very rational and sometimes very emotional; sometimes a person may be highly motivated by money and at another time quite oblivious to it. In any scientific approach to individual behaviour the total person needs to be examined.

Values are held by everyone. A value is something that has worth or importance to an individual; thus values shape human behaviour. Values are of various types, a useful classification is that due to Springer (quoted by Hodgetts, 1980, p. 87):

1. Theoretical — discovery of truth
2. Economic — what is useful
3. Aesthetic — what is beautiful
4. Social — love of people
5. Political — love of power
6. Religious — love of God

Different occupational groups tend to have different values, for example, scientists tend to have high theoretical values; business people high economic values; musicians high aesthetic values; and so on. Specifically the values of the employer may not be shared by the employees, or the values of top managers may conflict with those of their first-line managers; if the value differences between these groups widen, then the probability of industrial unrest increases. These differences may manifest themselves as behaviour which breaks the "rules" of an organization, and these rules may be described as "formal organization" or (at least) as a large part of it.

Formal Organization

"Formal Organization" means the grouping of activities and therefore of the people who carry out such activities (e.g., into departments) and the defining of relationships, responsibilities and functions, and hence the establishing of formal communication links. Put simply, the purpose of formal organizing is to produce an organization structure for an enterprise. A good organization structure should ensure that everyone knows who is to do what, and who is responsible to whom and for what, and that efficient communication, co-operation and decision-making are encouraged. An organization structure needs to change when the enterprise changes (e.g., by expansion or contraction, by the introduction of new products or technology, by changes in the site or buildings, by the change of personalities). Structure is shown by organization charts but these must be amplified by job descriptions.

Organization charts show the superior-subordinate and peer relationships in an enterprise and, hence, the formal communication network. A generalized organization chart of an enterprise with five levels in its hierarchy is as follows:

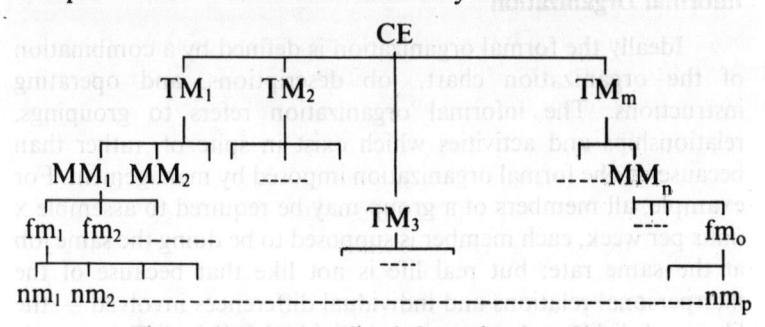

CE
TM_1 TM_2 TM_m
MM_1 MM_2 ----- MM_n
fm_1 fm_2 ------- TM_3 ---- fm_o
nm_1 nm_2 ---------------------------------- nm_p

Figure 1: A Generalized Organization Chart

In Figure 1 CE is the chief executive (the most senior full-time manager) and there are m top managers (TM_1 etc), n middle managers (MM_1 etc.), o first-line manager (fm_1 etc.) and p non-managers (nm_1 etc.). The following should be noted:

1. the lengths of the lines have no significance, e.g., the chart as drawn does not mean that TM_3 is inferior to the other top managers (he might be senior to them all);
2. a manager is anyone with subordinates, whatever the title attached to the post held;
3. a first-line manager is one whose subordinates are non-managers;
4. everyone in an enterprise is either a manager or a non-manager, all are workers;
5. it is important to differentiate between direct and indirect subordinates of the CE: only the top managers (TM_1 to TM_m) are his direct subordinates.

Important Relationships

Line relationships are those between any superior and his direct subordinates, e.g., between the CE and any TM or between TM_1 and MM_1, MM_2 or MM_3

Staff relationships exist between a person charged with a particular function (auxiliary to the enterprise's main activities) and those whom he advises, other than the CE. Examples are the relationships between the personnel manager, the public relations officer, the company accountant, or the company medical officer (on the one hand) and all others in the enterprise, except their own subordinates.

Informal Organization

Ideally the formal organization is defined by a combination of the organization chart, job descriptions, and operating instructions. The informal organization refers to groupings, relationships and activities which exist in spite of, rather than because of, the formal organization imposed by management. For example, all members of a group may be required to assemble x units per week, each member is supposed to be doing the same job at the same rate; but real life is not like that because of the interpersonal relations and individual differences involved — the likes and dislikes of the various individuals, their differing needs and their differing speeds. Sometimes, in a group with supportive interpersonal relations the slow workers will be protected by the fast ones restricting their output to avoid the others suffering by comparison (as in the Hawthorne Studies, see Roethlisberger and Dickson, 1939). In other circumstances slow workers who are unpopular may not be helped or protected; they might be insulted or ostracized.

Informal Leadership

In the formal organization leaders are appointed — they are called managers. In the informal organization the leader is chosen by the group — not by any formal procedure like an election but by many subtle pieces of behaviour characterized by deference and support. The group can dismiss its informal leaders at any time, and sometimes the leadership role shifts frequently; the essence is that the informal leader has power (i.e., the ability to influence or persuade others) but no authority (i.e., the right to command). All formal leaders have authority (whether appointed or elected) and, usually, power (otherwise their commands would not be obeyed). Informal leaders use their power to achieve group objectives (either imposed or informal; the latter includes protecting the group against superiors) and to maintain the role of leader. Note that informal leaders may be managers who, for instance, lead their peers against more senior managers.

Behavioural Control and Dependancy

The formal organization (i.e., the employer) has a system of rewards and punishments (e.g., promotion, salary increase, praise, are rewards; their absence, punishment). The informal organization has its own rewards and punishments e.g., praise by the group and inclusion in its social or sporting activities are rewards, and vice versa. Most people, even if they do not totally accept the informal group's norms (i.e., behavioural rules) depend on the group for social interaction and support. However the degree of this dependancy will vary from time to time (as a result of variations in the individual's needs) and the ability of the group (especially its leader) to satisfy them.

Informal Communications

The informal communications network in an enterprise is

commonly called "the grapevine" because it grows everywhere in all directions entwined around the formal communication structure (like morning glory on a trellis). The grapevine arises from social and work interaction and usually transmits oral messages, but some are written (marked "Personal and Confidential" of course). The grapevine can deal with social matters but is most frequently concerned with work, often in the form of rumour, or speculation, or gossip (malicious or otherwise). The grapevine is most active and powerful when:

1. information is lacking or stale;
2. people feel insecure;
3. personal interest is involved; or
4. the rumour-mongers have high prestige.

(For a discussion of prestige and persuasion, and on credibility and trust in human communication, see Aronson, 1980, pp. 64-79). Virtually the only antidote for rumour is the truth, given as early and as widely as possible. Used properly the grapevine can effectively supplement the formal communications system and this merits deeper examination here (for a fuller discussion of the dynamics of informal groups see Luthans, 1981).

Benefits of the Informal Organization

Provided that there is no significant conflict between the formal organization and the informal organization, the one supports the other and the following benefits should accrue:

1. the informal organization can often get things done more quickly than through formal procedures because it cuts "red tape";
2. participative management is encouraged through reduction in conflict (see Likert & Likert. 1976 for a detailed view);
3. increased job satisfaction by providing social interaction and the protection of the group, although both can be denied if the group norms are flouted too often or too much;
4. the relief of tension by the expression of doubts, fears, anger, disappointment, frustration, etc. to other members of the informal organization;

5. providing feedback to managers, provided the manager concerned has access to the informal organization (but there is the danger that such managers may encourage gossip and have favourites);
6. the opportunity to use the informal organization by disseminating the truth especially to counteract rumour.

Disadvantages of the Informal Organization

The following may occur when the informal organization does not support the formal organization:

1. resistance to change, especially if the group sees its members, norms, existence, power, security, or rewards threatened (e.g., by the introduction of automation);
2. restrictive practises (in the limit, strikes);
3. an increase in the number and intensity of rumours.

Individuals and the Organization

Interactions between the individual and the enterprise, and between individuals within the enterprise suggest many questions such as: Is interpersonal conflict increasing?; Do individuals change having worked in a particular enterprise for many years?; Should the enterprise change to accommodate an individual's characteristics?; Why do some people resent their jobs while others thoroughly enjoy them?; and so on. This chapter will not resolve all these questions but it may help to answer them. Hard-held assumptions need to be challenged, research is required to establish the facts. It is tempting to assume, for instance, that evidence on behaviour at work obtained in one country can be readily applied in another. Singapore, like other countries, is unique and needs solutions appropriate to its culture, history and environment.

All individuals play a series of roles, many of them concurrent. Roles at home (child, parent, sibling) are replaced or overlaid by roles at work (superior, subordinate; manager, non-manager; employee, employer) but it is difficult to believe that a caring, concerned, rational, supportive parent becomes a domineering, arrogant, cynical superior at work. Obviously no one leaves their troubles at home when they go to work (or vice versa); but most situations are complex in which the individual's experience, ability, aptitude, needs, values, ethics, ambition, and status are brought to the enterprise by that individual. These individual characteristics often produce conflict between competing individuals, and between individuals and the enterprise. The potential for interpersonal conflict may be strengthened or encouraged by the characteristics of the enterprise (e.g., formal organization, informal organization, working conditions, managerial attitudes). Conflict will always occur when the individual believes that individual needs are incompatible with enterprise aims. This lack of congruence is a major source of most problems a manager faces, if only because of the effects this mismatch has on performance and hence on productivity. The effects of the technical system used are also significant since the technical system will partially determine the individual's attitudes to the enterprise and how individual needs are satisfied. This may even be seen as a competition between men and machines, especially with computers and robots. (For a fuller discussion see Hunt, 1972).

Automation in Singapore is increasing rapidly reinforcing the national policy of moving towards high technology industry. Fears that this will lead to unemployment may surface. In fact increasing automation leads to reduced costs and higher quality, and hence lower prices and, more importantly, better value for money. This results in increased demand for goods and services generating higher output and higher employment. But these facts have to be demonstrated in Singapore. This should not be difficult especially when labour is short and willingness to learn from Japan's economic success is high. The need for mutual trust and understanding between employee and employer (the individual and the organization) is paramount, and increasing emphasis is being placed on this in Singapore especially since the National Conference of Productivity Committees in April 1978.

Organization-Society Interaction

Every enterprise exists within a set of external environments which are both national and international. One useful classification of these environments, due to de Greene (1982, p. 21) is:

1. natural environment (population, resources, pollution, etc);

2. technological environment (discovery, invention, innovation, research and development);
3. human resources environment (abilities, aptitudes, skills, values, attitudes, cross-cultural differences);
4. political environment (legislation, trade unions, international relations, defence);
5. social or socioeconomic environment (responsibilities to society, macro-economics, etc.);
6. market environment (consumer behaviour, competition, saturation).

Clearly these environments overlap and interact one with another, either reinforcing each other or conflicting, e.g., trade union activity (part of the political environment) has a continuing effect on the attitudes of employees (part of the human resources environment); at the same time these environments affect the enterprise which in turn affects the environments. Thus enterprises are open systems whose main purpose is to survive despite hostile environments.

The above classification depends on the properties of the various environments. There are many other methods of classification but another useful way (due to Emery & Trist, 1965) emphasizes the degree of change, or the relationship between enterprise and environment in causal terms. Their classification is a progression, thus:

1. placid, randomized environments — those where events affecting the system's survival are randomly distributed in a static situation. Such environments are rare (although the unborn child in the womb has been suggested as an example);
2. placid, clustered environments — here, although a static situation, events are clustered in logical ways; examples are the environments of a mining company, or of plants;
3. disturbed reactive environments — those where similar systems are in interaction and competition; examples are a market with limited competition between a few producers or sellers (i.e., oligopolistic), or situations characterized by deductive reasoning, or concentration of power at the top of a hierarchy — such environments appear disturbed because they have multiple directions and are reactive in the interplay of

tactics designed to counter the pursposes of the other systems competing for the resources;
4. turbulent field environments — those of constantly interfacing, multiple, mutual influences, i.e., the same types of fields studied by the ecologist — here not only do systems interact but also components interact within the systems resulting in complexity, rapidity of change and a multiplicity of interconnections; examples are, most situations in the real world.

An enterprise may exist in either "disturbed reactive" or the "turbulent field" environment, depending on the extent of environmental influences.

This discussion of the various environments and the conclusion that most enterprises exist in a "turbulent field" underlines the fact that change is normality, at least in Singapore and most other parts of the world. Changes in the physical environment are apparent to all since we are surrounded by them, but other changes are more subtle although no less real. Individuals and enterprises need to adapt to change otherwise stress results.

Adapting to Change

It is sometimes said that human beings resist all change yet it is unlikely that anyone will resist change which results in improvement for them, unless they are so suspicious of the decision-maker that any decision is greeted with cynicism, or the improvement is seen as unjust when compared to a greater benefit given to a co-worker. Clearly many subjective judgements are involved. Sometimes managers resist change more than non-managers (e.g., in some Singapore firms introducing Quality Control Circles). At a national level, Singapore (over the last twenty-five years) has seen vast political, environmental and economic changes — the change in emphasis from commerce to manufacturing has been dramatic but so has the increase in population and the creation of new buildings for living, working and leisure. People living in Singapore are familiar with change although little research has been done on the degree to which change is resisted, welcomed, or initiated.

The degree to which change will be resisted depends on many factors which can be classified as either logical, psychological or sociological (see Davis, 1981); but these factors are so inter-linked that classification tends to suggest frontiers between them that do not exist. Some common factors are:

1. experience — people who have suffered from change in the past are likely to resist further change;
2. ignorance, which breeds fear;
3. lack of notice of intended change and hence inadequate time to adjust to the new situation;
4. threats to economic security;
5. possibility of "loss of face" either through hard-won skills becoming redundant, or status being threatened.

Although all change tends to induce stress, the individual reaction to stress varies widely — many thrive on it provided it is not too strong. Thus reducing resistance to change is primarily the responsibility of the manager whose powers of persuasion, communication, and leadership are crucial. There is significant evidence (although it may not be conclusive) that the best way of resisting change is by ensuring that those involved participate in (or better, initiate) the decisions resulting in change, (see Rose, 1978). Certainly, mere exhortation will not persuade individuals to change, and this is true of enterprises too, (see Handy, 1976). Willing acceptance of change is essential on the part of individuals and enterprises and society — this will not happen by chance but only as the result of effective action by the leaders concerned. Progress means change; the reverse is also true.

Conclusion

An organization or enterprise is a group created and maintained for the purpose of achieving an aim. Unlike the family its members can join or leave it, but like the family it is part of larger systems, for example, the nation and the world. All these co-exist in dynamic situations and are subject to various interactions (e.g., the interactions within an enterprise), and the effects the enterprise has on society and the society on enterprises. Since change is normality, individuals and groups need to recognise the dimensions of the dynamic forces acting upon them and especially the necessity to adapt to change. This is particularly important in Singapore if only because Singapore is changing more rapidly than most other countries. A knowledge of human behaviour, formal organization and informal organization should help both individuals and groups to anticipate change and hence to adapt to it with minimum upset.

QUESTIONS

1. Should an enterprise change to accommodate a newly recruited individual's characteristics? Explain.
2. Why do some people enjoy their jobs while others dislike them?
3. Filial piety is characteristic of some cultures. If this conflicts with society's norms concerning right and wrong how should the matter be resolved? If "enterprise loyalty" was substituted for "filial piety" would your answer be different? If so, explain.

REFERENCES

Aronson, E. *The Social Animal*. 3rd ed., San Francisco: Freeman, 1980.
Davis, K. *Human Behaviour at Work: Organizational Behavior*. 6th ed., New Delhi: Tata McGraw-Hill, 1981.
De Greene, K.B. *The Adaptive Organization*. New York: McGraw-Hill, 1982.
Emery, F., and Trist, E. L. "The Causal Texture of Organizational Environments", *Human Relations* 18 (1965): 21-32.
Handy, C.B. *Understanding Organizations*. Harmondsworth: Penguin, 1976.
Hodgetts, R.M. *Modern Human Relations*. Hinsdale, Illinois: Dryden Press, 1980.
Hunt, J. W. *The Restless Organization*. Sydney: Wiley, 1972.
Likert, R., & Likert, Jane G. *New Ways of Managing Conflict*. New York: McGraw-Hill, 1976.
Luthans, F. *Organizational Behavior*. 3rd ed., New York: McGraw-Hill, 1981.
Roethlisberger, F. J., and Dickson, W. J. *Management and the Worker*. Cambridge: Harvard, 1939.
Rose, M. *Industrial Behaviour*. Harmondsworth: Penguin, 1978.

PART TWO

SOCIETAL PERSPECTIVE

3
Human Resource Management: Societal Perspective

CHONG LI CHOY

Summary

This chapter serves as an introduction to Section Two of this book. It relates human resource management to the vision of society and nation in the Singapore context and explains the appropriateness of human resource management to Singapore's development.

Human Resource Management and the Vision of Singapore Society

How should a society manage its human resources? The answer to this question depends very much on the society's vision of what it should become in the future, and what its goals and objectives are at present. Having a vision of the future or a utopia, is extremely important to societal planning and development.[1]

Singapore's vision of the future is as contained in the pledge. "We, the citizens of Singapore, pledge ourselves as one united people, regardless of race, language or religion, to build a democratic society based on justice and equality so as to achieve happiness, prosperity and progress for our nation." In other

---

[1]Chong Li Choy, "Utopias in Social Planning: Utility in Four Southeast Asian Nations", in *Southeast Asian Journal of Social Science* 3,2 (1975): pp. 65-72.

words, there is a common vision of the future.[2] This call for unity in a multiracial, multilingual and multireligious society is both hope for the future as well as a present reality. Such tolerance of the other races, languages and religions is part and parcel of the historical development of Singapore as a trading centre, which in times past brought immigrants of different races, languages and religions from all over the world. The building of "a democratic society based on justice and equality", is the political aspiration of a people who had once lived under colonial rule. The "struggle for independence" is no more than a struggle for justice and equality. Democracy puts the right to rule, and to decide on rulers, into the hands of the people. The attainment of happiness, prosperity and progress is certainly the hope of Singaporeans, whether in the past, present or future. This is the reason why the early immigrants came to Singapore — to seek fortune and a better living. This is the reason for wanting independence from colonial rule. This is also the goal of national development in Singapore.

These images of Singapore society have been variedly expressed in different forms over the last twenty-five years. This is the image of a prosperous society, that of a "global city" that is outward-looking and which sits at the crossroads of international economic activities. The development of Singapore as a modern financial, industrial and trading centre is consistent with this image. There is also the image of a "garden city" and the emphasis on "gracious living", both of which concern the quality of living, perhaps an operational definition of "happiness and progress" of the people in society. There are campaigns against social deterioration, such as against "drugs" and "long-hair", "pollution", "littering", and "crime" — all these being also possible operational definitions of increasing "happiness" and "progress" in society.

These images of society co-existed with another set of images, much emphasized in the early years of national independence. These images relate more to the realities of survival and nation-building. There is the image of a "rugged society", the exhortation to work hard and reference made to the

---

[2] For further discussion on this, and in relation to development planning, see Chong Li Choy, *Social Planning Strategies in Southeast Asia — Current Approaches to Planned Development in Four Nations*, M. Soc. Sc. Thesis, Department of Sociology, University of Singapore, 1974.

"pioneer spirit" of early Singaporeans. Meritocracy is also much emphasized. Mention has been made by the Prime Minister of a "technocratic society" with administrators at the top of the social hierarchy, and reference being made to Plato. National service gives a "spartan-type" image of society. Of interest too is the need to maintain genetic quality (talent) in the population — a point emphasized by the Prime Minister. This latter concern is expressed in relation to survival and to the continual future progress of the nation.

The Appropriateness of Human Resource Management to Singapore's Development

Today, after almost two decades of very rapid progress since achieving nationhood in 1965, the leaders in Singapore are emphasizing the need for good human resource management. This concern is appropriate since Singapore has a scarcity of natural resources other than its human population. However, this does not constitute a change in the direction or vision of the future of Singapore. On the contrary, the leaders are merely holding on to their original course and vision of what to expect of Singapore.[3] Good human resource management is consistent with the values of a "just and equal society" in its management of people. Making workers happy or giving them satisfaction at work is an important concern of human resource management. Good human resource management increases the productivity of the people, and the nation, and hence will contribute towards prosperity and progress.

The present emphasis on human resource management in Singapore (in the 1980s) is not only appropriate but also very timely. In the early days of Singapore's development (1960s), the problems of unemployment, the lack of proper housing and the need for nation-building, required the setting up of labour intensive industries, leading to the rapid development of cheap housing, and resulting in the creation of various other socio-economic structures and institutions. Management emphasis was

---

[3] For a discussion of the human orientation ("principle of satisficing") in development management in Singapore, see Chong Li Choy, "Economic Growth and Social Equity in Singapore: A Managerial Perspective", *Contemporary Southeast Asia*, 4,2 (1983): pp. 188-201.

obviously related to goal attainment, task orientation and structure creation. The solving of immediate and short-term problems was critical during the early period of Singapore's development. However, inspite of this, the need to improve human welfare has always been the goal of the government. The emphasis on goal attainment, task orientation and structure creation enabled the government to provide for society, in areas, such as housing, health and education. Although human orientation was not emphasized in management in the early days, the well-being of the individual was nevertheless the goal of the government.

Today the situation in Singapore is different. The poverty, unemployment and lack of proper housing have been replaced by a situation of relative wealth, where there is more than full employment (there being more jobs than Singaporean workers) and where people are properly housed. In other words, in terms of material well-being, the quality of life of Singaporeans has improved tremendously. Yet the continual improvement in the quality of life remains the goal of development in Singapore. "Gracious living" is continually emphasized as seen in improvements made in the physical environment, (such as making Singapore "clean" and "green"); improvements in the social environment, (such as neighbourliness and the need for the successful and able in society to participate in community service); improvements in recreation facilities, (such as public parks and gardens); and improvements in working conditions, (such as the high-wage policy, consideration of the five-day work-week and the call for good human resource management). Yet, "gracious living" must be financed and this requires continual rapid economic growth. Productivity must be increased in order to maintain this state in the economy. Better human resource management by all managers (of both the private and public sectors) will not only improve the quality of work life in Singapore, but will also increase the potential productivity of Singapore workers.

Moreover, the move to high technology industries in Singapore in the 1980s also means that labour will become more valuable as a resource. Good human resource management becomes therefore even more appropriate. It is within this societal context that human resource management is being emphasized in Singapore.

REFERENCES

Bell, Wu and James Mau. "Images of the Future: Theory and Research Strategies", in Bell and Mau (ed.), *The Sociology of the Future*. New York: Russell Sage Foundation, 1971.

Chong Li Choy. "Utopias in Social Planning: Utility in Four Southeast Asian Nations", in *Southeast Asian Journal of Social Science* 3,2 (1975): pp. 65-72.

———. *Social Planning Strategies in Southeast Asia — Current Approaches to Planned Development in Four Nations*, M. Soc. Sc. Thesis, Department of Sociology, University of Singapore, 1974.

———. "Economic Growth and Social Equity in Singapore: A Managerial Perspective", in *Contemporary Southeast Asia* 4,2 (1981): pp. 188-201.

———. "The Multinational Enterprises in Singapore's Development", in *Multinational Business and National Development: Transfer of Managerial Knowhow to Singapore*. Singapore: Maruzen Asia, 1983, pp. 61-76.

Mannheim, Karl. *Ideology and Utopia — An Introduction to the Sociology of Knowledge*. London: Routledge and Kegan Paul, 1936.

Mau, A. James. *Social Change and Images of the Future*. Cambridge, Massachusetts: Schenkman, 1968.

Moore, E. Wilbert. "The Utility of Utopias", *American Sociological Review* 31,6 (1966) pp. 765-772.

N.T.U.C. *Towards Tomorrow: Essays on Development and Social Transformation in Singapore*. Singapore: The Singapore National Trades Union Congress, 1973.

Polak, F. L. *The Image of the Future* (2 vols). New York: Oceana Publications, 1961.

4
The Singapore Context

TAN CHWEE HUAT

SUMMARY

This chapter defines the scope of human resource management and discusses the topic at three different levels: national, organizational and individual. It deals with the significance of HRM in the context of Singapore during the various stages of industrial development.

The importance of HRM in the restructuring of the Singapore economy is highlighted and the need for higher productivity as a national objective is mentioned. Emphasis on the human aspects of productivity as recommended by the Committee of Productivity and the implementation of Quality Control (QC) circles are also dealt with.

Scope of Human Resource Management

In recent years, the terms "Human Resource Management" (HRM) and "Human Resource Development" (HRD) have been used by many people in various contexts to mean different things. The economic planner and politician use it to mean the planning and developing of all manpower (including woman power) in the context of the economic and social development of the nation. The personnel manager, corporate trainer and human resource professional use it to mean recruiting, training and developing employees (including managers) in the organization. The career counsellor and the industrial psychologist use it to mean guiding, measuring and helping individuals to understand themselves and to seek a suitable career or a meaningful life. The community worker is concerned about the social well-being of the community.

Thus, HRM may be discussed at three different levels: (1) the national level; (2) the organizational level; and (3) the individual level.

At the national level, HRM involves the process of preparing the nation's human resources (in simple terms, people) through education and training, for productive employment and in enabling them to contribute their maximum potential in producing the goods and services needed by the nation. At the company or organizational level, it involves providing a conducive working environment and motivating employees to contribute their best to the organization. At the individual level, it involves understanding one's own self (personality, interest, talents, ambition, etc.) and seeking means to develop relevant interpersonal skills to interact with other people in the process of pursuing the most suitable career in an organization and to derive maximum satisfaction in life.

HRM at the National Level

At the national economy level, HRM extends into the realm of labour economics to understanding the factors affecting the supply and demand of labour. It examines the characteristics of the labour force and explains the determinants influencing its productivity. Within the framework of achieving planned economic development, HRM involves manpower planning by industries and sectors, thus affecting the education plan of the nation. It also examines public policies (such as prices and wages) that will affect activities in the labour market. The important role of trade unions, their organization and leadership are also of great significance to the national manpower planner. This is especially important in the context of Singapore where the National Trades Union Congress, the People's Action Party and the government are integral parts of the national leadership. Schools, universities, polytechnics, training institutes and professional bodies are all contributors in upgrading the national human resources. Agencies such as the National Wages Council, and the Skills Development Fund are instrumental in indicating the direction of human resource development. All these efforts must synchronize with national objectives through the manpower plan. Regular stimulation exercises (such as the productivity campaign) must be carried out to remind people of the national goal of maximizing the only resource the country has.

HRM at the Company Level

In many management books, the term Human Resource Management has often been used interchangeably with personnel management. It will be less confusing to the reader if we define some of these terms for the purpose of this discussion. In this context, personnel management is narrowly defined to include only such functions as recruitment, selection, salary administration, industrial relations, employee welfare, training, manpower planning and other "traditional" personnel activities. HRM is a broader concept which incorporates not only personnel management but also includes "human relations" or what is more popularly known as "people management". The latter is a function performed by *any* manager (including the personnel manager) or supervisor who has to deal with people. It involves understanding individual and group behaviour, and the acquiring of interpersonal skills in communicating, motivating, leading and coordinating the activities of subordinates. At the top management level, HRM involves human resource planning (or corporate manpower planning) and an analysis of how well all the human resources in the company have been utilized. Managers must be aware of the quantity and quality of employees, their abilities and skills, and how they perform in achieving company objectives. Deficiency in skills must be remedied by training programmes. Employees must be provided with opportunities to develop and identify with the growth of the company. All these may necessitate the introduction of a manpower system or human resource accounting system to justify the popular proclamation by many companies that people are their most important assets.

HRM at the Individual Level

For the individual, HRM begins with understanding one own self in terms of personality, interest, skills, ambition and preferred lifestyle. It implies that one must have a personal definition of career and the meaning of success. Only within this framework can one satisfy career, social and family needs. It entails a self-assessment process, followed by a realistic set of action plans to progress towards what one wants to become in the short and long term. The action plans must be realistic within the context of the organization, subject to its constraints and opportunities. To get along well with other individuals in the same organization, a person must acquire basic interpersonal skills for the purpose of communicating and interacting. The skills are necessary if a group is pursuing some common objective for the organization.

Meaning and Significance in the Singapore Context

Human resource development has always been of special significance in the economic planning of Singapore. This is exemplified by the emphasis placed on manpower development and training since the industrialization programme started in 1961.

A brief historical review of Singapore's economic development will enable one to better understand the significance of the country's manpower development. Before the industrialization programme was launched, the Singapore economy depended mainly upon entrepot trade. This sector was unable to generate enough jobs for the unemployed and the flux of school leavers entering the job market. It was decided that industrialization was the only solution. The EDB was set up to woo investors. During the initial stage of industrialization, the EDB was glad to welcome the investment projects involving assembly or manufacturing of simple products. Since then, industrial projects have reached new levels of sophistication.

Looking back, it can be seen that industrial success was brought about by ensuring the profitability of investments mainly through cost factors. Tax incentives were provided to investors to offset disadvantages such as increased transport costs and investment risks. These were further supported by fully serviced industrial estates, improved communications, transport facilities and expanded financial services. Industrial achievement over the last decade was impressive even by international comparisons. Despite the oil crisis and recession, the Singapore economy has grown at an enviable rate.

However success has created new problems. It became apparent to economic planners that the manufacturing sector depended heavily on low cost labour. With full employment in the 1970s, there was an increasing trend for higher wages and the phenomenon of job hopping among workers for a few dollars more. Externally, the economy was facing increased competition from countries with huge labour pools. Investors who came to Singapore because of low labour cost were beginning to look elsewhere for cheaper labour.

To complicate matters, the successful family planning programme has reduced the source of labour supply. Consequently, industries such as construction and shipbuilding have become dependent on foreign workers. This dependence was worsened by Singaporeans opting for softer jobs. Economic planners are left with only one feasible solution — to upgrade the skills of workers for the production of high value added products. This means that there is a need to increase productivity in order to remain competitive in the world market. The economy must move up the ladder into a second stage of industrialization.

HRM In the Context of Industrialization

The development of the nation's human resources in the context of industrialization may be analyzed in various phases:

1. Phase 1: 1959-1965 — This phase started with Singapore as a self-governing state, to when it became part of Malaysia, and up to 1965 when it achieved independence. During this period, the major economic objectives were to reduce unemployment and to reduce dependence on entrepot trade. For long term manpower development, the government continued its universal primary and secondary education policy with special attention on vocational and technical training. In the private sector, the emphasis was on-the-job training for operators and supervisors in the labour-intensive assembly industries. No difficulty was encountered in the training as most operations at this stage were technically simple.

2. Phase 2: 1966-1972 — With the loss of a potential Malaysian market, the economic objectives were to create more employment through export oriented industries; to expand trade; to develop Singapore into a financial centre; and to develop specialized technical services. Human resource development programmes aimed at providing supporting services and technical personnel. To this end the EDB set up the Light Industries Services Unit. The Technical Education Department on the other hand stepped up its technical and vocational training programmes. The National Productivity Centre was established. In the private sector, the Singapore Institute of Management was set up to upgrade local managerial skill.

3. Phase 3: 1973-1977 — In this third phase, the success of the industrialization programme resulted in an economy with

full employment. The main economic objective was to sustain growth by further expansion of the manufacturing sector with emphasis on skill-intensive industries. The programmes stressed on optimal use of human resources through training and development. The Industrial Training Board was formed and the Polytechnics were expanded. Training centres were jointly set up by the government and private enterprises. Examples were the Tata, Philips, and Rollei (now Brown-Boveri) centres. Industrial training grant schemes were introduced to encourage the upgrading of skills. The National Wages Council was formed to monitor the increase in wage levels.

4. Phase 4: 1978-present — This period sees an emphasis being placed on enhancing productivity as a national endeavour. The basic structure of the unions is thus examined in this new perspective. Labour laws that have become less meaningful in the new economic context have been amended. House unions have been encouraged in pursuit of company productivity through the encouragement of loyalty and company welfarism. Employees are encouraged to participate in small group activities such as Quality Control (QC) circles or Work Improvement Teams (WITs) in the practice of people-centred management. Organizations have been encouraged to learn from Japan in seeking an appropriate management philosophy for their long term growth.

Thus, in the restructuring of the nation's economy, human resource management has moved from the national level to the organization and the individual workers.

National Effort towards Productivity

In 1981, the Singapore Government appointed a national Committee on Productivity to formulate recommendations to improve work attitudes, productivity, and labour management relations. The Committee identified three areas where productivity gains may be achieved:

1. technology (e.g., process and equipment improvement);
2. management systems (e.g., computerized information systems, better management techniques);
3. human relations which embrace labour-management relations, company loyalty etc.

Whilst acknowledging the contribution of technology and systems in enhancing productivity the committee realized that sufficient emphasis had already been given in Singapore to harness these two factors for productivity gains. It then emphasized the importance of the human aspect of productivity.

Importance of HRM in Restructuring the Singapore Economy

In the 1960s, Singapore promoted labour-intensive industries to create employment. By the 1970s, full employment was achieved, resulting in a growing dependence on foreign workers in some industries. Wage levels have also increased over the decade. With competition from the labour-abundant developing countries, the only solution for Singapore was to move up the development ladder to produce high value products and to reduce its dependence on unskilled foreign workers.

However, the availability of cheap foreign labour can distort wage patterns and postpone the need of employers to introduce labour-saving devices. Workers from other cultures can further cause adjustment problems. They also compete for existing medical services and social facilities. The Skills Development Fund was thus established to accelerate the upgrading of skills in support of the economic restructuring.

Further measures include annual productivity campaigns, the emphasis on people-centred management, the encouragement of participating in QC circles and WITS — these all contribute to productivity consciousness.

This same objective can be seen in small group participation where workers are encouraged to be involved and motivated. They contribute through participation as a result of intimate knowledge gained and are rewarded with a sense of achievement.

Subsequent national measures to enhance productivity focused on people-management. In the workplace, QC circles were recommended as a specific course of action for management to seriously consider implementing. In the atmosphere of harmonious labour management relations, QC circles give to workers a sense of dignity and job satisfaction through participation and contribution to the company. The process is also viewed as an opportunity for workers to upgrade their skills thus enhancing productivity. The success of Japan and Korea and the productivity of their workers have been associated with the popularity of QC circles in their factories. In return, management places emphasis on company welfarism and the well-being of the workers.

The National Productivity Board (NPB) has been the main force behind the publicity and promotion of QC circles. Presentation by circle members, national conventions and other related events have been organized to sustain the momentum. These efforts have been supported by the mass media so that the message is brought to workers and managers alike. The NPB provides the necessary back-up training for QC facilitators and the steering committees.

The increasing number of QC circles formed over the last few years shows that such a concept has begun to take root in the life of a Singaporean worker.

Recent efforts have also been focused on upgrading the basic skills of individual workers. The Basic Education for Skills Training (BEST) programme was introduced after a survey disclosed that an alarmingly high number of workers were deficient in Mathematics and English.

Through the implementation of measures at the national, organization and the individual levels, it is hoped that the potential of the workforce can be harnessed in contributing to overall productivity.

QUESTIONS

1. Discuss the meaning of human resource management at national, organization and individual levels.
2. Discuss the development of human resource during the various stages of Singapore's industrialization.
3. Discuss the importance of human resource management in the restructuring of the Singapore economy.

REFERENCES

Lee Soo Ann. *Industrialization in Singapore.* London: Longmans, 1973.

National Productivity Board. *Report of the Committee on Productivity,* 1981.

Ng Kiat Chong. "Productivity Will through QCC", *Productivity Digest,* May 1983. pp. 42-48.

Ong Teong Wan. "The Training, Development and Utilization of Human Resources: A Singapore Perspective". Paper presented at the first Asia Training and Development Conference, Manila, 6-9 November, 1974.

Ong Wee Hock. "The Meaning and Significance of Human Resource Development in Singapore". Paper presented at the seminar on Human Resource Development in Industrial Training organized by ITB Training Staff Union on 17 March 1977.

Pang Eng Fong. *Factors which Hinder or Help Productivity Improvement: Country Report on Singapore.* Asia Productivity Organization, 1980.

_____. *Education, Manpower and Development in Singapore.* Singapore: Singapore University Press, 1983.

5
Productivity and National Development

CHONG LI CHOY

SUMMARY

This chapter provides a societal perspective to human resource management. It emphasizes the importance of increasing productivity to attain economic development, political stability and social well-being in Singapore. It points out the achievements of Singapore in economic, political and social development and how these have benefited the individual in Singapore. A brief discussion of the importance of international relations to Singapore in the acquisition of resources for its development is given. The relationship between productivity and economic development, and the need for individual and organizational cooperation to the nation's development efforts are also pointed out.

Development Attainment in Singapore

Singapore is today, the most developed nation in Asia next to Japan, and certainly the most developed nation in Southeast Asia. It enjoys a high standard of living in Singapore, and the currency is one of the most stable in the world. The achievements of the last two decades as summed up by the Minister of Trade and Industry, Dr. Tony Tan in Parliament last year were: "The per capita GNP increased from $2,649 in 1960 to $5,045 in 1970, and to $10,801 in 1981. Similarly, per capita private consumption increased from $2,266 in 1960 to $3,314 in 1970, and to $6,317 in 1980. Government expenditure on social services per person also increased tremendously, from $191 in 1960 to $368 in 1970, and to

$1,209 in 1981. The ratio of the number of persons to each television set also improved from 53 in 1963, to 13 in 1970, and 6 in 1981. Similarly, the ratio of persons per telephone also improved from 27 in 1960, to 13 in 1970, and 3 in 1981. The number of persons per public bus also improved from 1,230 in 1960, to 705 in 1970, to 352 in 1980. All these improvements took place with the population increasing from 1.6 million in 1960, to 2.1 million in 1970, and to 2.5 million in 1981.[1] All these statistics indicate the tremendous improvements in public welfare in Singapore since 1959. Although improvements in average welfare in society does not necessarily imply improvements in the welfare of every individual person, or even most persons, there is little doubt that most people did benefit from the economic growth in Singapore, because it did not result in greater inequalities in income distribution. This fact was demonstrated in a recent study by Professor Lee Sheng-Yi.[2]

Social Well-being

It should be pointed out that although economic growth is an important goal in Singapore, social goals like justice and equality are perhaps even more important. The very purpose of economic growth is to attain a more just and equal society in Singapore. This ideology of the ruling political party was expressed by the Prime Minister, Mr Lee Kuan Yew: "Every serious political party sets out to achieve certain ideological, economic or social objectives. To achieve these objectives, it must achieve power. As a political party, we will change our methods and styles. We will develop new strategies to achieve our objectives. But our abiding faith in equality of opportunities for all our citizens, in a more just and equal society, this faith cannot change . . . we must stand by our fundamental beliefs. We seek power because we want to change our society for the better."[3] (*Towards Tomorrow*, p. 143).

---

[1] *The Straits Times*, 17 March 1982.
[2] Chong Li Choy, "Economic Growth and Social Equity in Singapore: A Managerial Perspective", *Contemporary Southeast Asia* 4, 2 (1982): pp. 191-2. cf. Lee Sheng-Yi: "Income Distribution, Taxation and Social Benefits of Singapore", *The Journal of Developing Areas* 14, 1 (1979): p. 71.
[3] *Towards Tomorrow: Essays on Development and Social Transformation in Singapore*. Singapore: Singapore National Trades Union Congress, 1973, p. 143.

It is evident that the goal of economic development is merely a means to attain the more important social goals of justice and equality. This was also pointed out in an essay by Mr. K. M. Byrne, a stalwart of the ruling People's Action Party of Singapore in 1960.

> As a government inspired by socialist principles we do not believe in a policy of industrialization if it is to be achieved at the expense of the workers. As I have mentioned earlier, the pressure of our growing population has been such as to make it essential that we do industrialize if we are to survive. This does not mean to say that we will allow our young population to be exploited in the interests of achieving our industrialization programme and it was for this reason that we proclaimed our belief in a policy of industrial peace with justice.[4]

In other words, industrialization, a way to achieve economic growth, is necessary for Singapore's survival, but justice and the interests of the workers must be upheld under all circumstances. With this, we understand that the distribution of social benefits to the people is crucial in the development of Singapore.[5]

The social benefits enjoyed by Singaporeans also demonstrate the extent of social development that has taken place in Singapore. Singaporeans in the 1980s are better housed, better educated, better fed and better clothed. They enjoy better health, have more recreational facilities, and have more opportunities for employment. There is increasing concern for social well-being and gracious living, as opposed to the primary concern with the "rice bowl" which plagued the individual two decades ago. All these indicate progress in social development.

However, it should be noted that rapid social change has also resulted in the maladjustment of a greater number of individuals in society. For example: the sucide rates have increased from an average of 6 per 100,000 population between 1969 and 1977 to an average of 11 per 100,000 population between 1978 and 1981. The number of offences against persons and property per 10,000 population increased from 79 in 1971 to 107 in 1981. (Between 1971 and 1978, the figures ranged from 63

---

[4] *Ibid.*, p. 34.
[5] Chong (1982), *Op. cit.*; Lee (1979), *Op. cit.*

to 79 per 10,000 population. Between 1979 and 1981, the figures ranged from 80 to 107 per 10,000 population). The number of juvenile offenders arrested per 100,000 population also increased from 15 in 1977 to 42 in 1981.

Such maladjustments of individuals may be a result of their anomie, their feeling of alienation from society, or simply stress which they are unable to cope with. Anomie may be defined as lack of binding ties to conventional and shared values in society (norms), by groups or institutions, leaving the individual rootless and without norms. Alienation may be defined as an emotional separation from society or group which makes the individual feel powerless, normless and socially isolated. It should however be noted that should these problems become widespread, stability as well as productive capacity would be jeopardized.

Political Stability

The distribution of social benefits to the masses in society has led to political stability in Singapore.[6] Political stability is necessary for economic growth, particularly in the long run. Instability in the form of riots and strikes will not only mean the destruction of property and wealth and the decline in production, but will also discourage both domestic and foreign investments and threaten the survival of economic organizations in the country. As a result, the distribution of social benefits to the masses will also be disrupted.

Over the years, Singapore has evolved various institutions to promote and maintain political stability. National service is now generally accepted by most Singaporeans. The pledge of loyalty to Singapore is given daily at the schools. Community centres, the People's Association and Residential Committees are established all over Singapore not only to serve the community but also to enable the government to get in touch with the people. These are, to mention just a few, some of the efforts at political development.

Resources and International Relations

To develop, Singapore requires resources. However, Singapore has no natural resources beyond its strategically well-

---

[6] Chong (1982). *Op. cit.*

placed natural harbour and its people. International relations in the form of trade and investments are crucial to Singapore's development. A development theory which relates the availability of resources to international power and relations has already been discussed in several papers.[7]

In the conduct of business (whether as a commercial, financial, or servicing centre), Singapore must fulfil the needs of her clients better than all other competing countries. Efficiency and competitive pricing are therefore very necessary. The fact that Singapore is able to become a regional centre for trade (particularly entrepot), finance and communications, hinges on this efficiency and competitiveness. Similarly, the ability to serve the needs of foreign investors, such as in having a stable and sympathetic government, disciplined and educated labour force, good infrastructure and rapid economic growth, has led to considerable foreign investments (even high-technology industries) in Singapore. Foreign investments made by multinational enterprises are extremely useful to the country, not only in the provision of capital, managerial know-how and technology, and other scarce resources, but also in the provision of ready markets abroad for the locally produced goods. Both international trade and investments bring to Singapore resources which she otherwise would not have for her own development.

Productivity and Development

In order to serve the needs of others better and to produce more, the need to be even more efficient or productive is recognized. Productivity refers to a comparison of output with input in the production of goods and services. Productivity is said to have increased if the ratio of output to input is increased. A common measure of productivity is the value added per worker; i.e.,

$$\frac{\text{(total value of output)} - \text{(total value of input)}}{\text{total number of workers}}$$

---

[7] Chong Li Choy, "International Power and Southeast Asian Development", *Contemporary Southeast Asia* 2, 2 (1980): pp. 155-181; Chong Li Choy, *Open Self-Reliant Regionalism: Power for ASEAN's Development*. Singapore: Institute of Southeast Asian Studies, 1981; Chong Li Choy, "The Power Theory of Development: A Short Presentation", *Contemporary Southeast Asia*. 3, 3 (1981): pp. 286-300.

However, this measure of productivity is imperfect. An increase in this ratio could indeed reflect an increase in productivity (or efficiency) per worker. It could also be a result of inflation or even price-fixing.

A common measure of economic development (more appropriately economic growth) is the per capita Gross National Product (GNP), which in Singapore is the aggregate value of output produced by productive factors owned by Singapore residents irrespective of whether they are located within Singapore's geographical boundary or abroad, divided by the population. Its variant, the per capita Gross Domestic Product, (GDP), is the aggregate value of output produced within the domestic territory of Singapore per population in Singapore. It is clear from these definitions of GNP and GDP that these are essentially measures of total value added per population in the country, which therefore suffer from the same problems of inflation (which economists attempt to correct by use of price deflators, thus yielding "real incomes").

Individual and Organizational Responsiveness

That there exists a relationship between productivity and development is evident from the use of "value added" in both measures. An increase in productivity per worker would certainly under normal circumstances contribute to economic development, since national output would thereby have been increased. This calls for individual as well as organizational cooperation not only to the government's call for higher productivity, but also to the nation's overall development strategy.

Cooperation to Increase Productivity

It is recognized that it is important that both the individual and the organization, respond positively to increasing productivity in work. For the organization, higher productivity would mean higher profits or better services. For the individual worker, higher productivity should mean higher wages. For the nation, higher productivity would mean that there will be more goods for local consumption as well as for exchange with other countries (i.e., trade).

Attaining New/High Technology

Since new technology can lead to more efficient production, the willingness of the individual to acquire new skills and knowledge becomes important. Organizations should also help their employees by making training available for their employees.

Moving to Higher Value-Added Industries

The higher the "value added" of goods produced, the more of other goods one can gain in exchange (or trade), since one's own goods are worth more in relation to other people's. Business firms should therefore respond to the government's call to move into higher value-added industries, which are normally also technologically advanced. Similarly, individuals should be willing to acquire the necessary skills to work in these industries.

Conclusion

Social well-being is the goal of economic growth and development in Singapore. Political stability is crucial to long-term economic growth and development. Being a small nation with scarce resources of her own, Singapore is dependent on other countries for various resources. The ability to fulfil the needs of these other countries far better than other competing countries enabled Singapore to obtain considerable resources for her own development. An increase in efficiency in the production of goods and services would certainly help in this international competition. This calls for higher productivity in every sector of the economy. The introduction of new and better technology and the setting up of higher value-added industries will certainly help. All these require the cooperation of Singaporean workers as well as the organizations they work in. In this, better human resource management may help.

QUESTIONS

1. How is economic development related to political stability and social well-being in Singapore?
2. How is productivity related to economic development?
3. How and why should individuals and organizations respond to the nation's need for higher productivity and economic development in Singapore?

REFERENCES

Byrne, K. M. "On the PAP's Five-Year Plan", *The People's Action Party Sixth Anniversary Celebration Souvenir,* 1960.

Chan Heng Chee. Singapore: The Politics of Survival, 1965-1967, Singapore: Oxford University Press, 1971.

Chong Li Choy. "Economic Growth and Social Equity in Singapore: A Managerial Perspective", *Contemporary Southeast Asia* 4:2, 1982.

_____. "International Power and Southeast Asian Development", *Contemporary Southeast Asia,* 2:2, 1980.

_____. "The Power Theory of Development: A Short Presentation", *Contemporary Southeast Asia, 3:3, 1981 (a).*

_____. *International Development and International Dependence: A Study of Aid and Social Development in Southeast Asia.* Ann Arbor, Michigan: University Microfilms International, 1977.

Hans-Dieter Evers, (ed.). *Sociology of Southeast Asia: Readings on Social Change and Development.* Kuala Lumpur: Oxford University Press, 1980.

Lee Sheng-Yi. "Income Distribution, Taxation and Social Benefits of Singapore", *The Journal of Developing Areas,* 14:1, 1979.

N.T.U.C., *Towards Tomorrow: Essays on Development and Social Transformation in Singapore.* The Singapore National Trades Union Congress, 1973.

6
The Significance of Non-adversative Union-management Relationship in Singapore

V. ANANTARAMAN

SUMMARY

This article is developed on the premise that the Singapore government has succeeded in evolving a common ideology binding the actors in the industrial relations system in Singapore despite their divergent interests, and in winning their generalized commitment to this common ideology of "an open society committed to industrialization". The central behavioural manifestation of this common ideology in the industrial relations system has been the development of non-adversative union-management relationships. This relationship has been significant in contributing to the success of the government's efforts to industrialize Singapore in two stages: the first industrial revolution covering a period of two decades between 1959 and 1979, and the second industrial revolution beginning 1979 and extending into the eighties and the nineties of this century.

The rest of the analysis deals with how the government, relying mainly upon its legislative and institutional structures, has created a symbiotic relationship with the National Trades Union Congress (NTUC) and together produced its first industrial revolution strategy of world market-oriented industrialization from 1959 to 1979. The second part of the article analyses how the government's modified strategy of industrialization was to manage manpower and management with aid of the elaborate institutional infra-structure from 1979 to usher in the second industrial revolution.

This discussion of policies and strategies reveals that the stress is on establishment of house unions and the promotion of joint consultation in the high-technology industries. This is because the ideal employer-employee relationship for future success depends upon its efforts not only to transform NTUC into a technologically-oriented trade union movement, but more importantly, to integrate these Japanese innovations into the social fabric of Singapore.

Introduction

A national industrial relations system in a pluralistic society is said to be stable and mature when despite divergent goals and interests of the interacting parties within the system, a common ideology binds them together to subserve the national goals of industrialization adumbrated by its political elite. Ellison Chalmers, in his book "Crucial Issues in Industrial Relations in Singapore" argued that the industrial relations system in Singapore evolved its common ideology of "an open society committed to industrialization".[1] He pointed out that this ideology, due to various circumstances, gained the generalized commitment of the parties to the industrial relations system in Singapore. The central behavioural manifestation of the industrial relations (IR) system, as a consequence, has been the non-adversative union-management relationship. This relationship has been significant for the success of the government's efforts to industrialize Singapore in two stages: the first industrial revolution covering the period between 1959-1979, and the second industrial revolution beginning 1979 and continuing till today.

The First Industrial Revolution

The overriding economic factor of eradicating the mounting unemployment in the early sixties, and of achieving the goal of full-employment was responsible for the government's strategy of world market-oriented industrialization. This meant inviting

---

[1] W. Ellison Chalmers. *Crucial Issues in Industrial Relations in Singapore.* Singapore: Donald Moore Press. 1967. pp. 1-69.

foreign investments in low-value added, and labour-intensive industries like textiles and consumer electronics.

Foreign capital did flow into Singapore, not out of any love of Singapore, but motivated by the desire to make profits. The government was, therefore, quite seriously involved in ensuring the following pre-conditions to attract foreign capital — political stability; industrial peace; industrial discipline; low-labour costs; and an effective industrial infrastructure.

It is not difficult to analyse in detail how the government went about ensuring these pre-conditions through the use of changes in its legislative and insititutional framework, and the framework of government-NTUC relationships. Suffice to say that the government mobilized the NTUC unions vis-à-vis rival unions through the use of the deregistration and registration provisions of the Trade Union Act of 1941.[2] According to Federic Deyo[3], the initial total dependence of the NTUC on the PAP for both political and financial support led to the consolidation and the centralization of the trade union structure, and eventually to the incorporation of the trade union movement into the PAP hegemony. However the relationship which developed between the NTUC and the PAP became popularly known as a symbiotic relationship i.e., an association of dissimilar organizations to their mutual advantage. The spirit of this relationship has been articulated by Ban Kah Choon when he observed that "out of the early maelstrom of struggle, a cooperative mutually respecting bond between the government and workers has been forged, and as a result the ugly habit of confrontation between unions and employers, holding the society to ransom, has been overcome".[4]

This relationship explains many of the characteristic features of the Singapore trade union structure.[5] There was substantial personnel overlap between the party and the NTUC as Members of Parliament, including parliamentary secretaries, were active in union affairs as advisers and resource personnel. The Secretary-

---

[2] *Alex Josey. Industrial Relations: Labour Laws in Developing Singapore.* Trade Union Act, 1941, Sections 10-12. Singapore: Federal Publications, 1976, pp. 188-191.
[3] Federic C. Deyo. *Dependent Development and Industrial Order: An Asian Case Study.* New York: Praeger, 1981, pp. 42-50.
[4] Ban Kah Choon's review of "Our Heritage and Beyond", NTUC, Singapore 1982, in *Straits Times,* August 11, 1982.
[5] Frederic C. Deyo, Op. cit., chapter 3, pp. 41-51.

general of the NTUC was for instance a cabinet minister. Furthermore, PAP guidance of union activities is effected through the NTUC Research Unit, and in 1974 it was announced that all union negotiation claims had to be submitted for approval by the NTUC Dispute Committee. This committee was vested with powers to ask a union to withdraw a dispute against an employer in the dispute settlement process.

The government had the power to register or deregister a union, to freeze its bank account in certain circumstances[6] and to give wage guidelines through the tripartite National Wages Council. The Employment Act 1968 curtails indiscriminate demands for benefits and working conditions. The Industrial Relations Amendment Act of 1968 excludes from the scope of collective bargaining, personnel matters such as transfer, promotion, termination of service due to reorganization or redundancy, and assignment of duties. The Industrial Relation Act 1960 provides for a broader scope for the Minister of Labour in conciliation and in adjudication of industrial disputes by the Industrial Arbitration Court. This court has been vested with powers to ensure that the sectoral interests of the parties do not adversely affect the larger interests of the community, specifically the economy of Singapore. In the exercise of its discretion, the court has been enjoined by law to avoid unnecessary technicalities and legal forms. More important is the fact that the court is exempt from the supervisory jurisdiction of the higher courts. A bilaterally concluded agreement cannot come into force unless certified by the Industrial Arbitration court.

Although unemployment was curtailed in Singapore, the implementation of the government strategy of world market-oriented industralization has not been without considerable cost to the trade union movement. The labour movement lost its credibility in the eyes of its rank and file since its behaviour was, in a large measure, orchestrated by the government. The NTUC membership was steadily declining from its peak of 112,635 in 1965 to 85,422 in 1970.[7] In an effort to regain the lost status and membership of the NTUC, the government tried to bring about a

---

[6] Frederic C. Deyo, Op. cit. p. 50. The Ministry of Labour acquired power in 1977 through an act of Parliament to freeze the bank account of any union under investigation by the Ministry of Labour or the Registrar of Unions.
[7] Ministry of Labour Annual Reports, 1964-1982.

turnaround by shedding its traditionality and by going modern.

In the process of going modern, the trade union movement was required:

(1) to subordinate the sectoral interest of labour to the larger interest of the nation;
(2) to shed the traditional adversative value in preference to the modern value of consultation in union-management relationship;
(3) to open up a third sector in the economy, namely, the cooperative sector with its own enterprises like Welcome, Income, Fair Deal and Denticare; and
(4) to play an educative and socializing role in nation-building activities. True to the expectations of the government, the trade union membership registered a steady increase from 1971, to reach a peak of 236,699 in 1979.[8]

The second and more serious cost of the first industrial revolution was at the level of workers in enterprise. The stringent labour laws, particularly the 1968 Employment Act and the increase in assembly-line work brought about a growing feeling of anomie and alienation among the workers in Singapore.[9] This could be one reason why in 1978, approximately twenty-five per cent of the labour force was engaged in job hopping.

The government sought to solve this problem by promoting worker identification with enterprises through more vigorous efforts in house unions and joint consultations.

The Second Industrial Revolution

In the late seventies Singapore was facing an acute shortage of labour. This was further aggravated by employers hoarding labour as a hedge against a tightening labour market. Labour productivity was low. Increased protectionism and the lack of demand from the Third World further reduced the competitive position of Singapore's industrial products in the world market. All this called for a change in the government's strategy regarding industrialization.

---

[8] Ministry of Labour Annual Reports.
[9] Frederic C. Deyo, Op. cit. pp. 85-98.

The shift in strategy ushered in the second industrial revolution in 1979. This revised strategy was characterized by the effort to invite foreign capital into high value-added and capital intensive industries, such as, manufacturing of industrial electronic equipment, aircraft components, integrated circuits, computers, industrial robots, and specially pharmaceutical products. The restructuring of the economy, along with the massive efforts to train workers to upgrade their skills was expected to not only lead to an increase in productivity but to realize an equitable sharing of its gains through wages, better working conditions and improved quality of life.

The implementation of this industralization strategy called for planned efforts, on the part of the government, firstly, to manage manpower as well as the management, and secondly, to create an institutional framework which would support its efforts in these two directions.

The Management of Manpower

The circumstances in the late sixties required the NTUC to modernize and win back its membership, however, the eighties compelled the NTUC to transform itself into a technologically-oriented labour movement in order to be relevant for the next twenty years. It is in this context that one should view the appointment of a technocrat as the Secretary-general of the NTUC in 1979. He was given a mandate from the government to reorganize the two omnibus trade unions into nine industry-wide unions and to improve the organizational control by recruiting young scholars and professionals into key policy-making positions. The transformation of the NTUC did not progress well however, mainly because of the leadership style of its technocratic Secretary-general.[10] Policy papers from the Lim Chee Onn elitist team superceded the more traditional, informal way of deliberation and decision-making. Consequently, the union leaders felt that they were left out and displaced by the experts. Their seniority and experience had not been sufficiently appreciated. Lim was capable, but "has not been able to generate that sense of participation, that feeling of belonging to the movement".[11] As a result he was replaced by Ong Teng Cheong

---

[10] Ivan Lim, "The NTUC that is Left Behind", *Straits Times*, April 13, 1983, p. 8.
[11] Prime Minister's May Day address, *Straits Times*, May 2, 1983, p. 8.

because "by temperament and personality, he is more likely to succeed in welding together the professionals and union leaders with a minimum of friction".[12]

The role of the professionals and scholars in a technologically-oriented trade union movement is very vital.[13] This was clearly stated by the Prime Minister: "old guards do deserve respect, the right to consultation, but they have no right of veto for change. The labour movement must continue to adapt to changing circumstances. There is need for recruiting professionals direct into the NTUC to be groomed as leaders, not as back-up experts only because such infusion of fresh talent would only help the NTUC maintain the quality of its leadership and play an equal role in any tripartite consultation of government, unions and management. The professionals, on their part, should develop trust and confidence between themselves and the union grassroot leaders and convince them and the workers that there was an identity of purpose. The young professionals and the old guards must learn to work with each other. There can be no return to the past; you must prepare the workers for the future."

Generally, one can see two distinct stages in the restructuring of the NTUC in gearing the Trade Unions to face the new era of microchips and higher technology. In early 1982, Lim Chee Onn as the chairman of the NTUC Task Force was entrusted with the responsibility of restructuring two of its largest omnibus unions, The Singapore Industrial Labour Organization (SILO) and The Pioneer Industries Employees' Union (PIEU), with a combined strength of 93,000 members into nine national industrial unions. This move would enable the Trade Union officials to acquire specialized knowledge of the industry in its move to higher technology. The NTUC Task Force also undertook the training of Trade Union leaders to develop their expertise in the area of workers' education, retraining, health and safety, productivity, incentives, and collective bargaining. After having made the NWC abandon its conservative policy of the seventies in 1979 in preferance for a liberal wage policy, the government announced in 1982 its intention to play a new role in the NWC.[14] The government announced that it would not play its

---

[12] The Prime Minister's letter to Lim Chee Onn, *Straits Times*, April 13, 1983, p. 1.
[13] All the quotes are from the Prime Minister's May Day address, Op. cit. p. 8.
[14] *Straits Times*, May 18, 1983, p. 14.

role as a third party in its deliberations and negotiations but as employer representative from the public sector. The unions were also told that they would have to bargain over future annual increases in wages instead of looking to the government to settle their differences. The government's firm stand in restoring wages back to collective bargaining was further evidenced by its new policy to encourage employers and unions to negotiate wage settlements even before the announcement of NWC guidelines for the year. The new feature was that unions and employers were to be encouraged to work out sectoral wage increase guidelines which would reflect more accurately the performance, productivity and profitability of individual industries. Other developments further affirmed the government policy of restoring the unions the right to bargain directly with the employers on wages, hours, and other terms and conditions of employment. They include:

1. The active support given to unions to negotiate even a twelve-hour shift with reduced work week in some organizations;
2. The proposal to reduce the extent of state welfarism and switch over to company welfarism through a reduction of the employer's contribution to the central provident fund; and
3. The establishment in the Ministry of Labour of a preventive mediation machinery whereby its industrial relations officers would monitor work place relations through close rapport with management and union. This ministry was given the task of identifying and diffusing potential conflict and promoting a problem-solving approach to resolving differences.

As a consequence of this clearly enunciated policy, it was not surprising that the parties began equipping themselves to face the realities of the bargaining table. The NTUC conducted a three-day seminar in 1982 for 150 union officials with the help of a West German expert on how to fully prepare for wage negotiations.[15] Following the West-German model, the NTUC is already working on creating an institution to provide specialist backup service to union negotiators on matters such as precedents and cases to help deal with current issues. The secretariats of economic affairs and of industrial information/statistics jointly compiled

---

[15] *Straits Times*, Sept. 14, 1982, p. 9.

information on the economy, productivity, wages and fringe benefits to help unions negotiate objectively. The Singapore National Employers' Federation launched, in April 1983, a 143-hour certificate course over a period of five months followed by a six-week attachment programme with the Federation.[16] This course was meant to train managers who were new to industrial relations in grievance-handling, dispute settlement and collective bargaining. Based on these facts, it is safe to conclude that the government policy had set the stage for union management relationship, on a basis of free but mature collective bargaining on the terms and conditions of employment in Singapore.

The culmination of these efforts was the 1982 amendment to the Trade Union Act, 1941. Although the new Act has not denied the unions their right to strike, it redefines the basic role of trade unions as the promotion of good industrial relations between workers and employers, in contrast to the existing key objective of promoting, organizing and financing strikes. Under the new Act, trade unions will primarily be concerned with improving working conditions, and the economic and social status of workers and raising productivity.[17]

The second shift in the government policy of restructuring the trade union movement was evident in early 1982 whereby a proposal was made to split the large industrial unions into smaller house unions. This latter restructuring could, for several reasons, be interpreted as a reversal of the earlier. To begin with, it might have been prompted by the unwillingness of foreign capital to flow into the new industries until a more favourable industrial relations climate could be ensured. Undoubtedly Singapore has been recognized as a haven for foreign investment on the basis of the past experiences of foreign investors.[18] However, powerful industrial unions exercising free collective bargaining were a threat to foreign investment in high technology industries where capital expenditure is enormous. This could be the underlying reason why several American companies have been allowed to

---

[16] *Straits Times*, April 1-2, 1983.
[17] *Straits Times*, Editorial, Sept. 27, 1982, p. 14.
[18] *Straits Times*, April 9, 1983, p. 1. The Association of Risk Analysts, New York, on the basis of a survey of 100 of the 'Fortune 500' companies, listed Singapore among the top five countries as a safe haven for investment because of her political stability.

operate without unions for a fixed period of years.[19]

On the other hand, this shift toward house unions might have been prompted by a genuine attempt on the part of the government to overcome the problem of anomie and alienation among Singapore workers. House unions are more effective in promoting joint consultation[20] between workers and employers in order to encourage commitment on the part of workers to work and be loyal to their enterprises. In comparision, industry-wide unions pull worker loyalties away from their own companies.

The restructuring of industry-wide unions into house unions was recommended by the committee on productivity in June 1981 to help workers identify with the company and its future.[21] This will make it easier for workers to accept changes such as job enlargement, job redesign and multi-functional assignments. Again it was the Committee on Productivity that recommended work excellence committees or Quality Control Circles as a tool of joint consultation between workers and management, with the support of the unions. The government promptly acted on these recommendations.

As a result of recommendation of the twenty-member study team to Japan, an advisory committee was formed in 1983 to promote joint consultation at national level and monitor and advise on such activities.[22] It is on the initiative of the advisory body that the tripartite convention on Joint Consultation through Work Excellence[23] was organized, to promote joint consultation at

---

[19] The Prime Minister's May Day address. Op. cit. p. 1. "Several American companies have invested in Singapore only if they are allowed to operate without unions. And we have agreed, giving them a fixed period of years without unions. And if enlightened, management can persuade their workers that they do not need unions to defend them from abuses by management, I say, good for them."

[20] *Straits Times,* April 11, 1983. Joint consultation currently advocated in Singapore is a concept developed in Japan, and it is a forum for discussing anything relating to the well-being of the company and its employees, except collective bargaining.

[21] *Report of the Committee on Productivity.* National Productivity Board, Singapore, 1981, pp. 14.

[22] *Straits Times,* May 1, 1983. The idea of introducing joint consultation in Singapore became a reality only after the NPB led a twenty-member study team to Japan. The advisory body created, on its recommendation, comprised representatives from the Ministry of Labour, the Singapore National Employers' Federation, the National Productivity Board, and the NTUC.

[23] *Straits Times,* May 1, 1983.

all levels of the organization. The convention recommended companies to form a steering committee of labour and management representatives to spearhead the drive towards joint consultation in the organizations.

It soon became evident that the government's long-term policy and objective was to make the house union the union of the future in Singapore. It was made clear that the breaking up of unions into smaller outfits was in line with the industrial policy of promoting good industrial relations, improving working conditions, enhancing the economic and social status of workers and raising productivity. And, since house unions call for more experienced labour leaders, the NTUC had to identify and train the natural leaders at grassroot levels to take on greater responsibilities.

The second phase of the restructuring of unions started in October 1982 when several thousand workers in two companies, Metal Box and Jurong Shipyard, took a major step to organize the workers into house unions. Until then, the majority of workers were organized into industry-wide craft or occupational unions. Subsequently house unions were organized in the Post Office Savings Bank, Telecoms Board and the National Iron and Steel. The NTUC in its ten-year plan committed itself, among other things, to create model house unions in the public sector and to promote joint consultation with management through work improvement programmes.[24]

The tough line taken by the Secretary-General in the recent British Petroleum episode where leaders of the industry-wide union were contemplating disciplinary action against those who were trying to form a house union clearly spelt out the NTUC policy that it would not tolerate any obstacle to free and voluntary formation of house unions.[25]

At the same time both the Prime Minister, and subsequently the Secretary-General, allayed the fears of unionists against any possible exploitation of smaller unions by management by assuring them that NTUC and the Ministry of Labour would closely monitor the relationship for sometime and "if necessary, intervene".[26]

---

[24] *Straits Times*, April 21, 1983, pp. 12.
[25] *Straits Times*, July 30, 1983. Also *Straits Times*, July 19, 1983. Ivan Lim. "Dissenters of British Petroleum Press for a House Union". pp 11.
[26] The Prime Minister's May Day address, Op. cit. p. 8.

Perhaps in this context, we may understand the complementary change in government policy regarding its role in the new style National Wage Council (NWC). The government is not going to abdicate its role as a third party because (according to the chairman of NWC) both unions and employers in the NWC are against the government leaving the NWC — the government should not just play the role of an employer in the NWC; it has an important supportive role to play. "The NWC remains a tripartite partnership, except that the government representatives try to keep a low profile. this is the essence of the new style."[27]

The reorganization of the trade union structure was but one step in the plan to transform the NTUC into a technologically-oriented labour movement. More importantly, it has been assigned the more significant role of changing the attitude of workers to education, training and productivity, as well as their attitude towards their company and enterprise. To quote the Prime Minister, "they must be positive and cooperative, and not negative and antogonistic. The 'them' and 'us' division between workers and management must disappear. The NTUC must convince our workers that if the company they work for fails, then their interests must suffer; that if their company succeeds, they will be better off in term of job security, pay and fringe benefits."[28]

Generally speaking, the government strategy to manage manpower was directed at educating and training the labour force and to make workers perceive the immediate relevance of such education and training in order to promote their personal gains through increases in productivity. Many programmes and efforts established to prepare the labour force to meet the demands of higher technology are treated with high regard. Some of these are, the NTUC. Basic Education for Skills Training (BEST) programme launched in 1983, to teach basic skills in literacy and numeracy to the 600,000 workers in the labour force;[29] the establishment of the VITB in 1979 for vocational training in commerce and industry; the creation of the National Computer Board to oversee computer training; and the expansion of facilities and intake in the tertiary educational institutions,

---

[27] Straits Times, May 18, 1983, pp. 14. "What is New in the New Style NWC."
[28] The Prime Minister's May Day address, Op. cit.
[29] Straits Times, Aug. 12, 1982, pp. 13.

particularly for technical, engineering and managerial manpower. Since most of the statutory bodies are tripartite, and advisory bodies and councils have labour representation, the NTUC continues to have an indirect role in all efforts.

Promotion of productivity consciousness among workers and the general population is an integral part of the government strategy. Among the efforts undertaken for this promotion are, the National Productivity Board (NPB) with its three advisory committees on Safety, Health and Training, and Consultancy; the publication by NPB of a Productivity newsletter and the creation of the National Productivity Council with a commitment to create productivity consciousness among the various sections of the populaion within a time-frame. The productivity month launched in April 1983 with "Teamy" as the mascot was followed by another spectacular promotional effort in November 1983.

Finally, special mention must be made of the efforts aided by the NPB to include the Human Relations Programme in the National University of Singapore and the government effort to introduce Confucian ethics in the school curriculum to develop "good" work values among future workers and to contribute to the stability of society.

The Management of Management

In managing management, the focus of the government effort is to change the attitude of management towards labour in line with its policy of promoting house unions and joint consultation — the two key components of the emerging new industrial climate of Singapore.

The need for a fundamental change in management attitude has been expressed by the president of the NTUC soon after the tripartite convention on joint consultation. He criticised the negative attitude of management towards many aspects of the government strategy to promote healthy industrial relations in Singapore. He especially highlighted:
- (1) statutory contributions like CPF and the Skills Development Fund (SDF);
- (2) company welfarism;
- (3) Singapore workers compared to workers from non-traditional sources;
- (4) job-hopping; and

(5) joint consultation and the poor response to the BEST programs.[30]

It was significant that Mr Lim Chee Onn, at the tripartite convention on joint-consultation, emphasized the need for top management commitment to make joint consultation successful in Singapore[31]. Another reminder made to management was that smaller house unions were created to foster a spirit of teamwork and cooperation, not for exploitation of labour by management. It is not surprising that the Prime Minister went to the extent of cautioning recalcitrant management by saying, "if there are managers who do not realize what the change is for, both the NTUC and the Labour Ministry will intervene".[32]

Finally, in its efforts to manage management the government diligently plays the role of a model employer to publicly demonstrate that it practices what it preaches to others. We have already noted the successful efforts of the NTUC in starting house unions in the public sector and to promote joint consultation through work improvement programmes. The government is effectively playing this role by computerizing public sector operations, training and upgrading the skills of employees and even in accommodating part-time workers to meet the shortage of personnel. Moreover, salaries and working conditions have been revised and work improvement committees formed to help develop and retain an elite corps of administrators. Similarly, the starting of house unions and joint consultation machineries in the public sector, such as, shipyards, the Post Office Savings Bank, serve as gentle reminders to all workers, union leaders and management in the private sector that they cannot postpone the introduction of these Japanese innovations necessary for the restructuring of the economy in the years to come. On this point, the Prime Minister asserted that the Japanese managers have already demonstrated that higher productivity can be achieved even with British, American and Australian workers. He also stressed that many American companies which have employee-centred management like IBM, Texas Instruments, Hewlett Packard, and General Electric are highly successful. They have

---

[30] Press conference given by the president of NTUC, Mr. Vincent, *Straits Times,* Sept. 18, 1982.
[31] Report On the proceedings of the Tripartite Convention, *Straits Times,* May 1, 1983.
[32] May Day address, Op. cit.

excellent relations between management and workers and highly motivated and involved workers.[33]

Conclusion

I have discussed the strategy of the Singapore government to manage manpower as well as management with the aid of the organizational arrangements in order to pave the way for the second industrial revolution in Singapore. Whether or not such efforts will succeed in effectively integrating the Japanese innovations of house unions and joint consultation into the social fabric of Singapore is a matter for further analysis and debate. It is hoped that others, especially sociologists, would take an active part too.

However, there is much truth in the government's assertion that involvement in work and loyalty to the enterprise are necessary for organizational success, especially in high technology industries. This is testified by many positive outcomes of organizations following the Japanese management practices of total commitment to the development of its human resources and the establishment of collaborative and participative systems within the organization.[34] In his book, *Theory Z,* Ouchi explains how Theory Z organizations (modified American organizations) adapted Japanese management practices to suit the needs of the American society. The ideal type Z combines a basic cultural commitment to individualistic values with a highly collective, non-individual pattern of interaction. It simultaneously satisfies old norms of independence and present needs for affiliation. The traditional sources of affiliation in the American society have been the family, the church, the neighbourhood, the voluntary association and the long-term friendships. But urbanisation and geographic mobility have weakened these sources of affiliation. This gives rise to the anomie problem. When workers have unfulfilled needs for affiliation, they will experience anomie, the sensation that there are no anchor in life, no standards, and thus a feeling of being lost. It is interesting that traditionally the 'A' organization has included only a segment of the husband, in a sense leaving the rest of his family. Japanese organizations (J type) have integrated the workers with the organization leaving his

---

[33] *Ibid.*
[34] William G. Ouchi. *Theory Z.* New York: Avon Books, 1982.

family untouched because families in Japanese culture have deep rooted associational anchorage. But the Type Z organization, by contrast, includes the husband and his nuclear family in the organization. That means family members regularly interact with other organizational members and their families and feel an identification with the organization.

Another major adaption in Type Z organizations is that decision-making is consensual and in these companies there is often a highly self-conscious attempt to preserve the consensual mode. However, it is still the individual who is ultimately the decision-maker and responsibility remains individual. This procedure puts a strain on the individual and this is sought to be mitigated by modifying the type 'A' arrangement of immediate evaluation and rapid promotion by evaluating performance against explicit performance measures (not a J type practice) over a period of time (a J type practice)."[35]

One can argue that the concept of work organization providing a total associational tie for the worker and his family is not a Japanese idea. After all the military in every country in peace time provides this kind of total associational anchorage to uprooted families.

Ideally, "communitism" as opposed to individualism, as the ethos of a society, sustains these management practices more effectively. According to Dr Wong Kwei Cheong, Head of the National Productivity Board (NPB), "communitism is a natural moral value that Singaporeans already have. Traditionally such moral values have been passed down through word of mouth by our parents. We practice them unconsciously. Now we need to bring them to our consciousness, to build up this group system of togetherness and communitism."[36]

This will take time. Perhaps President Devan Nair is more realistic when he said that "the achievement of higher productivity will depend on the acquisition of new and positive work habits, which will call for an attitudinal revolution, not only throughout

---

[36] Dr Wong Kwei Cheong, "Link Between Moral Values and Productivity", *The Singapore Monitor*, Jan 26, 1983.

Perhaps Dr Wong was encouraged to hold this view on the basis of Prof. Fujita's observation, "After all, the Japanese management system and culture are based on Chinese culture. The five Confucian virtues of benevolence, righteousness, courtesy, wisdom and trustworthiness are the focal points from which not only Japanese culture but also traditional Chinese culture has sprung. The Japanese have merely adapted the Chinese culture to evolve a style of their own".

the labour-management spectrum, but in society as a whole. This attitudinal revolution must involve a total social and cultural effort, beginning with family units, continuing in schools, junior colleges, on into national service and in tertiary institutions. Thus ideally, a young person who begins his or her working life should already have been equipped educationally and psychologically to work as a member of a large team. But this will take a generation or so . . ."[37]

To conclude, when such a re-awakening or re-eduction takes place it will not be surprising to find future generations of students of industrial relations restating the common ideology of the Singapore Industrial Relations System to that of "an open society committed to industralization in a spirit of cooperation in union-management relations".

QUESTIONS

1. "Legislation in the domain of labour-management relations has amply aided the PAP effort at industralization of Singapore". Discuss.
2. What are the steps taken by the PAP and the NTUC to change the attitude of Singapore workers to meet the challenges of technology in the years to come?
3. Explain the significance of the symbiotic relationship between the PAP and the NTUC with regard to industrial relations in Singapore.
   or
   Attempt to predict the probability of success of the PAP effort at a second industrial revolution, analyzing the strength and weaknesses of its strategies and policies.

---

[37] *Straits Times,* April 1, 1982, pp. 4. For more information about the normative re-educative strategy see Robert Chin and Kenneth D. Benne, "General Strategies for Effecting Changes in Human Systems", in the *Planning of Change,* Warren G. Bennis, et. al. New York: Holt, Rinehart and Winston, 1976.

REFERENCES

Chalmers, Ellison W. "Crucial Issues in Industrial Relations in Singapore". Singapore: Donald Moore Press, 1969.

Deyo, C. Frederic. "Dependent Development and Industrial Order: An Asian Case Study". New York: Praeger, 1981.

Dunlop, T. John. "Industrial Relations Systems". New York: Holt, Rinehart, 1958.

Jayakumar, S. (ed.). "Our Heritage and Beyond", NTUC Singapore, 1982.

Legget, C., Wong, Evelyn, and Ariff, Mohammed. "Technological Change and Industrial Relations In Singapore", in Bamber, G., and Lansbury, R. 1983 (Ed) Bulletin No 12 Technolgical Change and Industrial Relations, Deventer, Holland: Kluwer.

Nair, C.V. Devan. "Not By Wages Alone", NTUC Singapore 1982.

Pang Eng Fong and Tan Chwee Huat. "Trade Unions and Industrial Relations", in Peter S.J. Chen (ed.), *Singapore Development Policies and Trends*. Singapore: Oxford University Press, 1983.

Pang Eng Fong and Leonard Cheng. "Changing Patterns of Industrial Relations in Singapore", in *The Role of Trade Unions in Developing Societies*, E. Kassalov and G. Damachi (ed.), London: Macmillan, 1977.

Wong, Evelyn, Sue. "Industrial Relations in Singapore — Challenge of the 1980s", Department of Business administration, National University of Singapore, Singapore Occasional Papers, No. 27, Sept. 1982.

"Why Labour Must Go Modern", NTUC Singapore, 1970.

7
Organizational Structure and Human Resource Development

EDITH C. YUEN

SUMMARY

This chapter considers the need for human resource development from the perspective of environmental demands on organizations. Included in the chapter are discussions on the influence of the environment on organizational structure and the human resource development implications of different structural types. The pattern of industrial development in Singapore and the kind of environment local industries are likely to face are also considered.

The Pattern of Industrial Development

In his thesis on the international division of labour, Wallerstein suggested that while advanced industrial societies tend to monopolize the kind of production which involves advanced technology, sophisticated skills and intensive capital investment, underdeveloped countries typically engage in labour intensive production which uses low-technology with low-skill requirements. As a country advances in the course of industrialization and joins the central league of developed countries, it gradually sheds low-technology, labour-intensive industries and adopts capital-intensive, high-technology industries. An interesting example of such a pattern of development is the textile/clothing industry. The production of textile goods is labour-intensive and does not involve advanced technology. The textile industry was one of the important industries in Britain in the early days of the industrial revolution. In the fifties and early sixties, Japan was one of the chief producers of textile goods and this role was then taken over by developing countries like Hong Kong, Taiwan and South Korea. At the moment, Hong Kong has moved "up-market" specializing in quality fashion garments and South Korea has diversified into heavy industries. In turn, developing countries like Sri Lanka, Malaysia, People's Republic of China and Algeria compete for the market.

While Wallerstein tried to explain this phenomenon of international division of labour in terms of a system of exploitation of the underdeveloped and developing countries by the developed ones (the one-way channelling of wealth from the peripheral to the centre), it is also possible to explain the pattern of development in purely economic terms.

Typically, underdeveloped and developing countries with low-living standards and education have an abundant supply of cheap, unskilled labour. Given also their lack of capital and technological know-how, it is logical that at their early stage of industrial development, they turn to industries which utilize their pool of cheap labour but which do not require much in terms of capital investment and/or technological know-how.

In labour-intensive industries, developing countries, with their cheap labour can produce at a fraction of the production cost of developed countries. With a large number of nations seeking to develop similar industries, keen competition forces the market value of the products down. For the advanced developed countries, given their high-labour cost, profit margins in these industries are gradually eroded. Should they continue to invest in these industries, their labour value and subsequently standard of living will have to be reduced.

Industries which utilize sophisticated technology and involve intensive capital investment do not face this dilemma. The value-added per worker in these industries is high and the higher salaries demanded by workers in developed nations can be afforded without making profit margins untenable. In consequence, large companies in developed countries establish subsidiaries in underdeveloped countries to tap their pool of cheap labour; while at home they concentrate on industries which involve high technology. Thus, while it is possible to explain the pattern of industrial development in terms of a system of exploitation, it is equally possible to suggest that developing countries have been forced out of labour-intensive, low-technology industries by market factors, perhaps against their own wishes.

It is not difficult to fit Singapore into this pattern of development. While the cost of unskilled and semi-skilled labour in Singapore is still low in comparison with those in developed countries like the United States, Japan and Australia, it is relatively high in comparison to wages in underdeveloped countries. In order to maintain a dynamic and viable industrial/manufacturing sector, Singapore has no alternative but to move to higher value-added, less labour-intensive industries.

This has indeed been the manifest policy of the Singapore government. Generally speaking, the policy is to move towards:
(1) the production of high quality, reliable products rather than cheap, unreliable ones in large quantities. Once again, this is because the value-added per worker for quality products is higher;
(2) production involving high technology;
(3) commercial services that require little physical handling of materials and resources.

Based on the general trend of development of industrial countries, it can be assumed that this is likely to be the direction of industrial development in Singapore in the near future. An analysis of the kind of environment which Singapore industries are likely to operate in will be discussed. However, it would first be necessary to introduce the variables used for the analysis of organizational environments.

The Analysis of Organizational Environment

Since the introduction of the open system view in the late fifties and early sixties, it has been commonly recognized that in order for organizations to be successful, managers must be able to structure their organizations in a manner best fitting a variety of environmental factors as well as fitting the requirements of their production technology.

An important piece of research which contributed significantly to this contingency approach to organizational design was a study by Burns and Stalker. The authors introduced a dichotomatic classification of organizational structures — mechanistic and organic — a classification which is still much in use today. The first type of organizational structure, the mechanistic structure, represents the traditional bureaucratic form with a high degree of specialization and centralization of decision making. Organizational members perform clearly defined tasks and are given specific goals to achieve. Such a structure typically has many hierarchical levels and vertical command is emphasized. The second organic type stresses horizontal communication and decentralized decision making. Not only are members involved in diffuse task activities, they are also responsible for planning and coordinating their activities to achieve organizational objectives. Organic structures tend to have fewer hierarchical levels and the span of control is usually wider. The two organization types represent the two extremes of a continuum of organizational design and organizations can be described as more or less organic/mechanistic.

What Burns and Stalker found in an analysis of twenty manufacturing firms in Britain was that each of these structural types can be successful in a different environment. An organic structure is more flexible and adaptable and can cope with a rapidly changing environment better whereas the bureaucratic, mechanistic type with its uniform procedures, provides administrative/productive efficiency in servicing large numbers. Hence it is particularly suitable in an environment of relative stability.

Subsequent research by Lawrence and Lorsch took the contingency approach even further. In their research across many industries, the authors found that even within the same organization, different departments face different environmental demands and people in different units acquire different orientations towards time, interpersonal relations and goals. These differences in orientations are in turn manifest in behavioural patterns as well as in structural forms. Thus, successful Research and Development (R & D) departments are typically organic in structure; production departments tend to adopt the mechanistic design whereas marketing departments usually lie between the two.

To help managers choose the appropriate structural type for their organizations, Schermerhorn, Hunt and Osborn suggest the use of environmental complexity and technology as the key contingency variables.

Environmental Complexity

In their analysis of organizational environment, the authors made a distinction between the general environment (which includes cultural values, economic conditions, legal-political conditions and educational conditions) and the specific environment. It is the specific environment which has more direct relevance to organizational structure. The term "specific environment" is used to refer to "the network of suppliers, distributors, government agencies and competitors with which an organization must interact to grow and survive".

The basic question in analyzing the specific environment of an organization is its complexity. "Environmental complexity" is a measure of the magnitude of the problems and opportunities in the organization's environment. Generally speaking, the more complex an environment is, the more responsive, innovative and adaptable an organization has to be. Environmental complexity is measured by the degree of richness, interdependence and uncertainty of a specific environment.

The specific environment is rich when a firm's suppliers, distributors, competitors and regulators are growing in numbers and resources. In a rich environment, opportunities abound, competition is keen, and change rapid.

Interdependence refers to the network of relationships which exists between an organization and outside groups. The critical question in such relationships is whether an organization is in a dependent position or whether it has the upper hand. If it is in control of its relationships with outside groups (for example, a company which produces its raw materials and is in monopolistic control of the market), it can afford to be less responsive to its environment.

The degree of environmental uncertainty is another critical factor. In a rapidly changing environment, investment, production technology, the market, etc., may be outmoded in a relatively short period of time and the successful management of such uncertainties is important for the continual survival of an organization. There is little disagreement among research findings that rigid bureaucratic structures are particularly vulnerable when dealing with a high degree of environmental uncertainty.

The degree of uncertainty, richness and interdependence provide a good indicator of environmental complexity. Generally speaking, the greater the richness, interdependence and uncertainty, the greater the environmental complexity.

The degree of environmental complexity affects an organization in two important ways: it affects the stability of its production goals and the stability of its production technology. (Production technology will be dealt with in greater detail later).

The Environment of Singapore Industries

While the political, social and economic conditions which an organization has to tackle are largely pre-determined and few organizations have the power or the resources to change them, organizations can in fact have substantial choice over its specific environment. An organization can choose the industry it moves into, the kind of products it specializes in; whether to emphasize on quality or quantity; the kind of market/clients it caters for. In fact, one of the key functions of managers is to make these strategic decisions. Thus the policy of the Singapore government to move into high technology and high value-added industries, to emphasize on manufacturing quality products has certain implications on the kind of environment which Singapore industries are likely to operate in.

Singapore as a Producing Nation

As a producing nation, Singapore is highly dependent on other countries. Being relatively deficient in natural resources, it has to rely on other countries for the supply of fuel and other raw materials. The need to import almost all the raw materials adds an element of uncertainty to the production process; there are problems of supply and reliability of supply, problems of organizing and scheduling the freight and delivery of the raw materials, etc. In some industries, it may be necessary to order supplies half a year in advance.

Given the need to pay for the import of raw materials and for products which Singapore does not produce and given the size of the local market, manufacturing industries in Singapore have to be export-oriented. In order to export to overseas markets, local organizations have to adhere to foreign government policies, regulations and quotas. Thus, in relation to its markets, Singapore does not have the upper hand.

In addition to being dependent on other countries for both raw materials and markets, Singapore has to depend on advanced industrial nations for the transfer of technology. The inability of a small nation to provide adequate resources, incentives and opportunities for research and development means that Singapore does not have an upper hand as far as this particular aspect is concerned. Singapore has to attract foreign firms with the technological know-how to produce in Singapore or to get them involved in joint ventures with local companies. To achieve this, it has to provide attractive investment terms to these companies.

The Move to High Technology

The picture presented about low-technology, labour-intensive industries was one of stiff competition between underdeveloped, developing and, to a certain extent, developed nations. It would be naive to assume that competition in high-technology industries is any less keen. The nature of competition, however, is different. Competition in labour-intensive industries using established technology is mainly along one major dimension — that of cutting labour cost. Innovative designs to make the products more attractive and marketing skills are the other dimensions of competition, but in view of the relative simplicity of the techniques involved, a lower-cost competitor can rapidly catch up with the product and market leaders.

Competition in high-technology industries is more dynamic and multi-dimensional. One factor which affects both the degree and the nature of competition is that competitors in high-technology industries are quite different from those in low-technology industries. In high-technology industries, Singapore will be competing with countries which have a lot of resources, experience, skills in aggressive marketing, and facilities to promote research and development. Competition with countries like Japan or the United States is quite a different matter from competition with underdeveloped or developing countries.

In high-technology industries, the major concern is not so much that of cutting labour costs as catching up with the rapid pace of innovation and technological developments. When the potential profit for innovative products is hugh, companies plough millions of dollars into research and development. An example is the electronics industry. The average amount spent by companies on research and development is 5-6 per cent of their total revenue. Companies which are anxious to maintain their lead in the market spend even more.

The lure of success and money attracts people with brains, innovative ideas and preserverence into the "modern gold rush". The electronics industry is crowded with major manufacturers with hugh research and development departments, small companies on the make, and inventors and researchers with venture capital support. They all compete to beat the others in introducing innovative products, to improve on the quality, reliability and/or compactness of their products through better technical designs, to introduce alternative technology or to cut costs by using technologically sophisticated components.

Examples of such technological competition abound in recent years. Products that come immediately to mind are pocket calculators, digital watches and personal computers. While pocket calculators have become increasingly compact, they perform more and more functions at the same time. Reliability has generally been improved and the price of these products has declined sharply as they come to be retailed in chain stores and supermarkets.

A more interesting example of competition in high-technology industries is that of the video-cassette recorder. Back in 1972, Philips introduced the world's first video-cassette recorder. However, even before the general public became familiar with the notion of videotape recording, Japan's Sony Corp. introduced the Betamax, a three-hour playing recorder which allows copies of television programmes or tapes of movies to be played on the T.V. screen. They achieved monopolistic control of the market almost immediately. Two years later, Matsushita announced a cheaper recorder that worked on a rival technology, known as VHS. This used different size tapes and made recordings for up to six hours. Matsushita then outmaneuvered Sony by adding extra features to its recorders and by concluding marketing pacts with companies such as RCA and General Electric. By 1978, barely three years after Betamax hit the market, Matsushita's VHS recorders out-marketed Betamax by about 6 per cent in the United States. Sony later improved the Betamax, but the company never regained its dominant position. In 1983, VHS recorders captured 75 per cent of the American market while Betamax had only 25 per cent.

The sheer number of competitors with hugh financial backing provides the major push behind the astonishing pace of technological innovation. Involvement in high technology industries can be rewarding but risky. "Front end" costs in R & D, in obtaining and training technical personnel are high, and switching out of outdated methods into new ones is as commercially difficult as it is technologically necessary.

While Singapore will not be competing with Japan, America, Germany, etc., at the research and development level, local manufacturers still have to tackle the rapid pace of technological innovation. Producers catering for high-technology industries (for example those involved in the production of semiconductors or printed circuit boards) have to monitor new developments in their areas closely.

An important implication for organizations which operate in high-technology industries is that they cannot count on manufacturing similar products using the same established technology year after year. Products such as tissue paper, bedsheets, kitchen utensils and baby clothing have a steady and stable market. Changes in product design are usually minor and require little change in production machinery and technology. For companies which produce newly developed products using high technology, the situation is quite different.

In terms of environmental complexity, the environment of the manufacturing industries in Singapore in the near future is likely to be complex. As a producing nation, Singapore is dependent on other nations and does not have the upper hand in its relationships with other organizations. The decision to adopt advanced technology and to move into high-technology industries means that the organizations involved will have to operate in an environment which is high along both the richness and uncertainty dimensions. While an environment which is complex along any one of these dimensions is difficult to manage, the combined effect of all three renders Singapore particularly vulnerable.

Implications for the Design of Organizational Structure and HRM

As mentioned before, the degree of environmental complexitiy affects the stability of an organization's production goals and the stability of its production technology. Both these factors have direct relevance to the choice of organizational structure.

Mechanistic Structures and their HRM Implications

Research on organizational structure suggests that an organization which has clear long-term production objectives and which utilizes a stable production technology tends to be more successful when it adopts a rigid mechanistic structure. The mechanistic design is based on two organizing principles: the extensive application of the principle of division of labour, and the separation of planning and coordination from actual production operation. Examples of mechanistic design include government bureaucracies, university and hospital administrative departments and in industries, assembly lines.

The advantage of a mechanistic structure is its productive and administrative efficiency. The centralization of planning and coordination at the top together with the extensive division of labour and standardization enable jobs at the bottom of the bureaucratic hierarchy to be designed in such a way that little skill is required in task performance — a process which Braverman referred to as de-skilling. Productive efficiency is achieved through a high degree of specialization and the extensive use of cheap, unskilled or semi-skilled workers in the production process.

Such a structure requires a high degree of formalization. It is necessary to provide the workers who may not understand the logic behind the design of their jobs with detailed instructions. In addition, since the goals and activities of individual workers are specific and often mutually exclusive, coordination has to be provided by managers at the top and this is achieved in mechanistic organizations through a complicated system of rules, regulations and procedures. The abundance of formal rules and procedures is an outstanding characteristic of mechanistic structures.

Communication in mechanistic organizations is typically one-way — from top to bottom and is usually in the form of orders and instructions. Further, in view of the critical function performed by top management in synchronizing the large number of highly differentiated activities, it is hardly surprising that heavy emphasis is placed on the absolute nature of position-based authority.

While the main weakness of a mechanistic structure is its rigidity and consequently, its inability to be responsive to environmental changes, this is also the source of its strength. In a stable environment when both production goals and production technology are highly stable, mechanistic structures have definite advantages over other forms of organizational design.

The adoption of a mechanistic structure has certain human resource implications. While top managers in such organizations have to carry the responsibility of "making the system work" and are handsomely rewarded for their performance, those at lower levels in the organizational hierarchy are supposed to be conformers and followers. They are supposed to take orders with demure obedience and follow rules and regulations without questioning either their purpose or the need for their existence. In evaluating the performance of a subordinate, emphasis is laid on whether the target/quota set for him by the management has been met or not. Loyalty is measured in terms of "fitting in" the system and not "making trouble" and innovative ideas to change the system are more often than not, conceived of as "rocking the boat". No wonder bureaucratic/mechanistic structures are often accused of stifling individual initiatives.

There are two reasons why such a system is unable to cope with unpredictable changes. First, organizational members are not oriented to change, and second, even if top management diagnoses a need for change, the system as well as its personnel are too rigid. The parts in a mechanistic structure are like bricks in a building, each of which has been fitted into a particularly position in the overall structure and held in place in relation to the other parts by a system of rules, procedures, and routines. To change such a system, one has to change the structure as well as the system of rules and procedures before remoulding the human parts. A major change is often a painful process in such an organization and often managers opt for minor readjustments.

The HRM Implications of Organic Structures

By contrast, an organic structure is more flexible but more expensive to operate. Hence, it is less efficient. The essential feature of an organic system is the relatively high degree of decentralization. Unlike their counterparts in the mechanistic system, members in an organic structure do not perform highly structured or clear-cut tasks. Their duties are less specific and more diffused. they are responsible for planning their activities so as to contribute to the attainment of organizational objectives and to coordinate their activities with those of other organizational members. Given the nature of individual tasks, an organic structure has fewer levels in its organizational hierarchy and a much smaller number of formal rules and regulations. In addition to two-way communication between superiors and subordinates, advice and information flow laterally as well. The flexibility of such an organization comes from the organizational members. Not only are they more flexible as individual parts — they can perform a wider range of duties, they contribute to the decision-making and coordination processes and can help facilitate changes as well.

The key to the successful operation of an organic system lies not in its structure, but in its human resources. In a decentralized system, many of the skills required only by top managers in a traditional mechanistic organization, are now required by people further down in the organizational hierarchy. An inventory of such skills includes:

(1) The ability to communicate effectively not only with other organizational members, but also with clients and other organizations.

(2) The ability to work effectively in groups as in an organic structure, team-work is important. Inevitably, people have to work in teams to design and implement change programmes.

(3) The ability to coordinate. With the relative lack of structure and coordinating mechanisms in an organic structure, organizational members have to take up more responsibility of coordination.

(4) The ability to lead and to influence. Since authority in an organic structure is less position-based, individual members have to understand more about the influence process.

(5) Skills in conflict management. As change often upsets the existing patterns of resource, power and/or influence distribution in an organization, a major change often causes conflicts. The ability to resolve conflicts, to channel the energy aroused in a conflict situation into constructive use, to prevent destructive conflicts are important skills to be mastered by managers and subordinates alike in an organic organization.

(6) Motivational skills. In a mechanistic/bureaucratic structure, minimum required behaviours are clearly set out in job descriptions and production quotas. Managers plan on the assumption that organizational members will only try to achieve the specified minimum (a pattern of behaviour described by Herbert Simon as "satisficing"). An organic structure relies on individual initiative and a high level of employee motivation for its success. Superiors have to apply both intrinsic and extrinsic rewards effectively to motivate their subordinates.

Apparently, the need for structural flexibility varies among high-technology industries. Even within an organization, the need varies between different units and departments.

However, if Singapore is to emphasize manufacturing quality products, even the production departments (which generally, are the most mechanistic) cannot be too mechanistic. In order to turn out reliable products of high quality, it is essential that the workers involved in the production process, that is, subordinates at the very bottom of the organizational hierarchy, are at least reasonably motivated, satisfied with their jobs and are responsible. It is also important to allow the workers a certain amount of discretion in task performance and to encourage horizontal communication between units and departments at lower levels. The structural and associated motivational differences between a highly mechanistic structure and a more decentralized one are often highlighted by the differences between the much publicized Volvo and Saab production systems and that of General Motors at Lordstown.

Conclusions

More out of necessity than by choice, Singapore plans to adopt advanced technology and to move into high-technology industries. The kind of environment which the manufacturing industries will operate in is likely to be more uncertain. To be successful in such an environment, the organizations involved have to be more innovative and flexible.

While providing organizational members with a higher level of education, and more advanced technical training will no doubt improve the flexibility of the overall system, this alone is not enough to cope with a turbulent environment. The organizations involved will have to adopt a more flexible structure and emphasize human resource development.

QUESTIONS

1. What are the differences between an organic and a mechanistic type structure? What are the human resource implications of these two structural types?
2. Describe how you as a manager might function in an organic organization. What might your day be like? Consider whether you might feel better or worse operating in a mechanistic structure.
3. Using the oil refinery and electronic industries as examples, describe the kind of environment which companies in these two industries have to face and comment on the amount of structural flexibility required.

REFERENCES

Burns, T. and Stalker, G. M. *The Management of Innovation*. London: Tavistock, 1961.

Braverman, H., *Labor and Monopoly Capital*. Monthly Review Press, 1974.

Lawrence, P. R., and Lorsch, J.W., *Organization and Environment: Managing Differentiation and Integration*. Boston: Harvard Business School, 1967.

Moritz, M., "Max Trouble for Betamax", *Time,* Jan. 16, 1984. Tagliabue, J., "If you can't beat them, join them", *Business Times,* Jan. 17, 1984.

Schermerhorn, J. R., Hunt, J. G. and Osborn, R. N. *Managing Organizational Behaviour*. New York: Wiley & Sons, 1982.

Simon, H., *Administrative Behaviour*. New York: Free Press, 1947.

Wallerstein, I. M., *The Modern World System*. New York: Academic Press, 1976.

8
Human Resource Management in Singapore: Some Current Issues in Singapore

TAN CHWEE HUAT

SUMMARY

This chapter discusses some of the current issues in human resource management especially those affecting Singapore workers. In restructuring the economy there is a need to reduce dependence on foreign workers with low-level skills. The Basic Education for Skills Training Programme has been introduced as a massive attempt to upgrade the basic skills of Singapore workers.

The concept of Quality Control (QC) circles is discussed and its rapid acceptance of organizations in Singapore is revealed. House unions have been suggested as a better organizational form to strengthen the relationship between union and management. Labour legislation is re-examined and amendments are proposed to reflect the realities in the labour market. Company welfarism is proposed as a management philosophy to shift the burden of state welfarism to the companies as a means to inculcate loyalty and commitment among employees.

Foreign Workers

When the industrialization programme was implemented in the 1960s, workers were happy to get a job to support their families. As few jobs were available, they were not concerned about the nature of the work nor the working conditions in the factories. However, as the industrialization gained momentum, more jobs became available promising higher salaries and better working conditions. This situation created opportunities for workers to choose the type of jobs they liked. With better education and skill, they also looked for better paying jobs which suited their qualifications and training. This resulted in more vacancies being created in hard industries such as construction and shipbuilding.

To meet this labour shortage, the government granted work permits to workers from Malaysia to fill the vacancies. When the Malaysian economy prospered many of these workers returned to seek jobs nearer their homes. The Singapore government then permitted employers to recruit from non-traditional sources such as Thailand, India and Sri Lanka to solve the problem in the tight labour market.

Problems Created by Depending on Foreign Workers

This policy of untightening the labour market by liberally allowing more foreign workers into Singapore can however only be a temporary measure. The experience from Western nations such as West Germany and Britain has shown that guest workers create economic and social problems. The Minister for Communications and Labour explained some of these problems:

> The first is the provision of housing. As more guest workers arrive we will have to build more houses to accommodate them. This will worsen the housing problems that we now face. Although it has not happened it is expected to make it difficult for us to provide housing in time for our own citizens. Secondly, it is inevitable that some of them will want to marry Singaporeans and settle down here. The longer they are here the more likely this would happen. Yet, it will be difficult to justify our family planning policy on the one hand and literally allow foreign workers to stay here permanently on the other, except perhaps for the highly skilled. Thirdly, the presence of guest workers will in turn perpetuate the continuing demand for them. Instead of phasing out factories which use large numbers of workers and provide poorly paid and low-skilled jobs, as we should be doing, the presence of such guest workers will only make it possible for such factories to continue to operate in the same old inefficient ways. This defeats our efforts to have better paid and high skilled jobs to raise our standard of living. Fourthly, guest workers require medical services. They need recreation too. We will therefore have to expand these facilities to meet the needs of guest workers as well. The burden on our nation will rise. It may have to be at the expense of our own citizens. While we benefit from their economic contributions we have to weigh these against the costs of providing the basic needs of guest workers. As the costs of these basic needs escalates, it will outweigh the benefits that we may derive from them.

(Speech by the Minister on 1 August 1982)

Phasing Out Foreign Workers

In view of the above problems the Singapore government decided on a plan to phase out all foreign workers by 1991. The basic objective is to create a wholly Singaporean work force that would better serve the national interest. This process would be gradually implemented to allow employers time to automate labour-intensive operations. Thus by 1984, workers recruited from non-traditional sources would be phased out, except for those in the construction and shipbuilding industries, and those in domestic services.

This decision to phase out foreign workers dates back to 1979 when the government implemented its wage correction policy. This policy was meant to restructure the Singapore economy by encouraging mechanization and thus replace labour-intensive methods. In effect the wage correction policy would raise wages to a level where employers would find it worthwhile to mechanize their operations. However, given the tight labour market situation resulting from fast economic growth in the late 1970s, the wage correction policy could cause a wage spiral affecting the costs structure of goods and services. As a temporary measure, the government decided to allow the entry of more foreign workers to increase the supply. This strategy was also meant to allow employers more time for mechanization and automation. A few employers have in fact made serious efforts to increase efficiency through mechanization.

In early 1982, the government decided to restrict the entry of foreign workers again. The recruitment of workers from non-traditional sources (NTS) is planned to be stopped by 1984 and all foreign workers would be phased out by 1991. From 1 April 1982, the Singapore Government introduced a Levy Scheme whereby foreign workers were exempted from Central Provident Fund (CPF) contributions but subject to a new levy. As CPF is meant for old age security, contributions by foreign workers would serve no purpose because they would not remain in Singapore permanently. Such an exemption meant lower labour costs for the employers who would then employ more foreign workers. It was thus necessary to introduce the levy scheme under which employers were required to pay a monthly levy of thirty per cent of the foreign worker's salary, subject to a minimum of S$150 a month. The objective was to discourage employers from hiring foreign workers.

The Basic Education for Skills Training (BEST) Programme

In May 1982, in his Report on the Review of Economic and Monetary Policies, the Minister of Trade and Industry expressed concern that there were 600,000 workers in the workforce who had less than secondary education. As the Singapore economy is restructured towards higher technology, many of these workers would not be able to acquire the new skills needed because of their low education.

In July 1982, a Committee on Basic Education was formed to work out a basic education programme to raise the level of literacy and numeracy of these workers. The estimated number of 600,000 included workers from the English stream who had completed PSLE but not "O" level. The number of workers who needed basic education was narrowed to 322,000 comprising:

(1) 106,000 from all language streams who had less than PSLE qualifications,
(2) 216,000 from the non-English stream with PSLE but less than "O" level qualifications.

The BEST programme aims at raising the standard of English and Mathematics of those who need this education in order to help them communicate effectively and prepare them for further training in other skill courses. This is necessary preparation for the future when more sophisticated industries would be established in Singapore.

In 1982, the first batch of BEST classes with an enrolment of 1,600 workers was started. At the end of the five-month module, only one-third remained to take the examination. The high dropout rate was due to inappropriate teaching methods and the unsuitability of the materials used for the course. By the end of 1982, the materials were revised and improved and the teachers had to undergo an orientation session on the skills involved in teaching adults.

After the revamped BEST programme was introduced in 1983, the results were encouraging. The first intake in January involved 7,380 participants in classes conducted as in-house programmes of 61 organizations and in 30 education centres. The dropout rate was low. The passing rate of the English and Mathematics classes ranged from 81 per cent to 95 per cent. In the second intake in July 1983, the number of participants doubled to 13,600. They were enrolled in 88 in-house classes, 39 NTUC/PAP centres, 5 VITB centres and 22 MINDEF units. A subsequent survey showed that participants joined the BEST programme to upgrade their academic qualifications in order to pursue higher-level courses.

Quality Control Circles

The concept of Quality Control (QC) circles was first introduced from the United States to Japan in the early 1960s. However, the current QC concept has gone beyond the original idea of quality control as its name seems to imply. It has become a process to encourage active participation by workers who are directly involved in the day-to-day operations of the organization. Workers get together in a small group to discuss shop-floor problems and suggest solutions to improve work efficiency. The QC concept is based on a few simple premises. First, the worker who handles the day-to-day operation has intimate knowledge of his job. Given the necessary encouragement, he can suggest ideas for work improvement. Second, a worker who is involved in this process is a more motivated and productive worker. Third, the worker must be given proper training to equip him with the knowledge and skill to improve on work performance. Participation in a small group is an effective means for communication and in building team spirit and for inculcating loyalty.

Since its introduction in Singapore a few years ago, the QC circles have been gradually accepted by many organizations as a result of the active promotion of the concept by the National Productivity Board (NPB). Management of companies realize that workers at the shop-floor can contribute to the increase of productivity through participation in QC activities. It has been accepted that QC members have the knowledge and ability to help solve workplace operational problems which are either neglected or ignored by people in the higher echelons. QC activities have also brought about intangible benefits like higher morale, better teamwork and innovation.

Within the QC organization structure, an important role is played by the QC facilitators. They act as middlemen for the Steering Committee and the circles. They also help to train QC leaders in the running of the circles. They have to ensure that the concept of QC is clearly explained to both the workers and potential members. The benefits of such activities and task within the circle have to be clarified so that workers who volunteer to be in the circle know what is expected of them.

The response to QC circles has been encouraging. In 1982, the National Productivity Board registry listed 42 companies with 330 circles. In 1983, there were 93 companies with 1,330 circles. The number has increased four times within a year. The register shows some interesting points:

(1) Forty per cent were manufacturing companies and the other 60 per cent were service companies.
(2) Sixty-two per cent were large companies employing more than 500 workers.
(3) Fifty-five per cent were local companies, while the others were foreign or joint ventures.

At the first National QC Convention held in November 1982, participation involved 465 workers from 60 circles representing organizations. The convention provided an opportunity for these workers to share their experiences. The response was good and NPB held 3 such conventions in 1983. In the May convention alone, 58 circles involving 458 workers from 23 organizations participated.

House Unions

In promoting company loyalty among workers, it is necessary to strengthen the direct relationship between management and workers. The Japanese experience suggests that in Singapore the formation of a company-based union or house union may be a more effective alternative to the present unions organized along the line of industries or trades.

Encouraging the formation of house unions is a major change from the traditional organizational structure of unions in Singapore. If this idea had been advocated ten years ago, it would have been met with unanimous resistance from all unionists. The company-based union was viewed as a company-sponsored organization safeguarding the interests of management. Its effectiveness or ability to look after the well-being of workers was doubted in view of the lack of external support from other unions. This suspicion was justified in an environment where there was no mutual trust between union leaders and management.

In contrast with the Japanese past, unions in Singapore have played a very different role over the last three decades. The situation in the 1950s and 1960s encouraged an adverse relationship between union and management. The strength of the union was equated with its effectiveness in confronting management. Cooperation was ridiculed as a weakness. Any joint union-management consultation would be looked upon with suspicion by workers and other unions.

In view of this past experience in Singapore, the older generation of union leaders who are at the helm today, have to be convinced that the time has come for a rethink of a new role. Thus there is resistance to the idea of a company-based union among some leaders who are skeptical of any suggestion that would soften the confrontative will of unions. In his speech at the Far East Levingston Labour Organization Inaugural Delegates' Conference on 29 July 1983, the Secretary General of the National Trades Union Congress revealed that when the idea of house unions was suggested, one of the existing unions passed a resolution in 1982 threatening to expel any member who advocated the formation of house unions.

The concept of a house union is not an innovation. Known as enterprise unions, they have existed in Japan and other countries for many decades. They have played an important role in maintaining the harmonious labour management relations in Japan. The key to success in such a relationship is mutual respect and joint consultation. Management has to accept union as an equal partner and view it as an important communication link with employees. It accepts the welfare and interest of the workers as its responsibility. The union has to cooperate with management to ensure the company's success. In seeking better terms and conditions for its workers, it must understand company performance and economic reality. It must be willing to make short-term sacrifice in bad times. Thus, in this new form of relationship based on mutual trust and respect, there is no need for the presence of an outside party.

This new structure can be a good framework for fostering espirit de corps. It is easier for workers to identify with the company and to see the direct nexus between their well-being and the performance of the company. Being involved in the daily operations, union leaders and their workers are in a better position to understand the particular problems of the company. They are also in a better position to suggest solutions and to help management explore ways of improving efficiency. This cooperative spirit would both benefit the company and the workers.

Amending Labour Legislation

In the process of reviewing the spectrum of labour market dynamics, the government noted that some provisions in the labour laws had outlived the realities of time and needed to be updated in order to reflect current developments. Two distinct examples are the Trade Unions Act and the Employment Act. Further, the definition of a trade union had to be changed to reflect today's cooperative approach in labour management relations and to set new directions to improve this trend.

Under colonial rule, employers generally exploited workers to maximize profits. As there was hardly any system to resolve industrial conflicts, trade unions had to adopt a confrontational approach towards employers. Their main role was to promote, organize, and finance strikes. In contrast, trade unions in economically successful countries such as Japan and Korea, adopt a cooperative approach.

Under the new definition, the objectives of trade unions are:

(1) to promote good industrial relations between workmen and employers;
(2) to improve the working conditions of workmen to enhance their economic and social status;
(3) to achieve increases in productivity for the benefit of workmen, employers and the economy of Singapore.

The government on its part, is reviewing the Employment Act to ensure that the provisions are relevant for the 1980s. The Act had served its purpose during the 60s and 70s; the new emphasis would be to strengthen the nexus between employees and employers in order to enhance company loyalty so that workers would continue to work with motivation and commitment. Employers would be given flexibility to deploy their resources and optimize production; facilities which may lead to disputes would be removed; and obsolete provisions which do not serve the needs of current situations would be amended.

An example of a proposed amendment deals with flexible working hours and shift duties. This is to provide flexibility for employers who have invested in costly labour-saving devices. As a result of this amendment, employers need not pay for overtime, provided the weekly limit of forty-four working hours is not exceeded and an employee still has his weekly rest day. The existing Act was passed when shift work was not relevant. It did not allow employers the flexibility to adopt shift to maximize the usage of expensive machinery without having to incur overtime pay. Amendments were thus proposed to deal with flexible working hours and shift work. It is envisaged that with improved productivity and performance, employers would be able to pay high wages and improve working conditions.

Another proposed amenedment deals with annual leave. Under the existing Act, employees become eligible for 7 days leave per year after 1 year of service and 14 days after 10 years of service. The proposed amendment would enable an employee to become eligible for one additional day of leave for every subsequent year of service after the first year until he qualifies for the maximum fourteen days after eight years of service. This would allow employees to take pro-rated leave as and when the employee earns the leave instead of having to serve twelve months before being entitled to such benefits.

Company Welfarism

Company welfarism as a concept is not new in Singapore. In the past, many business enterprises, including large companies and small proprietorships, have provided benefits to their employees in varying degrees of generosity and regularity. However, promotion and encouragement of company welfarism in a concerted way, as a matter of management philosophy among employers, is a recent phenomenon. It is more than an attempt by the government to shift the burden of state welfarism to business firms. It is a deliberate effort to gain loyalty and commitment from employees, in return for the concern and obligation on the part of the employer to take care of the welfare of the employees and their families. The implementation of company welfarism would work towards encouraging the employer to develop suitable welfare benefit schemes for the employees as part of the desired people-centred management philosophy. Hopefully, this would stimulate higher productivity. Encouragement from the government comes in the form of Company Welfarism Through Employers' Contributions (COWEC) to the Central Provident Fund (CPF). The government has given its approval to companies which have submitted proposals within the framework of COWEC schemes drawn up by the National Productivity Council.

Under COWEC, companies would retain ten per cent of the employer's CPF contributions to create a separate COWEC Trust Fund. The balance of the contribution and those of the employees would be paid to CPF in the usual manner. Only investment returns from the trust fund would be used for welfare benefits. Income earned by the fund would be tax exempted. The fund must however be secured by a bank guarantee and the benefits introduced must enhance the nexus between employees and the company. COWEC fund managers would be given a free hand in investments to secure the highest possible returns.

Among the ten pioneer companies which initiated the COWEC schemes was the United Overseas Bank (UOB) which introduced a retirement fund for its employees. The higher investment income in excess of prevailing CPF rates would encourage employees to remain in the bank. Another company proposed to provide medical benefits, education incentives, company-sponsored group activities and life insurance premiums. The emphasis of the COWEC scheme is thus primarily to establish a link between the performance of the company and the reward for its workers. The COWEC scheme is voluntary for existing employees but compulsory for new employees. Should an employee resign from the company, his share of the fund would be credited to his CPF account.

QUESTIONS

1. Discuss the rationale for the need to phase out foreign workers.
2. How does a house union foster better relationship between union and management?
3. Discuss the need to amend labour legislation.

REFERENCES

Jayakumar, S. "Revising Employment Act for 1980s". Speech by the Acting Minister of Labour at the Singapore Employers' Federation's third annual dinner on 27 September 1983.

Lee Yock Suan. "More and More Workers Are Getting Involved". Speech by Minister of State for National Development at the May National QC Circle Convention on 14 May 1983.

Ng Kiat Chong. "NPB's Perspective of the QCC Movement in Singapore". Speech by the Executive Director of NPB at the Second QCC Convention on 19 November 1983.

Ong Teng Cheong. "Shackles of Our Past Colonial Master". Speech by the Minister Without Portfolio at the Far East Levingston Labour Organisation Inauguration Delegates' Conference on 29 July 1983.

_____. "Singapore's Second Industrial Revolution". Speech by the Minister Without Portfolio at the Metal Industries Workers Union Joint-Union Management seminar on "Higher Productivity Through Joint Consultation" on 5-6 August 1983.

_____. "House Unions". Speech by the Minister Without Portfolio at the first anniversary dinner of the Union of Telecoms Employees on 8 October 1983.

_____. "A Company's Most Valuable Resource is the Workers". Speech by the Minister Without Portfolio at the launching of the Productivity Month on 5 November 1983.

Tay Eng Soon. "Educating Workers". Speech by the Minister of State for Education at the Inauguration of the Basic Education Advisory Council on 7 January 1983.

_____. "Basic Education". Speech by the Minister of State for Education at the Orientation Workshop for BEST Teachers on 10 January 1983.

Wong Kwei Chong. "Worker's Welfare". Speech by the Minister of State for Labour at the second East Asian Actuarial Conference on 21 July 1983.

9
How Singapore may Learn from Other Countries

CHONG LI CHOY

SUMMARY

As Singapore embarks on improving human resource management in the nation, and continues her economic development, it is important that she learns from the successes and failures of other nations. This chapter points out how Singapore may learn from other countries. It explains the cultural and situational constraints involved, and the processes involved in the transfer of know-how (including indigenization).

Learning From Other Countries

Being a young nation and a "late developer", there is much that Singapore can learn from the experiences of nations that have developed before her. One may think in terms of the more advanced technology, knowledge and skills which Singapore may acquire from these developed nations. One may also think of emulating them in terms of their development strategies and policies, in terms of their organization and management, and even in terms of their political structures and laws. However, it would be unwise to learn for the sake of learning or emulate for the sake of emulating. Indeed, the failure of so many Third World nations in their developmental efforts could be attributed, at least partially, to their blindly applying the strategies and policies peculiar to the model of development of their choice, whether "East" or "West". Learning from others should contribute towards the realization of one's own goals. In the case of Singapore, learning should contribute towards Singapore's progress.

If learning from others should not mean "blind application" of strategies and policies so formulated or implemented by others, and if mere emulation of others is unsatisfactory, how then should Singapore learn from other countries? To answer this question, it is necessary to point out the cultural and situational constraints, as well as the processes involved in the international transfer of know-how. It is also necessary to understand the peculiarity of Singapore as the "learner" nation.

Cultural and Situational Constraints

Cultural and situational constraints in learning from other countries exist because every nation has her own unique cultural heritage and history, her own peculiar economic, political and social structures and her own needs and relationships with other nations. The routes to national development which were taken in the past by the developed nations can hardly be emulated by less developed nations today given their different historical and cultural situations. It would be considered ridiculous if a developing country in the 1980s should try to recreate within her boundaries the historical, social, political and economic conditions which led to the industrial revolution in Britain, or to attempt to colonize other nations so as to build an empire to include one-fifth of mankind.

In comparing Japanese and American companies, William Ouchi in his book *Theory Z* arrived at the following two ideal types (see Figure 1, p. 88), each reflecting the culture of the society within which it evolved.[1]

As Ouchi pointed out, these differences in culture do not necessarily mean that Americans cannot learn from the Japanese. Indeed, there are American organizations which have evolved many of the features of the Japanese ideal type, for instance, Ouchi's *Type Z Organization*. This is a modified form of the pure Japanese type — it is still an American type of organization, still consistent with American culture and is an illustration of how a nation may learn from other nations. Discussion will follow concerning the international transfer of know-how and will explain what learning from other nations involves. The learning

---

[1] William G. Ouchi, *Theory Z*. New York: Avon, 1981, pp. 48-49.

Figure 1

Japanese Organizations	vs	American Organizations
Lifetime Employment		Short-term Employment
Slow Evaluation and Promotion		Rapid Evaluation and Promotion
Non-Specialized Career Paths		Specialized Career Paths
Implicit Control Mechanisms		Explicit Control Mechanisms
Collective Decision Making		Individual Decision Making
Collective Responsibility		Individual Responsibility
Wholistic Concern		Segmented Concern

process by which a nation acquires the know-how from another national is inseparable from the processes of the international transfer of know-how.

The International Transfer Process of Know-how[2]

Know-how (whether technical or managerial know-how) consists of two components, namely, personal skills and culture. Personal skills (whether technical or managerial) refer to that part of know-how which is inherent in people like technicians, engineers or managers. Culture, on the other hand, refers to the socio-cultural environment peculiar to the organization in which the skills may be effectively employed. It should be pointed out that skills are often inapplicable or not effectively applicable outside a specific organization or social setting, that is, technical and managerial skills are often organization or process specific. This differentiation of know-how into two components of personal skills and culture is in accordance to their different embodiments.

Skills are embodied in people even as culture is embodied in organizations and society (social groups and their artefacts). In

[2] Chong Li Choy, "The Indigenization of Foreign Technology and the Irrelevance of Technological Dependence and Inappropriate Technology", Occasional Paper 23, Department of Business Administration, National University of Singapore, May 1982. Also cf. Chong Li Choy, *Multinational Business and National Development: Transfer of Managerial Knowhow to Singapore*. Singapore: Maruzen Asia, 1983.

this way the transfer of know-how, which is an intangible resource, may be observed in the transfer of men and organizations, including machines and other capital equipment, which encompass technology. Although technology can be stored as knowledge in such media materials as books, manuals, tapes, and films, which are readily transferable from place to place, such knowledge cannot be readily applied, until they are retrieved and embodied in men and organizations. The different embodiments of technology (excluding storage) are extremely important when we consider the transfer of know-how to a new social setting, since know-how cannot exist outside men and organizations. In other words, the learning process involves not only men learning the new skills and thus embodying these new skills, but also understanding the necessary cultural elements in the social setting in which these new skills may be applied. These necessary cultural elements must be absorbed into the new social setting of the men with the newly acquired skills.

However, the mere replication of a foreign organization, together with its foreign culture, technology, management styles, and alien responses to be expected from members concerned, would mean that the newly established organization is culturally distinct from the rest of society. Such an organization is more an extension of the home society and is therefore not a part of the receiving society. This gives rise to the phenomenon of "economic and social dualism" which Boeke (1953), a Dutch administrator, observed in Indonesian society.[3] This dualism was the result of an imported social system clashing with a culturally incompatible indigenous social system. In Boeke's observation, the Western-type plantations, although physically present in Indonesia, were distinct and separate from the traditional sectors of the Indonesian economy and never part of it. As long as the "technological culture" (this includes both technical and managerial) of the Western-type plantation remained distinct and not integrated with the culture of their host (receiving) society, it remained foreign, and the transfer of technology and the learning process would therefore not be complete. A complete transfer of technology or the completion of the learning process can only have taken place if the physical transplantation of the foreign organization with its "technological culture" has been followed by

---

[3] J. H. Boeke, *Economics and Economic Policy of Dual Societies Exemplified in Indonesia.* Haarlem: H. D. Tjeenk Willink, 1953.

"cultural developments" which integrate the foreign know-how into the indigenous culture of the receiving nation. This is the process of indigenization (or assimilation) of the foreign technology, without which, the transfer or learning process is incomplete. The indigenization of foreign know-how must not only mean the continual development of this know-how (skills and culture), in its new cultural setting (in the host nation), but also its adoption, together with some cultural adaptation by some other organizations or in other social situations within the same (host) society.

This latter situation of foreign know-how being indigenized within the new socio-cultural context of a receiving society and it finding new cultural expressions upon indigenization, is expressed by John F. Embree in his well-known paradigm of the "loosely structured social system" in Thailand:

> Still another manifestation of the Thai way is found in cabaret life. In Singapore the Chinese have organized cabarets so that there is no dancing with the taxi dance-girls without tickets, and the whole procedure is well organized to give a steady financial profit to the management. Bangkok also has cabarets — but no manager has succeeded in running one Singapore-style. Each girl comes or does not come on a given night as she pleases, she may or may not require a guest to buy a dance ticket, and if she goes home with him afterwards she may or may not be mercenary about it, depending on how she feels. A man from Singapore with some experience in cabaret management commented unfavourably to me on the casual way in which these things are done in Bangkok. Cabarets are, of course, an innovation in Bangkok from the West, but the permissive behaviour pattern of managers and the individual behaviour of the girls are characteristically Thai. Even if the manager is Chinese or European he finds it necessary to adjust his management to the Thai way.[4]

In this case, a foreign enterprise is adapted to the "loosely structured" socio-cultural environment of Thailand, and finds expression in individual behaviour that is characteristically Thai.

It is clear from the above discussion that the transfer of know-how or the international learning process involves at least

---

[4] John F. Embree, "Thailand, a Loosely Structured Social System", in Evers, H.D. (ed.), *Sociology of Southeast Asia: Readings on Social Change and Development.* Kuala Lumpur: Oxford University Press, 1980, pp. 161-167.

two major processes. The first process involves the physical transfer of know-how, or their embodiments, to a new location or new socio-cultural setting. In this case, know-how like any other resource, is physically transferable from one place to another. The physical transfer of know-how therefore involves the transfer of people (technocrats, including technicians and managers) who embody technological skills, and the organization (including machines and capital equipment) which embodies the "technological culture". In the context of the multinational enterprise, this involves the setting up of a new firm in the host society, which has a similar technological culture as its parent, and one which would probably be manned by expatriate technocrats with the relevant skills.

However, this first process of the physical transfer of personnel and organization alone to a new social setting does not complete the transfer of know-how. This is because the new organization with its distinct "technical and managerial culture" may remain foreign and incompatible with the local society. "Dualism", as pointed out earlier, will continue to exist. Furthermore, expatriate technocrats do not belong to the host country and normally will not remain there forever. It is therefore necessary to indigenize both the technocrats and the technological culture of their organization.

The second process of the transfer of technology is therefore the process of indigenization, a process which normally takes place within the firm itself. This process involves, firstly, the indigenization of the technocrats; secondly the indigenization of the organization's "technical and managerial culture"; and, thirdly, the integration or assimilation of "skills" and "culture" to the larger society in the host country. The following may be noted:

(1) The indigenization of technocrats normally involves the training of local personnel leading ultimately to their taking over technical and managerial positions formerly occupied by expatriate technocrats. The other way is to indigenize the expatriate technocrats such that they would become naturalized local citizens or permanent residents of the host country. Since most expatriate technocrats would prefer to return to their home nations, their indigenization will not be emphasized in this discussion of the transfer of skills.

(2) The process of indigenization also involves the adaptation of the organization's technical and managerial culture to the culture of the host nation. This process of adapting to the

local culture is extremely important if local personnel are to work effectively in the foreign organizational setting. This has been illustrated in the case of the management of the Thai cabarets.

(3a) The indigenization process involves the integration or assimilation of technical and managerial skills and culture into the larger society. This latter, involves, firstly, the adoption and/or adaptation of these skills for use within other organizations in the larger society. This for instance, can happen through the resignation of skilled local technocrats from the firm from which they learned their skills, and who join some other (probably) local firms. Alternatively, they may be seconded to other firms by management contract or by some other arrangements, made normally with the original firm. In this case, it is really adapting technical and/or managerial skills to suit the larger culture of the host nation, in which the firm exists.

(3b) The integration and assimilation of technical and managerial skills and culture into the larger society also involve further assimilation of the technical and managerial culture. Such assimilation would enable the application of technical and managerial skills in a larger social context. Thus, the formerly foreign technical and managerial cultures have now become part of the local culture, and hence would find expression also within other organizations existing in the same (host) society.

It should also be pointed out that although learning from other countries normally involves the processes of the international transfer of know-how described above, it may also take place through understanding, creative thinking, and innovation. For example, by understanding the "principles" behind Japanese management, we can creatively evolve an outworking of these principles within our own social and cultural setting. The Japanese themselves have in the past learned from the United States in this manner. Professor Ouchi in his book *Theory Z* advocates this same kind of learning by the United States from Japan. The President of Singapore, Devan Nair, commented,

> Learning from the Japanese, or from anybody else for that matter, is both possible and desirable. But to become Japanese is neither possible nor desirable. The Japanese themselves learned from the Americans, but without finding it necessary to become Americans themselves. So it needs to be said, for the satisfaction of Singapore workers and managers, that Singaporeans do not intend to become Japanese or Germans. They merely want to become better

Singaporeans. To recall a wise remark made in Singapore a few months ago by Mr Goshi, Chairman of the Japan Productivity Centre, "There is nothing we can do today which cannot be done better." This wisdom is recommended to all workers and managers in Singapore.[5]

The Uniqueness of Singapore as a Learner Nation

Singapore is unique as a learner nation because of her historical roots in business, as well as her multi-cultural origin. Singapore was first set up as a commercial centre by the British because of her strategic position and her good natural harbour. As a result, traders and immigrants of various cultures and national origins were attracted to the island. Since these early days, Singaporeans have learned to adapt to the culture and ways of people of other cultures and nations, and have lived through the British period in Singapore. It is in this context that we realize the Singaporean's adaptability to other cultures and also their willingness to adapt to foreign ways.

Learning from other nations has also become easier for Singapore because of the modern education provided which is similar to that provided in the developed nations. Moreover, the government continues to actively promote and support the learning of higher technology and better techniques from other nations through bodies like the National Productivity Board (NPB), the Economic Development Board (EDB), and even the National Trades Union Congress (NTUC). Continual education of the workers is also actively supported. Equally important, is the government's ability to induce foreign enterprises and governments to transfer know-how to Singapore. A stable and strong government, and Singapore's smallness in size also means that it is much easier to change institutional structures to suit new technology and know-how.

Questions

1. Why is it not satisfactory for Singapore to blindly emulate the developed countries?
2. Learning from other countries involves the international transfer of know-how. What does the process of

---

[5] C. V. Devan Nair, "Singapore's Potential for Higher Technology: Plusses and Minuses", in Lim Chong-Yah (ed.), *Learning from the Japanese Experience;* Singapore: Maruzen Asia, 1982, p. 4.

indigenization of foreign know-how involve and why is it necessary?
3. Explain the unique capacity of Singapore in being able to learn from others.

REFERENCES

Boeke, J. H. *Economics and Economic Policy of Dual Societies as Exemplified by Indonesia.* Haaslem: H.D. Tjeenk Willink, 1953.

Chong Li Choy. "The Indigenization of Foreign Technology and the Irrelevance of Technological Dependence and Inappropriate Technology", Occasional Paper 23, Dept. of Business Administration, National University of Singapore, May 1982.

──────. *Multinational Business and National Development: Transfer of Managerial Know-how to Singapore.* Singapore: Maruzen Asia, 1983.

Embree, John. "Thailand, a Loosely Structured Social System", in Evers, H.D. (ed.), *Sociology of Southeast Asia: Readings on Social Change and Development.* Kuala Lumpur: Oxford University Press, 1980.

Hans Dieter Evers. *Sociology of Southeast Asia: Readings on Social Change Change and Development.* Kuala Lumpur: Oxford University Press, 1980.

Lim Chong Yah (ed.). *Learning From the Japanese Experience.* Singapore: Maruzen Asia, 1982.

Nair, C. V. Devan. "Singapore's Potential for Higher Technology — Plusses and Development.* Kuala Lumpur: Oxford University Press, 1980.

Experience. Singapore: Maruzen Asia, 1982.

Ouchi, William. G. *Theory Z.* New York: Avon, 1981.

Ouchi, William, G. and Jaeger, Alfred. M. "Type Z Organization: Stability in the Midst of Mobility", *Academy of Management Review* 3,2 (1978): 305-314.

Vogel, Ezra, F. *Japan as Number One.* Harvard: Harvard University Press, 1977.

10
Increasing Productivity

S. RICHARDSON

SUMMARY

Productivity is defined and the problems of measuring it discussed. The human and technological aspects of productivity increase are examined and people-centred management systems described. It is concluded that much may be learned from other countries but that the Socio-technical Systems Theory seems to be the most promising approach to maximizing productivity.

Introduction

The prime aim of this chapter is to examine the definition and measurement of productivity. Against this background the paper then attempts to discuss the various ways in which productivity can be increased, with special reference to Singapore.

Changing Society and Productivity

Since change is normality (and Singapore changes particularly quickly) it is important that individuals and groups are aware of the characteristics of dynamic situations and the various forces (social, political, technological, economic) causing change. More importantly, it is necessary for society and its components to adapt, otherwise efficiency will fall.

The idea of productivity was introduced in earlier chapters using the important concept of "value added" — this was related to the need for maximizing social well-being in Singapore. The government's call to move into higher value-added industries was stressed noting that this requires a manufacturing sector with increasingly sophisticated technology. An important measure of national productivity, and hence economic growth, is GNP per capita. It is thus appropriate to take a more detailed look at productivity.

Defining and Measuring Productivity

There is considerate ignorance (and hence confusion) concerning productivity, partially because the word can be defined in various ways. However, it is always true that Productivity $= \frac{\text{Output}}{\text{Input}}$ thus it is a measure of efficiency which can be used at any level in a society's hierarchy from the individual to the economy as a whole. It is not the actual volume of production nor is it a production rate. It is best thought of as the efficiency with which resources (e.g., people, time, space, materials, machines, money) are used to achieve the aim. Thus it is applicable to the production of goods and the production of services.

Since productivity can be defined in various ways it is not suprising that it is measured in various ways. The measurement of "labour productivity" is deceptively simple: it is the ratio of the number of "pieces" produced to the man-hours expended in their production; but even this ignores the payment made to the producers and it makes several assumptions (e.g., that the producer is never delayed through lack of materials). At the enterprise or industry level, overall productivity can be measured using a mathematical model relating all outputs to all inputs, but these models are based on assumptions which are often difficult to test. Often profitability is used to measure productivity despite the fact that their co-relation is usually poor. Thus all productivity measurements need to be treated with scepticism; it is necessary to know what is being measured, and what is not being measured (i.e., assumed constant or irrelevant), (see Richardson, 1973; National Research Council, 1979; Bailey & Hubert, 1980, for detailed discussions).

However, in some situations a simple approach is acceptable. e.g., where the enterprise is concerned specifically with the better use of manpower. On the other hand, output of a system is sometimes very difficult to measure (e.g., in research or in teaching, where the real value of the output may not be clear for years). The output of groups presents special problems too, not least because of the individual differences and human interactions within the group. Further problems arise when inter-firm comparisons are attempted but these are beyond the scope of this analysis.

Human Aspects of Productivity Increase

It is tempting to think that productivity can be increased just by making people work harder. In fact, the aim should be to ensure that people work more efficiently and this is primarily a managerial problem, but also a problem for society as a whole. It is a problem for society as a whole because the society's culture determines the attitudes of people at work and especially the relationships between superiors and subordinates and between employers and employees. These relationships are especially conditioned by society's legislation and the opportunities that society offers its members. Examples are legislation concerning trade unions, hours of work, security of employment, minimum wages, safety, etc. Lack of equality of opportunity in education is likely to create or reinforce class barriers which, in turn, will affect superior-subordinate relations at work.

What is clear from the research is that effective management is a complex problem depending on situation, technology and human factors. This paragraph will concentrate on human factors although some important ones (like health and safety) will be ignored and motivation emphasized. This is not to deny the importance of health and safety (which is well understood in Singapore) but rather to highlight the importance of motivation which is less well understood. There is a wealth of evidence which suggests that the best way to motivate people towards increasing productivity is by participative management (e.g., Likert, 1961, 1967; Bragg & Andrews, 1973; Richardson, 1980). However, participative management, although previously seen as culturally universal must now be regarded as dependant on a nation's culture and values, as recent research has demonstrated (Schaupp, 1978). The same research has also shown that most employees desire a participative form of leadership style (employees tend to be more satisfied with employee-centred managers than boss-centred managers). This is especially true for managers who practise a "joins" style, the most participative style of management, rather than a "consults" or "sells" style.

Cultural differences are thus significant, one example is Japan's "system" of life-time employment (even during depressions) which inspires loyalty and high productivity. Japan has its own type of participative management illustrated by its committment to Quality Control Circles (QCCs). Originally confined to the control of quality these circles (groups coming together voluntarily) now concern themselves with a wide variety of work problems. QCCs are being introduced into Singapore and preliminary reports suggest significant success. Participative management though, is much wider than QCCs. Effective participative management depends upon the attitudes held throughout the enterprise at all levels. It demands that managers have complete trust and confidence in subordinates; always get and use ideas and opinions from them; promote appropriate communication vertically and horizontally; and operate with their subordinates and themselves as a group, always encouraging supportive relationships. To those accustomed to autocracy (benevolent or otherwise) this will seem a counsel of perfection, even an unattainable goal. Certainly an enterprise which does not conform to the model described cannot change itself overnight. However if the chief executive and his senior colleagues are truly committed to the concept of participative management then they will ensure that managers and non-managers receive such assistance, support, and training, as are necessary to change their behaviour so that participative management is practised at all levels (but this can only be done gradually and it may take a few years). Some cautionary words are however appropriate.

Participative management does not mean that everyone participates in every decision, but that important decisions are made by groups at the lowest possible level in the hierarchy and that these decisions are supported at more senior levels; at the same time the climate of opinion in the enterprise should be such that when unilateral decisions are made (e.g., in emergencies) then these are accepted and supported too. It is also clear that the relationship between participation and productivity depends on the situation and the individuals involved — if the people concerned are not willing to take part in decision-making then managers must provide appropriate incentives, in order to change behaviour. Job redesign techniques such as flexible working hours, management by objectives, job enrichment, job rotation, and job enlargement should help. Steers (1977) quotes a number of studies and concludes "one way for managers 'to facilitate effectiveness is to bring about a climate that stresses the importance of goal attainment while at the same time encouraging mutual support, cooperation, and participation, in the activities that contribute to goal attainment". Another way for managers to facilitate effectiveness is to take advantage of technological improvements.

One continuing need in Singapore is learning from other countries, which is not to suggest that other countries should not learn from Singapore. The need to avoid blind emulation of others is important, as well as the requirement to induce overseas firms and other nations to share their knowledge (but not necessarily their culture) with Singapore. Learning from other nations is relatively simple because of the type of education that exists in Singapore, and government intervention through bodies such as the Economic Development Board (EDB) and the National Productivity Board (NPB).

The government has also been active in promoting a common ideology, binding itself with organized labour and management despite the divergent interests of these three parties. This long-term policy is bearing fruit. The government's reliance on legislative action and the creation of a symbiotic relationship between the People's Action Party (PAP) and the National Trades Union Congress (NTUC) are crucial. The importance of the EDB, the NPB, the Industrial Arbitration Court, and the National Wages Council (all tripartite bodies) is considerable, as well as more recent developments like the Skills Development Fund (SDF) and the Basic Educational Skills Training (BEST) programmes. The essence of government policy has been to ensure no confrontation between managements and unions, nor within the labour movement. The Prime Minister himself has stressed that the "them" and "us" approach of many employers and employees must disappear, naturally this requires attitudinal changes by both groups.

Technological Aspects of Productivity Increase

Changing technology affects the way in which goods are designed, made, distributed and sold. Changes in technology are seen in new products, machines, methods, materials, and services. Thus technology has a significant effect on productivity although new technology need not increase productivity, and it often does not improve the environment (witness traffic congestion, and air, water, and noise pollution). Nevertheless, properly used, new technology can increase productivity especially when the working population is being reduced (as in Singapore). Further, Lupton & Tanner (1980) found that job enrichment occurred mostly because of the introduction of new technology rather than the opposite. They found that in many well-known European job enrichment programmes new technology became the opportunity to enrich jobs, hence new technology not only increases productivity by making work more efficient, it also increases productivity by enriching jobs. Increasingly, in Singapore and elsewhere, automation (and especially robots) will take dull, dirty and dangerous tasks away from people and give them to machines. The implications of this have yet to be fully explored in the Singapore context. "However, increasing productivity will often reduce the number of people required in a sub-system resulting in re-deployment (not dismissal) within the enterprise, so that enterprise production can increase with the same number of people.

Increasing production is essential for economic survival in order that the maximum may be earned through the sale of exports. But these will not sell unless there is an appropriate demand which in turn is based on price and quality. Products exported must conform to internationally recognized standards. This implies a higher level of technology (in terms of human skills, techniques and equipment) and of quality control. More stringent quality control may mean an increase in the proportion of people employed in this activity. This (like the use of other productivity improvement techniques) will lead to an increase in the ratio of indirect to direct labour. The probability of such increases should be recognized and the implications (especially regarding selection and training) studied." (Richardson, 1973).

People-centred Management Systems

Increasingly Singapore needs to develop people-centred management systems. The historical background to modern management thought reveals that the focus of the Scientific Management and Classical Bureaucratic Schools concentrated on job performance whilst neglecting the human factors. This contrasts with subsequent thinkers who falsely assumed that by ensuring job satisfaction, job performance would be maximized. Thus concentration on job performance (the early "economic man" approach), and emphasis on job satisfaction (the human relations, or behavioural approach) are two extremes and both may be criticized. The socio-technical approach attempts to bring together these two extremes.

The Socio-technical Systems theory (SST) views job change in the broader context of the individual (as a social being) interacting with technology, and seeks to integrate the social and the technical aspects of a job. SST may be regarded as the latest development in participative management with its emphasis on autonomous (or semi-autonomous) work groups, wide job variety, individual decision-making with regard to the job, etc. SST theorists argue that group working has advantages in that many jobs require inter-dependant tasks beyond the capacity of one person and individuals are free to switch their efforts to where they are most needed. Further, maximum flexibility is gained by every group member being able to undertake every group task. It is noteworthy that the successful application of SST depends on the people involved having a high need for social interaction — those who do not are probably best employed on tasks not suited to group effort. The concept that technology affects people and groups at work is hardly new but the formulation of SST has helped to focus thinking and solve some problems resulting from the introduction of new technology. The term "socio-technical" was first used by members of the Tavistock Institute of Human Relations in London during the 1950s (see Trist et al., 1965), and originated from their work in the British coal industry. The most famous application of SST has been in the Volvo automobile plant in Sweden. In sum, SST holds that each socio-technical system consists of three sets of factors:

1. Technical factors — equipment, processes, materials and the physical environment;
2. Social factors — relationships among the people in the system and their individual and collective attitudes to work and each other;
3. Economic factors — the measures by which the efficiency of the system is evaluated and the individuals in it rewarded.

Conclusions

The definition and hence the measurement of productivity is a complex matter. Yet, unless productivity can be appropriately defined and measured with sufficient accuracy it is impossible to tell how productivity changes. The need to increase productivity is paramount and significant evidence exists demonstrating that participative management allied to appropriate technology will always increase productivity, provided that cultural factors are considered sufficiently. Singapore's commitment to increasingly sophisticated technology is too important to be prejudiced by industrial strife or a failure to adapt to change. Much may be learned from the mistakes and successes of other countries although Singapore's solutions to her problems will be unique. The Socio-technical Systems theory seems to be the most promising approach towards maximizing productivity.

QUESTIONS

1. "People-centred management systems require a special style of manager and these are in short supply." Discuss.
2. What are the hidden secrets underlying Japanese corporate success and what should Singapore learn from Japan?
3. "In the past people in Singapore were motivated by the need to survive. Now that survival is assured, complacency has set in and only a significant level of unemployment will provide the motivation which is needed." Discuss.

REFERENCES

Bailey, D., and Hubert, T. (eds.) *Productivity Measurement.* Gower (for the British Council of Productivity Associations), 1980.

Bragg, J. E., and Andrews, I. R. "Participative Decision Making: An Experimental Study in a Hospital", *Journal of Applied Behavioural Science.* 9 (1973): 727-735.

Likert, R. *New Patterns of Management.* New York: McGraw-Hill, 1961.

_____. *The Human Organization.* New York: McGraw-Hill, 1967.

Lupton, T., and Tanner, I. in Duncan, K.D., Gruneberg, M.M., & Wallis, D., eds. *Changes in Working Life.* London: Wiley, 1980.

National Research Council. *Measurement & Interpretation of Productivity.* Washington D. C. : National Academy of Sciences, 1979.

Richardson, S. "Productivity: Meaning & Measurement", *The Singapore Manager* 7, 1(1973): 30-33.

_____. "Managerial Attitudes and Productivity: Hongkong & Singapore Compared", *Hong Kong Engineer* 8, 7(1980): 29-32.

Schaupp, D. L. *A Cross-Cultural Study of a Multinational Company: Attitudinal Responses to Participative Management.* New York: Praeger, 1978.

Steers, R. M. *Organizational Effectiveness. A Behavioural View.* Santa Monica: Goodyear, 1977.

Trist, E. L., Higgin, G.W., Murray, H., and Pollack, H.B. *Organizational Choice.* London: Oxford University Press, 1965.

PART THREE

INTERPERSONAL PERSPECTIVE

11
An Interpersonal Perspective

V. ANANTARAMAN

SUMMARY

This chapter aims at providing students with a conceptual framework for people-centred management systems both in behavioural and organization structural terms. As such it includes the contributions of human relationists and behavioural scientists on motivation, leadership, communication and organization structure.

Motivation

A major focus of organizational behaviour literature is the ways and means of motivating employees towards effective behaviour geared to the achievement of organizational goals. Effective employee behaviour includes less labour turn-over, absenteeism and tardiness; greater inclination to discharge extra-role functions in organizations; and higher quantity and quality of job performance. Behavioural science research findings have opened up various possibilities of motivating effective employee behaviour through satisfying their needs on the job. Some of these well-known techniques of motivation include participation in decision-making; problem-solving and conflict resolution; job and work restructuring through job enlargement; job enrichment; job redesign and work reorganization; management by objectives; and behaviour modification.

Motivation and Job Design

In the realm of motivation through job-design changes, the contributions of behavioural scientists have been highly significant. Ever since Adam Smith pointed out the advantages of division of labour and specialization in terms of productivity, the structure of jobs has been undergoing changes. In the days of mastercraftsmanship, one person performed all the operations by acquiring all the skills needed to perform the various tasks that went into the making of the final product. The job design of the Scientific Management School fragmented the job and parcelled out the various parts of the job among a number of people. Management of mass-production industries preferred this job design for two reasons: primarily, such specialized division of work allowed people to learn skills and become experts at their individual tasks, thereby contributing to increased productivity; secondly, replacing one worker with another did not present them with any problem because minute subdivision of a job makes it possible to put almost untrained labour on to a job very quickly. No wonder the human relationists blamed Scientific Management for reducing labour to a status of spare parts in the industrial machinery!

While division of labour and specialization increased job performance, it worked against job satisfaction. By 1960, modern management writers like Chris Argyris, Douglas McGregor and Frederick Herzberg called attention to the problems that extreme work simplification was causing individuals. They pointed out that when jobs became highly specialized or fragmented, workers find their tasks to be unpleasantly monotonous and unsatisfying. It gave rise to the problem of worker alienation because the work made no calls on their intelligence and sense of responsibility. It was then that the spillover effect of mass production job design came to be realized. Thus, Emile Durkheim, the sociological theorist, writing even before the extreme job specialization of assembly-line production became widespread, expressed his fear that both the individual and society would be damaged by the demoralizing impact of dull and repetitive jobs. These apprehensions became widespread with the development of the assembly-line, which became the symbol of dehumanizing jobs, alienating the individual from the workplace. A worker, it was believed, could be driven to distraction as he mindlessly repeats the same task over and over again while the assembly-line moves at pre-set speeds.

Management also began to realize that at some point, worker dissatisfaction may become so great, and the work itself so meaningless that excessive absenteeism, careless performance and even sabotage may became rampant. These losses would overtake any increased technical advantages that may result from additional specialization. If employees insist upon increased financial payment to compensate for their reduced enjoyment, the combination of poorer work performance and higher wages may make increased specialization more costly than less specialization!

It is in this context that attempts of behavioural scientists at job redesign to promote both job performance and job satisfaction should be considered. This job redesign was based on the principle of integration, not fragmentation. The experiments in job redesign included efforts to increase both job-depth and job-scope. By job-depth is meant the extent to which an individual can control his work. When management sets rigid standards, organizes work to the last detail, prescribes methods and supervises the work closely, job depth is low. But, if after objectives and general rules are set, employees are free to set their own pace and do the job as they think best, then job depth is high. By job scope is meant the number of different operations a particular job requires and the frequency with which the job cycle must be repeated. For example, a hospital nurse who checks temperatures, dispenses medicines, and takes blood samples has more scope than the one who is exclusively assigned to collecting blood samples. Hackman and his associates have advocated job redesign beyond the dimensions of job depth and scope. To them, a job could include five core dimensions, such as, skill variety, task identity, task significance, autonomy and feedback. They argued that for many workers, meaningfulness, responsibility, and an understanding of the results of work would not only contribute to satisfaction but would also motivate them to perform.

Motivation and Leadership

Another way of motivating employees is through appropriate leadership style. However, the findings of behavioural scientists in the realm of leadership cannot be accepted without reservation. The supervisory-style approach, for example, has given insights but no easy answers. Although their recommendations stem from empirical findings, the leadership-style approach has no solid theoretical base on which to build and receive support from both academicians and managers. Fiedler's theory of leadership is a case in point. Whereas his model can predict leadership effectiveness, it has not provided a highly convincing explanation of the process by which such effectiveness results. This is because not much attention is paid yet in leadership literature to interpersonal influence, i.e., how people in interaction come to influence each other. Nevertheless, the insights gained from leadership research has enabled management to move away from appeals and fear of sanctions and appeals to material self-interest as ways of motivating subordinate behaviour. For example, the human relations advocacy of employee orientation and participative leadership can be viewed as a move towards appeals that are supportive of helping subordinates maintain a favourable self-image. As Rensis Likert claims, his principle of supportive leadership would ensure organizational members of a sense of personal worth and importance.

Behaviour Modification

Another fascinating approach to motivation is behaviour modification or the technique of operant conditioning through positive reinforcement. This school of B.F. Skinner and his associates sincerely believes that if we can specify behaviour in the work setting that leads to effective performance; identify reinforcers to control behaviour; dispense positive reinforcement upon evidence of desired behaviour systematically on a continuous basis at first, and intermittently later, we can improve organizational performance. Numerous successful experiments applying the principles of behaviour modification in many organizations point to the untapped potential of this motivational technique. It can be argued that the posited relationship between performance and reward in the expectancy model of motivation, underscores the principle of positive reinforcement, since by implication the model advocates a differential reward policy based on differential performance. To an extent the Management by Objectives (MBO) performance review is linked to performance appraisal, the positive reinforcement idea is operationalized even under MBO.

An attractive feature of behaviour modification as a technique of motivating desired behaviour is that its impact on behaviour is direct. Techniques like job restructuring, work reorganization, as well as leadership-style approach try to change the behaviour of employees only through attempting to change their attitude. It is equally interesting to note that the focus of MBO *per se* is not on behaviour but on job objectives — on the assumption that the desired behaviour would result from knowledge of goals, participation in goal setting and feedback.

Motivating Climate

Finally, another approach that is gaining ground in recent years is that of individualizing the motivating climate in the organizations. Because of differences among workers, no single way of dealing with individuals is ever the best way to deal with all or even most individuals. On the other hand, treating everyone the same invariably leads to treating some people in ways that are dissatisfying, dehumanizing and ineffective. Thus, this approach considers various alternatives to current practices of job design, selection, evaluation, methods of pay, working hours, and leadership styles in order to adapt to the needs of the individuals, thereby creating working environments that will be more effective, satisfying, motivating and less alienating.

Communication

Yet another area in which the behavioural scientists have made a mark is that of interpersonal communication. Many organizations are currently experiencing environmental forces that are rapidly changing and increasingly unpredictable. It is as if turbulence is now a stable state! Corporate attempts to cope with this turbulence through a process of adaptation and innovation have proved to be ineffective in the absence of involving the individuals in the organizational change process. As a result, the team approach has become a distinctive style of working, aimed at harnessing the collective talents and energy of people to achieve useful corporate results, and at the same time, respecting the needs of the employees. Nevertheless it should be emphasized that team-building efforts should not be undertaken unless the value orientation of the business organization is congruent with that of team-building. This refers to the value orientation of openness, trust, understanding, and participation as the basic tenets of management. It is not surprising that improving interpersonal communication becomes the central theme of organization development of which team-building is a crucial subset. As such, behavioural science techniques to improve interpersonal skills, such as, the Rogerian Counselling Approach; Lewin's Laboratory Training; Blake's Grid Training; Berne's Transactional Analysis; and even the transcendental meditation of Maharishi Mahesh Yogi could be accommodated within any organic system including the System Four model of Rensis Likert.

Organization Structure

Most management writers have, it appears, been concentrating their attention on the behavioural areas and not on the organization structure. The single exception to this general trend has been the contribution of Rensis Likert whose organizational model took into consideration the organization structure, besides the organizational behavioural variables like leadership, decision making, and communication. If we define organization theory as the study of the structure, function and performance of organizations and the behaviour of groups and individuals within it, then Likert's Human Relations Organizational Theory is the only behavioural science alternative to the traditional organizational theory. His is indeed a refreshingly new approach to organizational behaviour, both in terms of structural design and its implications for behaviour.

Supervisory leadership is usually measured in terms of the effect on productivity of the group being measured. Obviously this is a measure of interest to management though it does not necessarily capture the full extent to which a supervisor exercises leadership. Both Pericles in ancient Greece and John Stuart Mill in the nineteenth century argued that states should not only be evaluated in terms of their efficiency but also in terms of the types of citizens they produce and the opportunities they give their citizens for individual development. We find the same view echoed by some social scientists dealing with organizational climate. Foremost amongst them is Rensis Likert who succeeded in operationalizing this concept in organizations.

His approach to organization structure is deceptively simple. If problem sharing between superiors and supervisors and between supervisors and employees is an effective way of integrating work group goals and organizational goals, then each superior and supervisor should belong to two different levels of work group — the work group composed of his subordinates, and a work group which includes his own boss. Such considerations led Likert to suggest that management should build up work groups and link them to the overall organization by means of people who hold overlapping memberships. This has come to be known as "The Linking-pin Theory". Secondly, participation is the major mechanism suggested for reconciling work group goals with company goals. Greater goal consensus, by reducing conflict, improves cooperation and hence coordination without the need for elaborate control systems for checking and correcting deviant behaviour. This in turn allows more delegation and effective decentralization.

According to Likert, an organization integrated on the basis of group process, the principle of supportive relationships, and the philosophy of participation will be a social system made up of interlocking work groups with a high degree of cohesion among its members and favourable attitudes and trust between superiors and subordinates. Not only will the application of the principle of supportive relationships satisfy the social and ego needs of the members of the organization, but there is impressive evidence that economic motives will be tapped more effectively. As a result, a cooperative, reinforcing motivational system emerges in support of the activities and goals of the organization.

Likert further asserts that his new theory is based on the principles and practices of managers who are achieving the best possible results in American business and government. More importantly, he claims that it is appropriate to all conditions, personalities, culture or technology. This claim of proven effectiveness and of potential for universal application is indeed provocative.

The strength of Likert's approach lies not only in the favourable effect his system has on end-result variables such as profits, output, sales, costs, or earnings, but on the intervening varilables such as perception, motivation, communication, decision-making, attitudes, and in brief, in preserving and enhancing, not liquidating the human assets of the organization. Finally, his advocacy of the Human Asset Accounting System will prove that in the long run, not only will productivity increase but there will also be better showing on the intervening variables under the cooperative motivational system.

REFERENCES

Argyris, Chris. *Integrating the Individual and the Organisation.* New York: John Wiley, 1964.

Cass, Louis Eugene, and Zimmer, G. Frederick, G. Zimmer (eds.). *Man and Work in Society.* N.Y.: Van Nostrand, 1975.

Davis, E. Louis. *The Design of Jobs.* London: Penguin Ltd., 1972.

Davis, E. Louis, and A. B. Cherns. *The Quality of Working Life.* New York: Free Press, 1975.

Griffin, R. W. *Task Design: An Integrative Approach.* Illinois: Scotts, Forbsman Co., 1982.

Hackman, J. Richard, and Greg, Oldham. *Work Redesign.* Massachusettes: Addison — Wesley, 1980.

Hackman, J. R., and J. L. Suttle, eds. *Improving Life at Work: Behavioural Science Approaches to Organisational Change.* California: Goodyear Publishing, 1977.

Likert, Rensis. *New Patterns of Organisation.* New York: McGraw Hill, 1961.

Luthans, Fred, and R. Kreitner. *Organizational Behaviour Modification.* Illinois: Scott, Foresham and Co., 1975.

Miller, L. M. *Behaviour Management:* The New Science of Managing People at Work. New York: John Wiley, 1978.

McGregor, Douglas. *The Humanside of Enterprise.* New York: McGraw-Hill, 1960.

Steers, H. Richard, and Lyman, W. Porter. *Motivation and Work Behavior.* New York: McGraw-Hill, 1979.

Wofford, J. C., E. A. Gerloff, and R. C. Cummins. *Organizational Communication.* New York: McGraw-Hill, 1977.

12
Developing People-centred Management Systems

V. ANANTARAMAN

SUMMARY

People-centered management systems are not overnight creations but essentially they are evolving systems, their evolution being a function of experimentation with behavioural science concepts, ideas, techniques and models. This chapter considers the seminal contributions of Douglas McGregor and Abraham Maslow, and points to the futility of exclusively production-centered systems to achieve results by making use of Chris Argyris' analysis of traditional management systems. In the domain of evolving behavioural science techniques, attention was primarily focused on job and work reorganisation techniques evolved by Frederick Herzberg, Louis Davis and Robert Ford. Finally, the celebrated Volvo experiment on work reorganization is described to illustrate the recent attempts to minimize the feeling of worker alienation through improving the quality of work life. In the context of large-scale efforts that are being undertaken both in the United States and in Europe to improve the quality of work life by designing work environments to minimize worker alienation and improve job satisfaction, the chapter concludes with Edward Lawler's comment that one of the greatest contributors to alienation is the collective treatment of individuals without regard for their distinctiveness and sense of unique identity.

Introduction

If a core cause has to be fixed for Japan's economic miracle, it is the greatest attention Japanese organizations have paid to human resource development. The secret weapon of Japanese management is people and how they are treated. Humans are

Japan's most abundant resource and instead of considering its large population, (in terms of other resources) a handicap, Japanese managers have capitalized on it to make it their main asset by making their systems people-centered and by concentrating their efforts on manpower development. This has yielded bounties in the form of a high-growth rate in labour productivity and a very low incidence of industrial strife, absenteeism, indiscipline and labour turnover.

In practical terms this strategy involves treating people as members of the organizational family whose participation in ensuring the well-being of the organization is total and whose potential is constantly upgraded. All the practices that are associated with the Japanese system of management — lifetime employment; democratic and decentralized decision-making; seniority favouring promotion and wage-scales; frequent training for almost all; the line-worker being his own quality inspector; the Quality Circle Movement; job rotation; the suggestion system; enterprise-based unions; management-union consultation on all important issues; directors selected from within the organization; bonuses that keep real incomes ahead of the price-line etc. — arise from this concern for capitalizing on and developing human resources.

In fact, unlike the West, the Japanese corporations' primary loyalty is to its employees and not its shareholders. This does not mean dividends are given a "go-by" but that the first claim of profits is to the employees and the organization, before the shareholders get their cut. By Western standards dividend rates of Japanese companies are low. On the other hand, investment rates, employee morale and cooperation and productivity are very high.

If other countries copy any aspect of Japanese management, it should be this commitment to human resource development. Some Singapore companies are experimenting with certain Japanese management techniques, e.g., Quality Control Circles (QCC). The success of such ideas like QCC hinges upon being committed to treating employees as full partners in the enterprise. It should be emphasized that the Japanese Human Resource Development effort was built on the fundamental behavioural sciences ideas and concepts of the Western world. It was Douglas McGregor who stressed the vital importance of human resource as an input in industry and advocated that it should not be assumed that employees worked because they had to but because they wanted to. This chapter will aim to trace the contributions of behavioural scientists in the Western world which culminated in the Japanese management systems, wherein we find, with the continued improvement in production management, a more creative integration of the work force in the production process.

Milestones in Management Thought

Analysis of the developments in Western management thought reveals that managers in the West have travelled a long distance from their traditional approaches to management. The main focus of the Scientific Management and Classical Bureaucratic approaches to management has been on job performance or the productive efficiency of the worker to the total neglect of the human side of the enterprise. The Human Relations Movement that took shape in the forties and fifties of this century was a reaction to the excesses of Taylorism and Bureaucracy. This turned out to be a movement spear-headed by visionaries with a missionary zeal, and understandably zealots of this movement brought discredit to the founding fathers of this movement (e.g., Douglas McGregor) by overemphasizing the human element to the neglect of job performance. Their assumption that if you ensure job satisfaction, job performance would automatically follow, is a result not borne in reality.

It was during this process of development in management thought that the celebrated performance-satisfaction controversy emerged. It was the contention of the Human Relations School that job satisfaction (equated to morale) caused job performance through affecting the motivation to effort. Lyman Porter and Edward Lawler in their attempt to prove that performance caused satisfaction through the medium of rewards could not ignore the circular relationships involved between the variables, job performance and job satisfaction. The socio-technical systems approach claims both job performance and job satisfaction as the twin results of their approaches to job redesign without bothering which causes which. This controversy is not settled due to the present focus on the concept of quality of work life, a concept much broader in scope than the limited concept of job satisfaction, and current research concentrates on the relationship between the quality of work life and job performance, with an implied causal relationship.

Scientific Management

Different approaches to human resource management may be distinguished on the basis of their assumptions about human nature. Essentially, the assumptions that Scientific Management has made about human nature are negative; man inherently dislikes work and wants money. Behind his desire for money is his physiological need for food, clothing and shelter; and the fatigue involved in work explains his dislike of it. These assumptions about human nature make it possible for the organization to enter into an exchange relationship, with the individual exchanging his work for money and overcoming his dislike of work through minimizing fatigue at work. Scientific Management, therefore, relies on two organizational principles: maximizing monetary payment and minimizing fatigue at work. These principles, when translated into action, have resulted in various schemes such as overtime; shift allowance; institution of incentive schemes; retirement schemes like pension; provident fund and gratuity; bonus payments and indirect payments like paid vacation and holidays; subsidized food in the canteens; and product discounts and stock options.

Concurrently, Scientific Management attempts at reducing fatigue at work have taken many forms, like reduced working hours and work week; introduction of lunch intervals; rest pauses; coffee breaks; leave schemes of all types; provision of company transport; canteen and recreational facilities; the special attention paid to working conditions such as ventilation, lighting, noise and pollution control, toilets, showers, water fountains, coffee vending machines; and supply of milk for workers during the third shift.

Classical Bureaucracy

The assumptions classical bureaucracy has made about human nature were not any less negative than those of scientific management. According to this school of thought, man is essentially irrational and unpredictable, and cannot be depended upon to do a job the same way twice. Furthermore, he is typically a power seeker and, as a result, clearly reveals a tendency to personalize relationships in the organization. An organization manned by such people obviously cannot realize its objectives unless constraints and restraints are imposed on its members with a view to make them less irrational and less unpredictable and to impersonalize their relationship with the others in the organization.

These constraints and restraints under bureaucracy took two forms, namely, the principle of formal discipline and the principle of impersonal power. The principle of formal discipline when translated into organizational plans has resulted in many well-known bureaucratic devices to control the behaviour of organizational members. These include manuals; job descriptions; policies; procedures; methods; rules and regulations; standardization; routinization; task specialization; training; and strict supervision buttressed by a system of punishment aimed at preventing irrational behaviour and channelling individual behaviour along predictable paths.

Further, impersonalization of interpersonal relations was thought to be achieved through the definition of authority. Authority is the power given to an individual to direct the work of others not because of his expertise, not because of his charisma or friendliness, but because of his position in the organizational hierarchy. Two points are worth emphasizing at this juncture. Authority is power, and this power is given to the individual by virtue of the position he occupies in the organization and, secondly, it is given to the individual not to boss his subordinates (exercise of personalized power) but to produce results. Hence, positional power becomes legitimate power because of its basis and purpose, and in bureaucratic organizations one respects the chair, not the person, and in the military, one salutes the rank, not the man!

Human Side of Enterprise

Management schemes and action plans based on negative assumptions about people have not inspired motivated performance but have resulted in minimum acceptable performance. An authoritarian climate provokes resistance from employees in the form of absenteeism, tardiness, negligence, misuse of machinery, sabotage, and high turnover.

This has led Chris Argyris to argue that traditional approaches to management are likely to liquidate the valuable human assets in the organization. The surest way to destroy an organization is to continue to treat workers as digits who are to be forced to work in return for economic gains and as spare parts to be replaced with ease to suit the immediate needs of the organization.

This type of analysis of the traditional organization is based on Chris Argyris' postulated assumption about human nature. The positive assumption made about human nature centered around the actualizing aspirations possessed by an individual as his innate characteristic. Specifically, Argyris says that man wants to become what he is potentially capable of becoming, i.e., man wants to develop from being dependent to becoming independent, from being passive and submissive to becoming active and creative, from being controlled by others to exercising a greater degree of self-control, and from using single skills to using multiple skills as he grows. This immaturity-maturity theory of development of human personality from infancy to adulthood posits, as the first step into the analysis, that when organizations employ workers they employ them as adults and not children. But managements believing in the principle of the traditional approach treat workers as immature children, not mature adults. Traditional organizations effectively stifle man from becoming what he is potentially capable of becoming. Argyris eloquently asks how man can become what he is potentially capable of becoming in an atmosphere of control and authority; exemplified by rigid rules and procedures; by attempts at standardization, rountinization and task specialization; and by strict supervision. As a result there ensues a conflict between the organization and the actualizing individual within it, and the conflict becomes irresolvable and leads to frustration of organizational members in the context of the power imbalance between the organization and the individual. A frustrated worker, naturally accommodates himself to the frustration either by fighting the organization, or yielding to the organization, or by striving to overcome the organization by moving up in the hierarchy to enhance control of his situation.

If the worker fights, he will absent himself a lot; often be tardy; become a militant union man; slow down on the job; submit grievances; sabotage products, material or machine; turn in poor work with a lot of scrap; or leave the organization. If he yields, he will become apathetic, indifferent, submissive, a "yes" man who emphasizes off-the-job fun and recreation. He will become a maintenance-oriented man remaining on the job with minimum acceptable performance, or become fatalistic and give the impression of a passive defeated man who is "just waiting it out". If he strives to overcome the organization he will try hard to move up in the hierarchy by foul means rather than fair, become highly competitive and be overly driven to succeed through any means. Such men carry tales against their bosses, would not hesitate to tread on the "dead bodies" of their colleagues, and no wonder they are known as the "organizational knife artists".

Whether or not the reason for the frustration is the self-actualization assumption about human nature, no one can deny that organizational members invariably fall under one of these three categories of behaviour which in the long run have a debilitating effect on both the individual and the organization.

What is the cost of this frustration? Regardless of whether an employee is fighting or yielding or overcoming the organization, he is in constant tension, and typically attempts to reduce tension through drinking, chain-smoking or drug addiction; the anxiety endangered by this tension leads to nervousness, nervous debility and in some cases nervous breakdowns. Furthermore, the incidence of allergy in the form of blisters or rashes, asthma or headaches or other forms of psychosomatic illnesses are very common. As a consequence, the morale of employees will decline and this can seriously affect production, and eventually, profits.

Unfortunately, traditional management believing as it does in Scientific Management and bureaucratic principles and practices will react to this state of affairs by resorting to the same means which in the first instance gave rise to the morale problem. As a result, the deterioration of the human assets of the organization becomes progressively worse and the vicious cycle continues till the organization faces liquidation. Judged from the great number of organizations going into liquidation every year in all countries, Argyris' explanation of the process of this liquidation of human assets and the consequent destruction of the organization sounds plausible.

What can be done to cut this vicious cycle? There have been many attempts by behavioural scientists to propose explanations and suggest remedies. Before accepting explanations it is better to sound a note of caution. Many of these explanations fall under the category of "proposed explanations" lacking empirical validity. Some are essentially situational theories, and the temptation to claim generality for their application should be overcome. A few of these fundamental postulations are nothing but philosophical speculations on plausible causation of behaviour. Though these postulations, concepts and ideas of behavioural sciences appear to have surface validity, repeated failures to predict and control behaviour make us hesitate to accept their claim for universal validity. Yet this caution need not unduly discourage one from considering behavioural science ideas and concepts. This is because untiring efforts are continued in certain academic circles to validate behavioural science models as alternatives to traditional models of management systems. As will be seen later, the longitudinal studies launched by Rensis Likert to validate his System Four model, which is essentially people-centered, is one such attempt to prove the validity of the concepts and techniques of the behavioural sciences.

In a sense, most of the techniques of managing people in organizations owe their source of inspiration and innovation to two such philosophical speculations — the postulations of Douglas McGregor and the theory of Abraham H. Maslow.

Douglas McGregor

In this celebrated work, *The Human Side of Enterprise*, McGregor summarizes the beliefs of managers following the traditional approaches to managing people and expounds the "Theory X" assumptions about human nature. According to him these assumptions are essentially negative and include deeply ingrained beliefs such as: work is inherently distasteful to man; he is incapable of assuming responsibility and he has to be directed and controlled by others; he is not capable of creativity in solving organizational problems; and he is interested only in satisfying his physiological and security needs and hence you can motivate him through money. Central to McGregor's ideas was his concurrence with managers on workers being lazy, irresponsible, incapable of creativity, and desirous of money. However, he differs from them in asserting that the workers were not so originally but they have become so because relationships and behaviours between manager and workers were based on these negative assumptions. Thus the theory of self-fulfilling prophesy inexorably worked out the currently widespread characteristics of workers in organizations.

The theory of self-fulfilling prophesy is a double-edged weapon — while it can provoke behaviour to make negative assumptions come true, it can also encourage positive behaviour, if only managers would proceed to base their relationships and behaviour with their subordinates on a set of positive assumptions. This is what McGregor does in postulating his "Y" theory assumptions about human nature: work is as delightful as play, if conditions are favourable; man is capable of assuming responsibility and self-direction and self-control. Creativity in solving organizational problems is thus not the sole possession of managers but it is more widely distributed in the organization. Finally, man seeks satisfaction not only of his physiological and security needs but also his social, esteem and self-actualization needs.

On the surface, it sounds very naive to expect managers steeped in suspicion and mistrust of workers to believe sincerely in the new set of positive assumptions about human nature on the basis of the infallible theory of self-fulfilling prophesy. However, a dispassionate analysis of the reality of organizational life will unmistakably reveal elements of truth in these positive postulations. For example, all of us will agree, regardless of whether our work is delightful or not, that we are not looking forward to retirement with an anticipation of unalloyed happiness. The deleterious effects of retirement on many people have been too well recorded to require any repetition. Secondly, if man is really incapable of self-direction and self-control we should be witnessing our bureaucracies spelling out volumes of rules and regulations to cover every situation and to govern every kind of behaviour leaving little room for discretion. We know we cannot make rules that comprehensively, we do rely on people to willingly discharge any extra-role function, something which is strictly beyond the call of their duty as spelt out by rules. It is amazing that "work to rule", has ably demonstrated the extent to which an organization, however bureaucratic it may be, depends upon man's capacity for assuming responsibility, self-direction and self-control. The same is true of the creative potential of workers in solving organizational problems. Creativity is not absent in non-managers, it is the absence of commitment to organizations and their management that kills creativity in them. Finally, McGregor argues that Maslovian postulations on human needs clearly point to the possibility of employees being motivated by needs other than mere money.

The "Y" theory advocates that traditional managers base their relationships with their subordinates on the basis of trust and confidence as opposed to suspicion and mistrust. However, any attempt at overnight adoption of these attitudes would be foolish because it takes time for managers to incorporate these postulations into their belief systems. It has to be through a process of internalization, not compliance nor even identification that such a change in the belief system can be brought about. Furthermore, as Douglas McGregor and his student, Warren Bennis learnt by experience, adoption of relationships and behaviour with subordinates along the "Y" theory postulations is recommended only when there is an agreement between the manager and his subordinates on goals or objectives that are measurable or at least verifiable. Goals and goal-setting buttressed by feedback are integral to applications of "Y" theory practices in management. Management by objectives, as we shall see later, has come to be recognized as a management technique incorporating these three ingredients essential for the "Y" theory application in organizations.

Abraham Maslow

The basic postulation of Maslow is that needs motivate behaviour, and that motivated behaviour is always goal-directed. When one is hungry, one may consume food. Food is the goal, hunger is the need and going to the canteen is the motivated behaviour which is directed towards the goal of taking food. It is obvious that goal attainment is need satisfaction. If needs motivate behaviour, naturally, we would like to know what the human needs are. Instead of listing human needs, an impossible task, Maslow classified human needs into five categories and arranged them in an order of hierarchy with physiological needs occupying the bottom position, i.e., physiological needs; security needs; social needs; esteem needs; and self-actualization needs.

In an organizational context, physiological needs include the need for food, clothing and shelter. This need is reflected in the demand for wages since money can procure them. When one level of need is satisfied the next level of need emerges and becomes prepotent (powerful) to the extent that it assumes the form of an urge and dominates the entire thinking and feeling process of a person. It is not necessary that physiological needs should be completely satisfied for the security need to emerge and become prepotent. An employee may not be satisfied with a job and a salary adequate enough to meet his physiological needs but he wants security. Security in the organizational context refers not only to job security but also to post-job security like retirement benefits. Satisfaction of security needs for a worker is management's assurance that the employee will continue to get food, clothing and shelter not only up to retirement but beyond. It is thus not difficult to understand that both the physiological and security needs, (the basic human needs) can be satisfied through the medium of money since they express an actual and potential need for food, clothing and shelter. When a worker has a job with a satisfactory salary and job security his social needs will emerge and the need to have a good boss, good colleagues, good working conditions becomes prepotent. The worker will feel deprived if the need that has emerged is not satisfied. Deprivation of a need makes that need all the more desirable and it is in this sense that it becomes powerful enough to assume the form of an urge and makes the individual feel that satisfaction of that need is the sole aim of life. This explains why someone having a decent job with assured security goes in search of another employer because he cannot work with his boss or co-workers.

The next level of need to emerge after the social need in the hierarchy is the esteem need. Esteem needs are sub-divided into self-esteem needs and other's esteem needs. Self-esteem refers to a good estimate of oneself or self-worth or self-respect, and it is the result of an individual's competence to do the job and the confidence arising out of that competence. One may have good self-esteem but sooner or later there will be a need to seek the esteem of others. Esteem from others takes different forms, like the individual's need for recognition, prestige, praise, compliments, autonomy, and pats on the back.

The final need to emerge is the self-actualization need or the need to become what one is potentially capable of becoming. It can be equated to an urge which says "What I can be, I must be." It is self-realization in the sense of realizing one's unused potential, and it is the highest order of self-motivation. Maslow also postulated that a satisfied need ceases to be a motivator in the sense that when an individual is not in a state of deprivation in relation to that need, promised satisfaction of that need fails to provide the motive force for behaviour. If satisfied needs do not motivate, obviously, unsatisfied needs alone can motivate behaviour. More specifically the most prepotent among the unsatisfied needs at any given time for a given individual will motivate him. This is the central postulation of the Maslovian theory of human needs. If one wants to motivate an individual, he has to find out his unsatisfied needs and promise the satisfaction of the most prepotent among them. This postulation effectively explodes the deep-rooted belief in money as the sole motivator of organizational behaviour because any want in any other need category can be equally effective as a motivator of behaviour. In other words, an individual can be motivated to perform in response to a promise of recognition as being the best worker in the organization.

The next postulation of Maslow is known as the "continued need gratification theory", i.e., we cannot maintain an individual at the level of a higher order need unless his lower order needs continue to be satisfied. And, finally, we could interpret Maslow to mean that if an individual is in a state of deprivation at any level of need in the hierarchy he will not be a normal human being. If one is deprived of his physiological need satisfaction he will suffer from malnutrition, disease and starvation, though not death. If his security needs are not satisfied, he will suffer from anxiety and uncertainty. If his social needs are deprived he will tend to be a maladjusted individual. If he lacks self-respect not only is he incapable of seeking others' esteem but he will suffer from a compulsive sense of discouragement in the company of others.

Having understood the potential application of the Maslovian postulations in an organizational context, the human relationists (and later, other behavioural scientists) concentrated in evolving techniques to motivate employees by satisfying their needs at different levels of the need hierarchy. Behavioural innovations like participative management and management by objectives owe their emergence, during the sixties, to these efforts. During the seventies, new techniques emerged, like job enrichment and job redesign, culminating in job development and work reorganization and the potential to enhance the quality of work life in organizations.

Although widely accepted, Maslow's Theory on human needs (postulated in 1943) was empirically tested only in 1968 and research failed to support his concepts. The hierarchy according to this empirical study exists at the level of basic needs and not at other levels of needs. This does not invalidate the Maslovian postulations because the postulated need hierarchy was only the natural state of needs in people and can be changed through learning and cultural conditioning. For example, in Japan, group needs seem to emerge before any substantial satisfaction of basic needs. Similarly, the Hindu religion can make people perceive the lower-order needs to be relatively unimportant.

Apart from jumping the order of hierarchy a more serious violation of hierarchy can take place — people can become preoccupied with horizontal movement rather than vertical movement. They could become concerned with more and more satisfaction at the same level. When this occurs at the lower levels we call it materialism, a shallow development of personality that has failed to grow in other directions. Such people who get stuck at this level of needs may never reach the higher levels unless something pulls them vertically.

Alderfer's Theory

After studying the major theories of personality and the religions of the world, Maslow came up with this hierarchy as a general framework and not as a model applicable to every individual. Alderfer modified the Maslovian hierarchy in order to make it more consistent with his postulations. He brought the basic physiological and security needs under existence needs. Social needs and others' esteem needs were categorized as relatedness needs, and the self-esteem and self-actualization needs were catagorized as growth needs. His theory of human needs retains the notion of hierarchy of needs without requiring it to be strictly ordered. Alderfer suggested a continuum more than a hierarchy. Accordingly to him, neither satisfaction of a need nor deprivation of a need is the only way to activate a need or motivate an individual. A person's background or one's cultural environment may dictate that relatedness needs may take precedence over unfulfilled existence needs.

Suppression or sublimaton of lower-order needs rather than satisfaction of lower-order needs may be responsible for the emergence of higher-order needs. Growth needs may increase in intensity the more they are satisfied. Finally, while Maslow postulated that a satisfied need ceases to be a motivator, Alderfer stresses that it will continue to be a motivator so long as the attempt to have the higher-order need is thwarted. The less the relatedness needs are satisfied, the more existence needs will be desired. The less growth needs are satisfied, the more relatedness needs will be desired. Be that as it may, despite many criticisms and attempted modifications, Maslovian postulations still remain the bedrock of all behavioural science techniques of management.

Frederick Herzberg

This section will focus on job design and job satisfaction. The contribution of Herzberg in establishing the cause-effect relationship between job design and job satisfaction is the result of his attempt to upgrade the human relationists' emphasis on the cause-effect relationship between need satisfaction at all levels of

Maslovian hierarchy and job satisfaction. The human relationists believed that job satisfaction for an individual was a function of need satisfaction along the Maslovian scale. The dual factor or Hygiene-Motivation theory postulated by Herzberg effectively modified this relationship between need satisfaction and resultant job satisfaction.

Based on his controversial research, Herzberg claimed that anything an organization does to satisfy the lower-order needs of employees — physiological, security and social needs — comes under the category of hygiene factors. In other words, hygiene factors on the job, such as salary and allowances, job security and retirement benefits, and working conditions and work relations, have the potential only to prevent dissatisfaction and not to promote satisfaction. Hygiene factors are called dissatisfiers because their absence will cause dissatisfaction. Motivatiors or satisfiers are what the organization can provide to satisfy the higher-order needs of employees, i.e., their esteem and self-actualization needs. Since absence of dissatisfaction is not presence of satisfaction, mere provision of hygiene factors on the job will only remove dissatisfaction and not lead to satisfaction. Therefore to ensure job satisfaction one should have hygiene adequately provided for on the job and motivators should be built into the job over and above hygiene. Job enrichment, is an innovation that affords ample scope for satisfaction of higher-order needs by making the job itself a motivator.

Herzberg dismissed the human relations technique of participative management as a hygiene factor without any great potential as a motivator. Generally speaking, he was convinced of the futility of job *context* factors as potential motivators. At best they could prevent dissatisfaction on the job. He advocated job *content* factors as contributing to motivation, and his much publicized technique of job enrichment is indeed a brilliant attempt to make the job itself more meaningful by deliberately building into the job greater scope for achievement and recognition, making the job more responsible and challenging and providing opportunities for advancement and growth.

Herzberg pursued his thinking along a line hitherto unthought of in the domain of organizational behaviour, and with empirical evidence to back up his theory. Although his research findings were doubted as method-bound, the seminal nature of his contributions cannot be questioned because, in course of time, it gave rise to the Job Development Approach, merging the

American innovation of his job enrichment with the socio-technical job redesign of the London Tavistock School.

Job Development

Job development has proceeded along two tracks — the job enrichment track of Herzberg (based on his dual-factor theory); and the job redesign track of Louis Davis (based on the earlier socio-technical ideas of the Tavistock School). The early experiments of Herzberg and Davis illustrate the difference between these two techniques. In summary, Herzberg's job enrichment is a technique of vertically loading the job by tasks taken from above in order to make the job more meaningful, whereas Davis' job redesign is a technique of horizontally adding activities to the existing job in order to enable the whole individual to do a whole job. Finally, there has been the successful attempt by Robert Ford in combining these two techniques in order to develop a job at the American Telephone and Telegraphs Company. What follows is a description of all the three experiments in order to clarify the concepts underlying them.

Job Enrichment

When called upon to solve the morale problem of experimental officers working under scientists in a research and development organization, Herzberg enriched the job of experimental officers by loading the job with tasks taken from the scientists. Before the job content change was affected, it was the responsibility of the scientists in the organization to conceive of research or development ideas and develop a research framework representing the experimental design and methods of data collection to be given to the experimental officers. It was the responsibility of the experimental officers to collect data, strictly according to the prescribed research framework, with the assistance of Laboratory Assistants working under them. They purchased the required raw materials and ordered supplies and services with the approval of the scientists. Once the data were collected they were handed over to the scientists who wrote he research report with the privilege of authorship to themselves.

The changes in the job content of the experimental officers brought about by this experiment included the following: the experimental officers were asked to write the research report and authorship was given to them, including the privilege of answering

DEVELOPING PEOPLE-CENTRED MANAGEMENT SYSTEMS 127

questions and queries arising out of their research reports. They were allowed to order supplies and services on their own without having to go through the scientists. They were made responsible for selection of laboratory assistants; the appraisal of their performance; and the designing of their training programme. These were the responsibilities formerly discharged by the scientists. Finally, the experimental officers were given the freedom to pursue their own research arising out of the initial ideas of the scientists. This freedom had not existed before.

Herzberg reported an all-round improvement in productivity with the experimental officers approximating around twenty-five per cent of the improvement. He further claimed that the changes brought about in the job content of the experimental officers provided the needed motivation, satisfying their needs not at the hygiene level, but at the level of higher-order needs. Specifically, the changes afforded the experimental officers greater scope for achievement; the privilege of answering questions and queries, and authorship of the research reports gave recognition to them. The power given to independently order supplies and services made their job more responsible and challenging. Finally, membership in the selection committee for laboratory assistants and the authority to appraise their performance and institute their training programme meant advancement in their status; the freedom to prusue their own research provided the opportunity for growth.

Herzberg and his associates defend their techniques against criticism on many counts. Most importantly, they argue that so long as we can overcome our current "holy cow" attitude to job content and the natural tendency to consider a job as containing only a fixed finite number of tasks, and approach every job with a conviction that job content could be changed, experiments in job enrichment would offer a formidable challenge to traditional thinking in management. Furthermore, job enrichment of the experimental officers does not lead to job impoverishment of the the scientists because nothing prevents the organization from enriching the scientists' job by loading their jobs by tasks taken from one level above. Also it is not impossible to consider the possibility of adding some new dimensions to the job of the chief executive when job enrichment touches him and he has to shed some of his original tasks to one step below.

In response to the question as to what would happen to the man on the lowest rung of the organizational ladder (groaning under the weight of the tasks shed by others above him), Herzberg's answer was — if you cannot enrich a job, eliminate the man on the job by automating it.

Job Design

Herzberg's job content changes were made by adding newer responsibilities to existing ones on a given job without altering the technology that determined it. In other words, Herzberg's brand of job enrichment, involved only changes in the social dimensions of the job and not its technical dimensions. Davis' innovation of job redesign altered the technology to give the individual a whole job instead of a fragmented job. Herzberg's job enrichment modified the job of supervisory and managerial cadres whereas Davis' redesign succeeded in making the job of the assembly-line worker more meaningful. One experiment in job redesign was the redesign of an assembly-line job in a Pharmaceutical Appliance Manufacturing Company. In this company each worker performed one of nine operations spaced at stations along the conveyor line. The operators were not responsible for material preparation and removal, inspection and supply. In the experiment, the new job design eliminated the conveyor (and pacing) and all nine operations. Final inspection and the securing of materials were combined into one job and performed by workers at individual work stations.

In other words, this job redesign involved configuration of tasks and assignments. Now the job included all tasks inherent in productive work, namely, auxiliary or service (supply and tooling), preparatory (set up), processing or transforming, and control (inspection). The job redesign permitted development of identity with the product. It introduced task variety in the form of larger numbers and introduced different kinds of tasks and skills, as well as more complex tasks. And finally it enabled self-regulation of speed of work, and self-determination of work methods and sequence. In sum, it provided for comprehensiveness in the work role while at the same time it imposed greater responsibility. The research asserts that job redesign promotes responsible autonomous job behaviour and this in turn improved organizational performance in terms of both quality and quantity as well as attitudes, perception and satisfaction of members of the organization. In short, the job redesign achieves the twin objectives of socio-technical systems, namely, job performance and job satisfaction.

Incidently, it should be noted that job redesign brings the concept of job design to where we were orginally before the advent of Scientific Management. Scientific Management, coupled with division of labour and mechanization, designed the job by fragmenting it and naturally the concern was exclusively technical, whereas job redesign designed the job not by fractioning it, but by integrating it into a meaningful whole. This concern is both social and technical, for job performance as well as for job satisfaction. The cycle has turned a full circle indeed.

Job Reorganization

Job reorganization is a process by which one adds responsibilities vertically, and activities horizontally to a job under review, thereby providing the whole person with a whole job (see Figure 1). A whole job consists of three basic elements:

(1) Planning the job;
(2) Doing the job;
(3) Evaluating the job or obtaining feedback at the first two steps and taking appropriate corrective action.

Figure 1 Steps in Improving the Job

```
                    ┌─────────────────┐
                    │ Pull down       │
                    │ responsibilities│
                    │ from above      │
                    └────────┬────────┘
                             │
                             ▼
┌──────────┐         ┌─────────────────┐         ┌──────────────┐
│ Pull     │         │ To              │         │ Pull later   │
│ prework  │────────▶│ improve this job│◀────────│ work stages  │
│ into the │         │ rearrange       │         │ back into    │
│ job      │         │ present parts   │         │ the job      │
└──────────┘         └────────┬────────┘         └──────────────┘
                             │
                             ▼
                    ┌──────────────────┐
                    │ Push work on down│
                    │ to lower job     │
                    │ classification or│
                    │ automate it      │
                    │ completely       │
                    └──────────────────┘
```

According to Fred Luthans, job restructuring is concerned with designing jobs that include a greater variety of work content; require a higher level of knowledge and skills; gives the worker more autonomy and responsibility for planning, directing and controlling his own performance; and provides the opportunity for personal growth and meaningful work experience. Hackman and his associates have, through their research, not only given operational meaning to these basic job elements and measured the extent to which a job contains them but has also explained the process by which a restructured job motivates a worker to improved quality of performance, resulting in job satisfaction.

In summary, Hackman and Oldham identified five core dimensions at work. Their Job Diagnostic Survey measures whether a given job is high or low on these five core dimensions. If the job is high on these five core dimensions, it will produce or create three psychological states in the employee, which in turn would result in both personal and work outcomes, provided the employee is high also on his growth need strength as measured by another questionaire. In detail, the five core dimensions are the following:

(1) Skill variety refers to the degree to which a job requires the worker to perform activities that challenge his skills and abilities.

(2) Task identity refers to the degree to which the job requires completion of a "whole" or identifiable piece of work, i.e., doing a job from beginning to end with a visible outcome. For example, task identity can be improved by requiring an employee to assemble an entire hotplate rather than just to attach the electrical cord to the hotplate.

(3) Task significance refers to the degree to which the job has substantial and preceivable impact on the lives of other people in the immediate organization or world at large. For example, a worker is more likely to perceive that he is doing a significant task when he assembles an electronic blood testing instrument or tightens nuts on aircraft brakes rather than when he is filling small boxes with clips — even though skill levels involved are comparable.

(4) Autonomy refers to the degree to which the job gives the worker independence, freedom, and discretion in scheduling work and how he will carry it out. Greater autonomy leads to

a greater sense of personal responsibility.

(5) Feedback refers to the degree to which a worker, in carrying out the work activities required by the job gets information about the effectiveness of his efforts. Feedback is most powerful when it comes directly from the work itself. For example, when a worker builds an instrument and is able to test it himself, he gets prompt feedback. On many jobs there is little or no feedback.

The three psychological states experienced by the employees are:

(1) *The experienced meaningfulness.* The individual must perceive his work as worthwhile or important by some system of values he accepts.

(2) *The experienced responsibility.* He must believe that he personally is accountable for the outcome of his efforts.

(3) *Knowledge of results.* He must be able to determine, on some fairly regular basis, whether or not the outcome of his work is satisfactory.

When these three conditions are present, a person tends to feel very good about himself when he performs well. And these good feelings will prompt him to try to continue to do well so that he can continue to earn a positive feeling in the future. This is what is meant by internal motivation or being "turned-on" to one's work because of the positive internal feelings that are generated by doing well, rather than being dependent on external factors such as pay for the motivation to work effectively.

The relationship between the three psychological states and on-the-job outcome is illustrated in Figure 2. When a worker feels high on these three psychological states, then internal work motivation, job satisfaction, and work quality are high, and absenteeism and turnover are low.

The above theory, however, will not work for everybody. Even where the motivating potential of a job is very high not everybody is able to become internally motivated in his work. Only people who have strong needs for personal accomplishment, for learning and developing, for being stimulated and challenged, would be influenced by the motivational potential of the job. Hackman's questionnaire identifies these people who are high on their "growth need strength". Job enrichment, job redesign, or job reorganization will be for them, not for others.

Figure 2 Core Job Dimensions, Critical Psychological States and on the Job Outcomes

Core job dimensions	Critical psychological states	Personal and work outcomes
Skill variety task identity task significance	Experienced meaningfulness of work	High internal work motivation
Autonomy	Experienced responsibility for outcomes of work	High quality work performance
Feedback	Knowledge of actual results of work activities reassures worker	High satisfaction with the work Low absenteeism and turnover

Employee growth needs strength

Volvo Experiment

Of all the work reorganization experiments, the innovation implemented at the new auto assembly plant of Volvo at Kalmar won worldwide recognition. The problems faced by Volvo in their various plants were high turnover, absenteeism and poor quality of work. It was assumed that the routine and repetitive jobs in auto factories were responsible for the worker's feeling of alienation from their work. Worker alienation indices were high in Volvo: 40 per cent labour turnover; 20-25 per cent absenteeism, and the quality of work turned out was poor.

It was significant that the managing director of Volvo announced unequivocally that "a way must be found to create a work place which meets the needs of modern working men with a sense of purpose and satisfaction in his daily work. A way must be found of attaining this goal without an adverse effect on productivity".

The wholehearted commitment of the chief executive was primarily responsible for the successful Swedish innovation in work reorganization along the following lines:

(1) Kalmar Factory assembled car bodies onto finished chassis. The assembly line was completely done away with.

(2) The work was organized so that teams of 15-20 workers would have the responsibility for different sub-systems installations like the electrical sub-system, the wheels and the brakes.

(3) Each team, for example, the work team in-charge of installing wheels, would have its own area and would totally be in-charge of allocation of work and of determining their work rhythm. Each work team had the freedom to do the work either way — either each member assembling the entire sub-system or the work could be divided among the members of the work team.

(4) The cars moved on self-propelled electrical trolleys from the storage area to the work bay. The team members were to move the cars and also be responsible for managing their own spare parts inventory.

(5) The three-tier development groups consisting of managers and staff specialists, supervisors and operatives were responsible for improving existing methods and planning new systems.

(6) The architecture of the plant directly supported the new innovation. Work areas were physically separated from each other by walls. Each team had its own entrance, changing and rest rooms. Extensive use of windows made the working environment very pleasant.

Work reorganization experiments of the Swedish kind cannot be undertaken elsewhere unless organizations are fully aware of its far reaching impact on managerial functions. For example, the introduction of autonomous work groups puts the supervisory role in transition. His traditional role of getting work done from operatives is eliminated, and he has to assume the new role of a team-leader facilitating the functioning of the autonomous production groups and ultimately he may have to acquire newer responsibilities transferred to him from those above. This in turn calls for involvement of the workers in the selection of their team leader — either direct selection of the supervisor by the work group or work group approval of management selection. Secondly, supervisors have to acquire new skills to play the role of effective team leaders in areas such as communication, interpersonal relations and group decision-making.

The three-tier development group comprising managers, staff specialists, and operatives, calls for a fundamental change in the staff specialists' orientation and way of functioning. Staff specialists are affected because shopfloor employees begin to look to the experts as a source of information, and not of legislation or of prescription. Furthermore, they expect to get information in the form and language that they can understand.

In the process of improving existing systems and planning new systems, deliberations in the development groups lead to the questioning of roles and functions of managers, staff specialists and other members of the supervising cadres. This naturally reveals the superfluous quality of the organizational jungle — duplication of work, overlapping areas of responsibility, and proliferation of staff departments. In one organization such questioning finally led to the abolition of a supervisory cadre altogether.

Finally, the traditional justification for the increase in the employment of expensive "managerial inspectors", in whole or in part, rests on the assumption that shopfloor employees are incapable and/or unwilling to accept greater responsibility for the work they physically do. The work reorganization innovation successfully demolishes this convenient management folklore.

Person-centered Systems and Behavioural Science Concepts

It is worthwhile illustrating how the experiment in Volvo's work reorganization at Kalmar is the direct result of the application of behavioural science ideas and concepts.

(1)   The Kalmar experiment, in the language of Organizational Development, falls under the category of techno-structural interventions, since by definition such interventions attempt to alter the organizational structure/technology and hence influence individual satisfaction and performance.

(2)   Participation in decision-making increases the commitment and involvement of employees.

(3)   People have a complex set of motivations. These include not only needs for material rewards but social needs also, needs for self-recognition, and needs for using their skills and abilities in stimulating and challenging ways.

(4) The core unit of improving employee satisfaction and performance is the work group, not the individual, not the manager nor the individual worker.

(5) A sense of completion and satisfaction is enhanced when the individual participates in a total task.

(6) Tasks should be so organized to give teams maximum control over them. The autonomous work groups have complete control over allocation of work and for setting the work rhythm.

(7) Physical architecture is important in affecting satisfaction and productivity.

(8) Public commitment to innovation, with a definite purpose, makes genuine efforts for successful implementation imperative. This last point was important in the context of the Volvo experiment because the entire industrial world was watching this experiment with great interest.

Quality of Work Life

Though morale can be enhanced through humanizing jobs through job reorganization and humanizing the work environment through work reorganizations, it is being increasingly realized that the needs and aspirations of employees cannot be adequately met by these limited concepts, and the only way it can be met is through improving the quality of work life.

The earliest to spell out certain dimensions of quality of work life was Richard Walton. In his article *(Harvard Business Review)* he listed the following criteria for quality of work life:

(1) Adequate and fair compensation.

(2) Safe and healthy working conditions.

(3) Immediate opportunities to use and develop human capacities; non-routine, non-repetitive work; abolition of current separation of planning and doing; autonomy; use of multiple skills; access to information on total work process; feedback; and the concept of "whole job for the whole person".

(4) Future opportunities for continued growth and security.

(5) Social integration in the organization, egalitarianism and the absence of undue status symbols.

(6) Constitutionalism in organization: Does a worker have privacy, freedom of speech and right of dissent? Does he perceive a sense of equity and fairness in compensation, security and status, besides due process for discipline? Does he have a share in the decision-making which affects him both in the organization and his union?

(7) What are the conditions of the work and total life space? What is the impact of work on the worker's life outside the work situation? Is it debilitating or enriching? What is its impact on his relationship with his family and other reference groups?

(8) The social relevance of work life: The role played by the employing organization is important — is it socially beneficial or socially injurious? Is his organization socially responsible in its products, waste disposal, use of resources, market techniques and employment practices?

While the criteria give a fairly clear idea of the concept of the quality of work life, it is more precisely described as a process by which all members of the organization, through appropriate channels of communication set up for this purpose, have some say about the design of their work. In this kind of participative and responsive organizational climate, suggestions, questions and criticisms that might lead to improvement of any kind are encouraged and welcomed. In such a setting, creative discontent is viewed as a manifestation of constructive caring about the organization rather than destructive griping. Management encouragement of such feelings of involvement often leads to ideas and actions for the upgrading of operational effectiveness and efficiency, as well as environmental enhancement.

The innovative work reorganization programme at the Kalmar plant of Volvo is an outstanding example of organizational effort to enhance some aspects of the quality of work life. The second outstanding effort has been made in four of the General Motor plants where the research conducted by the Michigan Institute of Social Research established a close relationship between an organization's performance and how employees felt about the work climate, how they felt about the quality of management, and how they felt about employee-employer relationships. Furthermore, it was shown that performance and human satisfaction can be improved by creating conditions in which people could become more involved, work together and experience personal growth and development. These findings have led to the establishment of a National Committee to improve the quality of work life at General Motors. It is amazing to note that it is the result of a contractual agreement made in 1973 between General Motors and United Auto Workers.

Recently, General Motors has come out with a system for measuring the success of Quality of Work Life (QWL) in its plants. This provides a bench mark against which progress or the lack of it, in the implementation of QWL can be judged. Measurement is based on a survey, aimed at employees which attempts to measure sixteen dimensions of QWL. The survey form has ninety items and uses a five-point scale to record employees' response. The sixteen dimensions of QWL in the survey relate to: employee commitment; apathy; on-the-job development; employee involvement and influence; advancement based on merit; career goal progress; relations with supervisor; work group relations; respect for the individual; physical working environment; confidence that management understands individual's concerns; economic well-being; employee state of mind; absence of undue job stress; impact on personal life; union-management relations.

Many organizations within General Motors use the survey as a springboard for involving more of their people in identifying problems and developing solutions. At follow-up meetings, employees share their ideas on why certain areas have high or low scores.

It should be noted that several QWL improvement experiments have failed, for various reasons. Both external and internal forces influence new ways of organizing work. In a recent study at Volvo, it was shown that redesign strategies within the company vary with such factors as management style, social relations, democratic structure and technology. Some conclusions drawn from the study are:

— That QWL programme will fail if management tries uncritically to copy solutions from one country to another, from one plant to another within the same country, and from one department to another within the same plant.

- That when management has a deeply rooted understanding of the local characteristics, the chances of success increase.
- That an active and positive management attitude towards change is a pre-requisite for positive results.
- That management has to be sensitive to the fact that the change process will sooner or later affect several organizational levels, independent of where the change was initiated.
- That changes in the work situation must include a "package" of activities introduced over a period of time. The "package" should include the following: delegation of responsibilities; integration of jobs; job rotation; participation in decision-making concerning job situations; and changes in physical working conditions.
- That many changes are undertaken spontaneously without the aid of the projects, without scientific sophistication, without their being reported to anybody. These changes occur simply on the initiative of keen and interested individuals.

Developing a Motivational Climate

In the context of large-scale efforts that are being undertaken both in the United States and in Europe to improve the quality of work life by designing work environments to minimize worker alienation and improve job satisfaction, Lawler laments that these approaches to organizational design are not treating employees as individuals but as indistinguishable parts of an aggregate, or with the satistical averages to whom most of the innovations should apply. Unfortunately, not every worker is average.

One of the greatest contributions to alienation, according to him, is the collective treatment of individuals without regard for their distinctiveness and sense of unique identity. Because of differences among workers, no single way of dealing with individuals is ever the best way to deal with all or even most individuals. On the other hand, treating everyone the same invariably leads to treating some people in ways that are dissatisfying, dehumanizing and ineffective.

Viable alternatives to currrent practices are available for organizations to change their job designs; selection; evaluation;

methods of pay; working hours; and leadership styles in order to adapt to the need of individuals, thereby creating environments that will be more effective, satisfying, motivating and less alienating.

Job Design

The job design in a Motorala plant allows the product to be produced in two different ways — on the assembly line or on a bench where one worker puts the entire product together. This option enables workers who prefer routine and repetitive jobs to do what they like, and those who prefer enriched jobs to also do what they prefer. In Non-linear systems and in Scandinavia, managements have left the option to be exercised by the autonomous work groups.

The use of work modules represents another approach to giving individuals greater opportunity to determine the nature of their work. Khan has defined work module as a time unit equal to approximately two hours of work at a given task. A normal 44-hour a week job would then be defined in terms of four modules a day, fives days a week, for between 48-50 weeks a year. Through the use of work modules it would be possible to increase diversity as opposed to monotony in work. Undesirable work could be spread out having everyone to take, for example, a module or two of such work every day. The result would be that workers would change activities through changing work modules. If some work modules have enriched activities, individuals could pick their work settings taking into account their needs and preferences.

Individualized Pay and the Benefit System

The cafeteria kind of plans come under this category. Under this plan, management would tell the employee the amount of money he would get on account of both pay and fringes and let him decide on the division between cash payments he would like to receive, and the fringe benefits he would like met. Under the cafeteria benefit scheme, the Thomson Ramo Woolrich (TRW) organization has offered a choice of four Health plans. Lawler reports a successful experiment in which employees in four work groups designed four different pay plans to suit their needs. Lump sum salary increase plans, for instance, allow individuals a choice of how they receive their pay increases, in one lump sum or in many instalments. Similarly, a choice could be given for employees to receive their salaries either monthly, fortnightly or weekly. Finally, the much publicized Topeka Wage System (General Foods Corporation) paid the workers on the basis of skills and abilities possessed, not necessarily utilized, after providing them opportunities to be trained to do multiple jobs.

Realistic Job Preview

Traditional selection methods assess whether the individual possesses the required ability to perform the job; not whether he will be satisfied on the job. Job preview is expected to overcome this serious omission. Realistic job preview at the time of selection gives the prospective employee realistic job information. It is not just a job description but includes results of job satisfication surveys in the organization; employees description or rating of the prospective supervisors; data on turnover; and absenteeism and grievance problems associated with particular work settings. In addition this approach advocates that the applicants should be given feedback on the psychological tests they had undergone during selection. The job preview could also include job-site inspection, descriptive books and films on working operations and conditions.

Given accurate information, people are able to determine whether a particular job situation would fit their needs and abilities. The reduced gap between expectation and reality minimizes disappointment and contributes to stability in employment in the organization.

Individualized Hours of Work

The innovation of flexi-time or flexible working hours with a set of core hours, perhaps four a day, meets the differences in individual needs by allowing some people to come to work early and leave early and others to come late and leave late. Moreover flexi-time can be extended to enable individuals to work weeks of different lengths. For example, some employees can work a 40-hour week while others may prefer a 20- or even a 10-hour week. Again it would make it possible for husbands and wives to share a job.

Flexible working hours is preferred to reduced work week in many industries. Above all, it has demolished the traditional assumption that organizations can be efficiently run only when everyone comes to work at the same time and leaves at the same time.

Individualized Leadership Style

It is increasingly realized that a standardized approach to leadership will not lead to employee satisfaction because some prefer to be directed and controlled while others prefer self-direction and self-control. It is suggested nowadays that management should train supervisors and superiors to diagnose the situation and individuals, and use the resulting information in selecting an appropriate leadership style.

These innovations are just the forerunners of other practices soon to be articulated. However, they drive home an important lesson in the people-centred management system. Meeting individual needs is certainly a positive approach to enhancing the quality of work life and the commitment and involvement of workers to organizational goals.

QUESTIONS

1. The theoretical contributions of Maslow, McGregor and Herzberg provide the base for building people-centered management systems all over the world. Discuss.
2. Clearly explain the Behavioural Science concepts underlying the celebrated Volvo experiment in work reorganization.
3. Explain the concept of "Quality of Work Life" and consider the possibilities of improving the quality of work life in Singapore.

REFERENCES

Davis, Louis E. "The Design of Jobs", *Industrial Relations*, (California) Oct. 1966, pp. 21-45.

Ford, Robert N. "Job Enrichment Lessons From A. T and T", *Harvard Business Review*, Jan-Feb 1973, pp. 96-106.

Gibson, Charles S. "Volvo Increases Productivity through Job Enrichment", *California Management Review* 15(4), Summer (1973): 64-66.

Hackman, J. Richard, Creg Oldham, Janson Robert and Purdy Kenneth. "A New Strategy For Job Enrichment", *California Management Review*, 17(4) 1975: 57-71.

Herzberg, Frederick. "One More Time: How do you Motivate Employees", *Harvard Business Review*, Jan-Feb 1968, pp. 53-62.

Lawler III, Edward E. "Developing a Motivating Working Climate", *Management Review*, July 1977, pp. 25-38.

Steers, Richard H. and Porter, Lyman. W. *Motivation and Work Behaviour*. New York: McGraw-Hill 1979.

Tichy, Noel M. "Organizational Innovations in Sweden", *Columbia Journal of World Business*, Summer 1974, pp. 18-28.

Walton, Richard E. "Quality of Work Life: What is it?" *Sloan Management Review*, Nov-Dec 1972, pp. 70-81.

_____ . "How to Counter Alienation In the Plant", *Harvard Business Review*, Nov-Dec 1972, pp. 70-81.

13
Group Dynamics and the Human Relations Organizational Model

V. ANANTARAMAN

SUMMARY

An individual as a member of a group is different from what he is outside the group. This is because the group has a tremendous influence on his personality, attitudes and behaviour. As such a knowledge of group dynamics is necessary for managers and supervisors not only to understand the functioning of informal groups but also to learn to integrate the goals of the informal groups with those of the formal organization.

Group dynamics is concerned with gaining knowledge about the nature of groups — how they develop and their effect on individual members and the larger organization. This chapter begins with a brief analysis of the properties of a group, such as, group goals, structure, norms and cohesion, with a view to understand how Rensis Likert developed his System Four Human Relations Organizational Model, applying the principles of group dynamics.

The System Four model based on the principle of the group as the basic building block of an organization includes other principles like that of integrated organization; supportive leadership; interpersonal climate conducive to decision-making; problem-solving; and conflict-resolution in participatory groups. This model of human relations is claimed by Likert to be superior to the traditional pattern of organization because of its better showing in the long-run, not only on the end-result variables as profits or sales or market share, but also on the intervening variables such as motivational, perceptual, behavioural, communication and decision-making which essentially reflect the enhancement of the value of the human assets in the organization. The chapter concludes with a critical assessment of the human relations model.

Introduction

The new human relations organizational theory proposed by Rensis Likert is largely the offshoot of the group dynamics approach to organizational behaviour. The influence of the European "wholistic" approach which states that the group is more than the sum of the individuals within it, gave rise to the conviction that the work group, not the individual, is the basic building block of the organization. Something new emerges with the group that did not exist with individuals. In other words, the effect is different from what one is individually. Many examples can be given to illustrate how group membership influences the personality, attitude and behaviour of individuals. For instance, an introvert joining a combat group may soon get over his inhibition because a recluse cannot last long in combat without friends; the leader of a street gang, mean and nasty in his group, behaves like a gentleman when he goes out with his girl on a date. Many parents have been pleasantly surprised at the exploits of a rather quiet child in group situations like the school picnic.

In this light, managements have been familiar with frequent instances of a very needy worker on incentive wages, resorting to practices of output restrictions as a result of being influenced by the members of his group. If a group has this potential to influence the attitude and behaviour of its members, there thus arises a need for managers to know and to understand group dynamics and the informal relationship in an organization.

Group Dynamics

Group Dynamics is concerned with gaining knowledge about the nature of groups, how they develop, and their effect on individual members and the larger organization.

Formation

Face-to-face interaction is basic to group formation, and human interaction characteristically involves communication in one form or another, written, verbal and non-verbal. Interaction and communication are not unique to group formation because in many togetherness situations, like when a few passengers on a train journey get together, one finds interaction and communication, not any group formation.

Informal organization of group takes place through the interaction of individuals with common goals conducive to interaction. This implies that the individuals perceive, even though dimly, that others also face the same problem and that co-operation with them has some relevance to the problem even if that of only providing mutual solace. It is true that initial goals which bring individuals together in the first place frequently remain as important factors in the continuation of group activities. But once the group gets stabilized, new goals may arise and these may account for the persistence of the group.

Structure

Without a structure, a group cannot achieve its goal. Structure refers to how the members of the group are related to each other with reference to the achievement of the goals of the group. Naturally, structure refers to the status and role relationship between the members of the group. Group structure tends always to be hierarchal along some dimension central to the realization of group goals. For example, the toughest and the strongest become the leaders of street gangs which are functioning in competition with other street gangs.

Status refers to the relative position in the power or influence hierarchy in the group, and the status of different individuals in the group, leader, lieutenant and follower, evolves through a process of consensus and stabilizes itself over a period of time. The same can be said of roles, and the necessary condition for stabilization is interaction among individuals over a period of time. Role is the expected behaviour of individuals in the group in relation to the goals of the group. Many roles can be identified among the individuals in the group. The major role is that of a leader performing the task facilitation role and/or the group maintenance role. The former is an intellectual role and the latter is an emotional role. Only leaders who are great men have performed both these functions. Often we find the group-maintenance role performed by a different person in the group, the trouble-shooting lieutenant for example. Groups seem to function better when two members of the group fill these two different roles.

A good number of other roles may also emerge in a group, and Paterson has identified the following roles in informal groups — the initiator who contributes ideas or sets group norms; the spokesman, who is the group's external representative, highly intelligent and adept at communicating the ideas of the group to others; the trouble-shooter who controls and reconciles internal relationships; the synthesizer who in the process of discussion in the group sums up at appropriate stages to keep the discussion purposeful; the historian who evaluates all present actions in the light of what was done in the past; and the mimetic who follows others' roles.

The role of the eccentric is unique. He is the one who represents a different point of view but who can play the role of a scapegoat, clown or joker. He may even function as a devil's advocate raising a stream of objections to a suggested course of action. The role of the eccentric is not widely understood; many aspirants for this interesting role fail the casting test because they imagine that the first and the only behaviour required is that in breach of group norms. Group loyalty is a necessary correlate of eccentricity. He is accepted by the group in spite of, or rather, because of his maintenance of a dissonant position. Eccentrics are needed so that others can conform while he provides the reserve of change options. Curiously, other members of the group often make their roles conservative to facilitate the work of the eccentric. He is willing to be this type and this is a condition of his group membership.

Group structure emerges through a process of consensus and stabilizes due to interaction among individuals with common goals over a period of time. It does not emerge as a result of a single episode. It is the result of a series of episodes, one episode following the other that helps evolve the various status and roles and achieves consensus for the structure.

Thus these relationships, status and roles, link a given individual to every other individual in the group in definite ways. In other words, an individual is related to another in the group by the relative position he occupies in the status hierarchy of the group and the role he plays in contributing to the achievement of its goals.

Group Norms

A norm is an idea in the minds of the members of the group

as a whole; an idea that can be put in the form of a statement, specifying what the member should do, ought to do, or is expected to do. Norms refer to standards of behaviour evolved by the group through consensus prescribing behaviour to its members under given circumstances. Norms are not formed by the group in relation to every kind of behaviour and every possible situation. They are formed in matters of consequence to the group. A working group has norms about its productivity, about its relationship to a supervisor, about behaviour among members of the group themselves and about non-work activities like attending weddings, celebrations, etc. In other words, norms serve to define how a member in good standing should behave in relation to (1) an outsider; (2) its own members; (3) the job; and (4) the emerging non-work activities.

Conformity to Norms

The concept of non-conformity is a little complex. Any deviation from the norm becomes a violation of the norm only when the deviation is beyond the limits of tolerable behaviour. A norm always permits a range of tolerable behaviour. The range of tolerable behaviour varies in extent, specificity and permissiveness, both in terms of the importance of the matter a norm pertains to, and in terms of the position of a particular member in the group hierarchy. For example, in matters crucial to the group such as identity of the group, major goals of the group and the continued existence of the group, the range of tolerable behaviour is proportionately narrow. Secondly, the leader is subject to a narrower range of tolerable behaviour than the other group members in matters of consequence to the group. A norm has a sanction pattern — conformity to norm is rewarded, non-conformity punished.

Ensuring Conformity

Depending on the importance of the norm to the group and the degree of deviation, non-conformity is reacted to by various measures, such as ridicule, scorn, silent treatment, avoidance, ostracism, use of invectives, physical punishment and even with death as in criminal gangs. The celebrated Hawthorne experiments revealed informal groups resorting to binging as a form of physical punishment to enforce conformity in informal groups. Binging is hitting a man with the edge of the hand on the upper arm when a member disapproves of something another has done, such as working too fast on the machine.

Rewards of Membership

The reward for conformity comes through the benefits of group membership to the individual. The group serves as a source of satisfaction, support and information.

As a source of satisfaction: It reinforces one's value system because it comprises of people sharing similar values. It helps establish one's identity in the vast impersonal wilderness of a formal organization. Identification with the group enables the individual to psychologically incorporate the strength of others in himself. Further, membership in a group confers on the individual the status of belonging to a distinct little organization which is more or less exclusive. A group further provides a forum of sympathetic listeners because all the members share common motives, values and goals, and thereby provides opportunities for self-expression. Finally, groups in general tend to meet the power needs of dominant members and the belonging needs of the rank and file.

As a source of support: Groups effectively serve the members as a protest and protective organization, through, for example, restriction of output. If they protest, it is usually against tight industrial engineering standards of output or other aspects of working conditions, like strict or overbearing supervision. If they are protective, such restrictions are used frequently to maintain the status quo and to resist change due to fears of a change in output standards, rates of renumeration, lay-off or retrenchment due to over-production. No wonder such informal groups are an embryo of larger and more formal organizations like the trade union.

As a source of information: Apart from the basic needs, an individual, according to Maslow, has two basic desires — the desire to know and the desire to understand. The desire to know is to be aware of reality, to get to the facts, to satisfy curiosity, and to see rather than to be blind. The desire to know is not sufficient. We have to understand what we know. The desire to understand is to systematize, to organize, to analyze, to look for relations and to search for meaning. These desires can be satisfied through information, in the absence of which, they cause anxiety and uncertainty in the minds of the individuals. In the absence of effective authentic channels of commnunciation within the organization, the grapevine becomes important to satisfy man's need to know and to understand. Gossip groups in highly centralized bureaucratic organizations are a case in point. People tend to join such groups in an effort to cluster around the individual who is the focal point in a communication network.

Such are the benefits of group membership that the individual derives, and the very fear of losing them serves as a powerful influence for individuals to conform to the group norms even though such conformity may conflict with certain other needs and values held by the individuals. No wonder the reward system operating within the group makes the individual different from what he is individually!

Social Control

Conformity is encouraged and non-conformity discouraged through social control. Social control operates through the medium of interaction and sentiment. This may be illustrated by two forms of punishment — avoidance and binging. Avoidance as a reaction to breach of a norm by an individual member will lead to a decrease in interaction of other members with him. As long as his interactions with other members of a group is a pleasure, any decrease, is in effect, a punishment. Binging is punishment of the offender for breach of a production norm. Punishment will not only bring the offender back to conformity with the norm but also keeps the norm alive in the minds of the other members of the group. The offender is chastised and the norm vindicated.

Social control becomes effective only when an individual gets integrated into the group and develops the sentiment of belonging to the group. This integration takes place when a person joins a group, occupies a definite status and role within it, and then forms attitudes appropriate to the norms relating to the roles, status and goals. Then only would the group values become one's own cherished values and the achievement of group goal is experienced as personal victory, and injury to another member becomes a personal concern.

Group Cohesion

Obviously social control is effective in cohesive groups. Group cohesion may be defined as the attractiveness of the members to the group or resistance of the members to leaving it. A cohesive group is one that provides satisfaction for its members or one that has a high probability of doing so. Anything contributing to member satisfaction with the group also leads to cohesion in the group.

The factors contributing to group cohesion are the following:

(1) proximity
(2) size
(3) similarities and attractiveness in terms of work activity, shared values or interests
(4) complementary personalities of members
(5) social rank, class and position
(6) supervisory practices
(7) external threats and pressures
(8) homogeneity of members in terms of race, religion, language, caste and community.

If cohesion is viewed as resulting from member satisfaction with the group, then the presence of status consensus, perceived progress towards group goals and perceived freedom for members to participate, contribute to member satisfaction with the group. A strongly felt need to maintain the identity and integrity of the group; a minimal level of divisive friction with the accompanying confidence that it can be sorted out; an adaptability to change through interpersonal readjustments; a strong in-group feeling; a shared consensus of goals and values; open interpersonal communication; and the pride of belonging to the elite group, characterize cohesive groups.

Management of Groups in Organizations

Many guidelines are available in the human relations literature on how to manage groups in organizations. However, Rensis Likert's approach is by far the most meaningful synthesis of group dynamics research and the most comprehensive, in the sense, that it views the organization as a whole. His approach is unique in behavioural science as it attempts to clarify the principles of organizational structure and organizational behaviour, especially the principles and practices of leadership that are responsible for both high productivity and high job satisfaction in the organization. A logical sequencing of knowledge on group dynamics can lead to an understanding of Likert's new theory of organization.

Management Attitudes

There are many steps in this logical sequence, foremost among which is the fact that management must have a positive attitude towards informal groups, for three good reasons.

(1) A formal organization contains the seeds of viable group formation. According to Delbecq, the technical, socio-technical and social dimensions of a position facilitate, over a period of time, the emergence of viable groups.

(2) An informal organization has a distinct advantage in the sense that it supplies a whole range of satisfactions which the formal organization cannot provide in order to maintain the morale of its employees.

(3) Groups are powerful is achieving their goals, whatever they may be. If management is able to bring about an integration of the goals of the group and the goals of the organization, groups would then achieve organizational goals.

Andre L. Delbecq analyzing the three dimensions of positions in a formal organization, namely, the technical, the socio-technical and social requirements, illustrated their interactions as follows:

> John Doe joins XYZ Corporation as a personnel management trainee. He is assigned to an office on the sixth floor within the personnel management department (proximity). He finds that most of the staff in personnel have been similarly trained in several nearby graduate schools (common training leading to shared concepts, values and attitudes). In carrying out his early work assignments he must converse with colleagues, primarily within the department (shared-work activities and socio-technical interactions). After several months, he is asked to play golf with the other members of the department, and soon the bi-weekly golf game is a standard recreational item (social dimension of the position). Interactions between persons (due to technical work requirements) leads to sentiments of liking (reinforced by shared professional norms arising out of training in a functional specialization) and this leads to new activities (social) and these, in turn,

mean further interactions. The more frequently persons interact with one another (ecological proximity and socio-technical requirements) the stronger their sentiments of friendship for one another are apt to be; the more frequently persons interact with one another, the more alike in some respects both their activities and sentiments become. The inter-related technical, socio-technical and social dimensions of John Doe's formal position as a personnel trainee, therefore, create all the necessary conditions for a viable group formation. This sub-group structure, in turn, results in behaviour patterns and normative concepts (norms, values and attitudes) which may or may not be congruent with the organizational objectives and the official decision system.

Integration of Goals

This step naturally relates to the possible ways by which an integration of the group goals and organizational goals can be brought about. Highly effective groups reveal the following three variables as responsible for group effectiveness: leadership, cohesion and communication. Any integration of goals has to come about through these variables. Quite interestingly, the influence of leadership on the other two variables is considerable. Not only can cohesive groups function more effectively with capable leadership but effective leadership, through its group building and maintenance roles, can contribute substantially to group cohesion.

Despite the independent effect of known behavioural science techniques to promote better interpersonal communication, the role of leadership in promoting better interpersonal understanding is very crucial. The leader has a greater responsibility in understanding the background, values and expectations of the members and in initiating openness and trust in interpersonal communication. It is no wonder then that leadership has become the focus of the human relations approach in order to bring about the integration of the goals of the group and the goals of the organization.

The Process of Integration

The employee-centered orientation enables the designated supervisor or manager to become the acceptable leader of his work group. However, integration of the goals of the group and the organization cannot be brought about by the superior being employee-centered alone. Besides being employee-centered, he should be goal-oriented and possess a capacity to spread a contagious enthusiam among his subordinates about the importance of the goals of the organization. In other words, the employee-centered supervisory style may produce favourable attitudes towards supervision, but the conversion of favourable attitudes into high performance does not automatically follow.

Employee-centered orientation may make the employees like their workplace much as they like a country club, and in fact may lead to less absenteeism and probably less turnover but not necessarily high performance. But employee-centered supervision does one important thing besides bringing about the transformation of the designated leader into an acceptable leader of his work group. It creates a climate conducive to convert the favourable attitudes toward supervision into high performance among members of his work group. The conversion of favourable attitudes into high performance is actually brought about through the technique of supportive relationships, namely, management by participation.

Supportive Relationships

The leadership principle enunciated by Rensis Likert is termed the principle of supportive relationships. Supportive leadership has both an orientation and a technique. The orientation is employee-centered and the technique is management by participation. The employee-centered orientation at the first level of supervision is called the employee-centered supervisory style and at the higher levels may be termed as subordinate-centered managerial style. This style of supervision or management is characterized by a genuine interest and unselfish concern on the part of the superiors for the success and well-being of their subordinates.

This orientation involves general supervision as opposed to high pressure close supervision; a concern for the personal problems of the subordinate; a keen desire to train able subordinates for higher jobs; the pursuit of constructive discipline with an educative, corrective or reformative orientation; a willingness to stand by the subordinate; an inclination to give recognition and credit to the subordinate for his contributions instead of taking the credit; keeping subordinates informed about how well they are doing and what is happening in the organization.

Lest the impression should be gained that the human relations approach takes a lenient view of discipline, the right emphasis should be given to the concept of constructive discipline. Apart from the positive orientation required, constructive discipline incorporates Douglas McGregor's Red Hot-Stove Rule of discipline, which demands that discipline should be with warning, immediate, consistent and impersonal. If this approach is followed there will not be any need for the supervisor to lose his temper nor the subordinate who is disciplined to feel hurt. Whatever the level, supportive leadership will be perceived by subordinates as unselfish, cooperative, sympathetic, democratic; it shows an interest in the success of workers and a willingness to help them.

Participative Management

Participation of subordinates in the decision-making process has essentially two dimensions — the extent of participation and the scope of participation. Invariably, bosses allow their subordinates to participate in decisions that they have themselves made. Ideally, participation should be extended not only to decision-making but also to defining the problem to which solution is sought. Participation should be real in the sense that it should not be confined to insignificant and innocuous areas, such as canteen and recreational facilities; nor should it be confined to nagging areas like safety, absenteeism and discipline where management solutions are hard to come by. Instead, it should be extended to vital production areas such as change in technology and timing of its introduction, production planning scheduling, and even performance appraisal.

Decision-making in participatory groups is through a process of consensus. Consensus is not necessarily a unanimous decision, more often it means that those who continue to disagree or have doubts about the decision will nevertheless publicly say that they are willing to support the decision. It connotes always unanimous support for the group decision. Success of decision-making by consensus in participatory work groups cannot be ensured unless the following three pre-conditions are perceived to exist by the members of the group:

(1) perceived freedom to express one's views in the group;
(2) perceived freedom to express opposition to views expressed by others in the group; and
(3) a feeling that he has been listened to and understood whenever he expresses his views or opposes the views expressed by others.

If these three pre-conditions can be ensured, the benefits of participation would be forthcoming. Thus:

(1) Participation leads to better decisions because decision by consensus is a synergistic decision arrived at by pooling the talents and resources of all members of the group;
(2) It leads to individual ownership of the group decision because everyone feels that he has contributed to the decision-making;
(3) It leads to commitment and involvement of members in implementing the decision as a natural consequence of their owning the decision; and
(4) Finally, follow-up becomes an eagerly sought after activity because of ownership, commitment and involvement of the group members in the decision-making process.

Among the many barriers to participation as a method of decision-making, problem-solving or resolving conflict, two of the managerial barriers deserve special emphasis:

(1) fear of loss of managerial authority over subordinates; and
(2) lack of managerial confidence in the subordinates' capacity to participate.

These barriers are not real because they are either the result of misconception about authority or the ambivalent attitude of managers to participation. Authority is power, and this power is given to the manager by virtue of the position he occupies in the organizational hierarchy, and secondly, it is given to him not to boss his subordinates (to exercise personalized power) but to produce results. Positional power becomes legitimate not only because of its basis but also because of the purpose, and this logic inevitably leads to the conclusion that the manager's authority is enhanced and not diminished or diluted by participation since the participatory group under his leadership produces better decisions and better results!

The ambivalent attitude of managers to participation has been established by research by Raymond E. Miles. The typical modern manager generally accepts and broadly endorses participation but they tend to rate themselves equal to, if not higher than their superiors, on such traits as creativity, ingenuity, flexibility and the willingness to change. They therefore expect their bosses to consult them. They frequently doubt their subordinates' capacity for self-direction and self-control and their ability to contribute creatively to departmental decision-making. Unless they change their attitudes, participation cannot become a reality in their organizations.

Furthermore, participation has the potential of satisfying the higher order needs of employees in the organization. It immediately satisfies the individual's need to belong since he is now an integral part of the team. His esteem needs are also satisfied because the fact that his ideas are sought after, accepted and implemented, means high ego involvement. Finally, the manager's capacity to motivate others to participate, brings out his potential for initiating creative contributions that would help solve organizational problems.

Interpersonal Climate

Success in decision-making by consensus in participatory work group is possible only when the interpersonal climate in the group is characterized by openness, trust and authenticity in interpersonal communication. As such, behavioural science techniques to improve interpersonal skills such as the Rogerian Counselling Approach, Bennis' Laboratory Training, Blake's Grid Training, or Berne's Transactional Analysis could, without any contradictions, be accommodated within the Likert's scheme of participative management.

Integrated Organization

Supportive leadership comprising an employee-centered orientation and management by participation will be effective only when two conditions are fulfilled. It is not enough that bosses at every level claim that they are following the principle of supportive relationships, the relationships must be perceived as being supportive, by subordinates at every level in the organization. These perceptions can be effectively assessed through the measurements of Liker's intervening variables. More importantly, the supportive relationships should not be confined to the relationships between the first level supervisor and the members of the work group, but should be extended to cover the relationships between all levels of management.

Through his advocacy of the principle of an integrated group pattern of organization, Rensis Likert has ensured the permeation of supportive relationships and an employee-centered orientation through the entire length and breadth of the organization. His advocacy of the principle takes into consideration organizational structural variables and results in a revolutionary restructuring of the organization. According to Likert's postulation, the organization will not derive the full benefits of its highly-effective groups, unless there is a link to the total organization by means of equally effective overlapping groups. The superior in one group is a subordinate in the next group and so on throughout the organization. This is Likert's celebrated linking-pin device to integrate the groups in the organization.

Figure 1 Integrated Organization: The Linking Pin

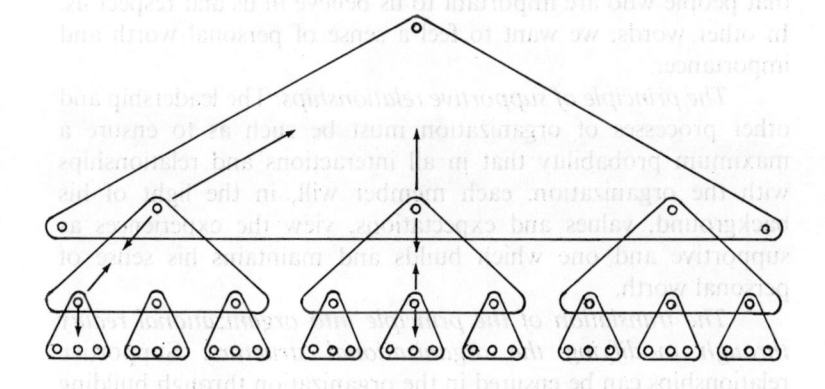

Note: The arrows indicate the linking-pin function

In sum, given the positive attitude of management towards informal groups, the goals of the group and the organization can be integrated through the twin principles of supportive relationships and integrated group pattern of organization. The logic of this integrating process is deceptively simple but far-reaching in its effects. The ideal organization as conceived by Likert would enjoy substantial congruence of objectives. It would have a high degree of harmony between individuals and their bosses; and between groups, individuals, and the organizations. In his scheme of things, the informal and formal organization will become one and the same; hence all social forces will support efforts aimed at achieving organizational goals.

The New Human Relations Organizational Theory

In his context, the formal statement of Rensis Likert's new human relations organizational theory can be readily appreciated. Like any other organizational theory it has three components:

(1) assumptions it makes about human nature;
(2) the principle of organization it derives from these assumptions; and
(3) the translation of this principle into an organizational reality.

Assumptions about human nature: This theory is based on the assumption that each one of us wants appreciation, recognition, influence, a feeling of accomplishment, and a feeling that people who are important to us believe in us and respect us. In other words, we want to feel a sense of personal worth and importance.

The principle of supportive relationships: The leadership and other processes of organization must be such as to ensure a maximum probability that in all interactions and relationships with the organization, each member will, in the light of his background, values and expectations, view the experiences as supportive and one which builds and maintains his sense of personal worth.

The translation of the principle into organizational reality through modifying the organizational structure: Supportive relationships can be ensured in the organization through building and maintaining highly effective work groups and linking them up into an overall organization by means of people who hold overlapping group membership.

Elements of the Theory

To reiterate, the four dimensions of this theory are:

(1) the validity of the group as the basic building block of the organization;
(2) organizational effectiveness flowing from linking groups through overlapping group memberships;
(3) supportive relationships emphasizing the relations between people in different hierarchal levels as it is within the group; and
(4) a conducive interpersonal climate characterized by openness and trust that would put into operation the principle of supportive relationships.

An organization integrated on the basis of group process, the principle of supportive relationships and the philosophy of participation will be a social system made up of interlocking work groups with a high degree of cohesion among its members and favourable attitudes and trust between superiors and subordinates. The application of the principle of supportive relationships not only satisfies the social and ego needs of the members of the organization but there is impressive evidence that economic motives will be tapped more effectively. As a result, a cooperative, reinforcing motivational system emerges in support of the activities and goals of the organization.

Likert not only asserts that his theory is based on principles and practices of managers who have achieved the best possible results in American business and government, but also that it is appropriate to all conditions, personalities, culture or technology. This claim of proven effectiveness and of potential for universal application is indeed provocative. Further, the strength of Likert's approach lies not only in the favourable effect his system has on end-result variables such as profits, output, sales, cost, or earnings, but on the intervening variables such as perception, motivation, communication, attitudes, and in brief, in preserving and not liquidating the human assets of the organization. He is highly critical of the present accounting system which fails to expose the short-run spurious earnings (achieved by pressure-oriented, threatening supervision) by liquidating some of the company's investment in the human organization. The Human Asset Accounting System that is being evolved will clearly prove, according to Likert, that, in the long run, not only are there productivity increases but there is also better showing on intervening variables under the cooperative motivational system.

Critical Assessment of Likert's Theory

George Strauss has subjected Likert's postulations to a critical assessment. Quite interestingly the criticisms he advances are not aimed at totally disapproving Likert's theory but are pleadings for refinements and modifications in order to make it realistic and workable in all conditions, as is claimed. Emphasis on face-to-face interpersonal relations is the foundation on which Likert's theory has been erected. Face-to-face orientation is a small group concept, but is the knowledge of the principles of small group effectiveness adequate for running a large complex organization?

The emphasis on ideal interpersonal relations is consistent with the emphasis on face-to-face relations. Failure of behavioural science techniques to promote openness, trust and authenticity in interpersonal communication will inevitably threaten the decision making process. The concept of group, not the individual, as the building block of the organization seems to ignore the potential of the individual to actualize alone. This seeming hostility on the part of Likert to individual effort seems to be uncalled for. Likert's theory is primarily personnel-oriented. It is concerned with only one factor, the human one, and the bulk of its attention is focused on a single human problem — leadership. The primary functions of the manager are not confined to relational areas alone but include conceptual, technical and administrative areas. A theory which entirely focuses on a single factor cannot represent a complete theory of organization.

The role of harmony is central to Likert's model. A complete congruence of goals between individuals and the organization may be envisioned in normative organizations like churches but not in economic organizations like businesses. In an organization, there is bound to be overlapping as well as conflicting goals between individuals and organizations. Likert's optimism of integrating the goals of the parties is not realistic. At best, the incongruence between the individual and the organization can provide the basis for continued challenge, but it cannot be assumed to disappear.

Likert, as is the case with other human relationists, does not ignore conflict in interpersonal relations but attributes its existence to immature, non-authentic interpersonal relations. Conflicts can therefore be resolved through a problem-solving approach, equipping managers with attitudes and skills necessary to resolve them and to eschew a win-lose approach. Though it may be argued that most of the conflict situations are not win-lose situations it cannot be assumed that objective zero-sum gain situations are non-existent. So long as zero-sum gain situations exist, issues can be resolved only through compromise, via bargaining, regardless of the amount of goodwill involved through authentic interpersonal relations.

The under estimation of zero-sum-situations naturally leads Likert to side-step the issue of labour management relations in his model. True, with his System Four Management, labour management relations have shown an improvement, but his model is not an answer to the power relationships between organized labour and management in the context of conflicting goals of the parties. This brings us back to the question of harmony, and the assumption that complete identity of interest between labour and management is utopian, at least in this century.

Likert's model takes into consideration organizational structure and its behaviour variables. However, the potential for universal application of this model of integrated group pattern of organization and participative management can be questioned. Technology, personality and culture may limit the application of this model to all economies and cultures. Only extensive experimentation can disprove these limitations with regard to universal application.

Conclusion

Despite these limitations, Likert's theory is deeply insightful and constitutes a single potent guide for management action. Likert has in fact demonstrated his propositions with insurance agents and a pajama company in his own country. The longitudinal studies he and his associates had undertaken in the United States have yielded results confirming his theoretical formulations.

Likert, however, thoughtfully observes that in the years ahead, management systems superior to any now envisioned will be developed as the science-based body of knowledge grows both in scope and accuracy. However, firms which wish to make full use of science-based management, both as we know it at present and as it evolves, can start now by moving towards something like System Four. Likert's confidence is tempered by scholarly modesty.

QUESTIONS

1. Explain the following properties of informal groups:
   - (i) group goals
   - (ii) group structure
   - (iii) group norms
   - (iv) group cohesion
2. Clearly explain the process of integrating the goals of the informal groups with those of the formal organization.
3. The principle of supportive relationships includes an orientation and a technique. Explain.

REFERENCES

Anantaraman, V. *Human Relations in Industry.* New Dehli: S. Chand and Company, 1980.
Bennis, Warren G. *Changing Organizations.* New York: McGraw-Hill, 1967.
————. et al., *The Planning of Change.* New York: Holt, Rinehart and Winston, 1976.
Blake Robert R. and Mouton, Jane S. *The New Managerial Grid,* Houston, Texas Gulf, 1978.
Delbecq, Andre L. "How Informal Organization Evolves", in Fred Luthans, *Contemporary Readings in Organizational Behaviour.* New York: McGraw-Hill, 1972.
Harris, Thomas A. *I Am Ok — You Are Ok.* New York: Harper and Row, 1974.
Homans, George C. *The Human Group.* London: Routledge and Kegan Paul, 1962.
Kelly, Joe. *Organizational Behaviour.* Illinois: Irwin-Dorsey, Homewood, 1969.
Lewin, Kurt. *Field Theory in Social Science.* (D. Cartwright, ed.), New York: Harper and Row, 1951.
Likert, Rensis. *New Patterns of Management.* New York: McGraw-Hill, 1961.
————. *Human Organization.* New York: McGraw-Hill, 1967.
Likert, Rensis and Jane Gibson Likert. *New Ways of Managing Conflict.* New Yorks McGraw-Hill, 1976.
Marrow, Alfred J., Bowers David G., and Seashore, Stanley E. *Management by Participation.* New York: Harper and Row, 1967.

Maslow, Abraham H. *Eupsychian Management*. Massachusettes: Irwin-Dorsey, Reading, 1965.
Miles, Raymond E. "Human Relations or Human Resources", *Harvard Business Review*, July-Aug 1965, pp. 148-163.
Rogers, Carl R., *Client Centered Therapy: Its Current Practice, Implications and Theory*. Boston: Houghton and Mifflin, 1965.
Sherif, Muzaffer and Sherif, Carolyn W. *An Outline of Social Psychology*. New York: Harper and Row, 1956.
Strauss, George. "Human Relations — 1968 Style", *Industrial Relations* 7, 3 (1968): 262-276.

14
Leadership

S. RICHARDSON

SUMMARY

The nature of leadership and some classical studies of leadership are examined. Various leadership theories are discussed as well as the various roles of leaders. It is concluded that no one theory of leadership has been demonstrated to be the best, but it is clear that a leader should choose a style suitable both to the situation and to the followers.

Introduction

Leadership involves interpersonal relations, and such relations are affected by the amount of conflict between the people concerned and the power held by them. There can be leaders of completely unorganized groups but when people are appointed leaders (and this implies of organized groups) we call them managers. An examination will be made of leadership against a background of research findings and various theories.

The Nature of Leadership

In Singapore everyone is familiar, at least at second hand, with a wide variety of current political, military and religious leaders because television, radio and the press constantly bombard us with news of their doings and sayings. Provided we understand the language they use we can follow their lives directly, and sometimes their deaths (violent or otherwise) by simply watching television. We can also read the vast literature that exists, not only about leaders of today and how they exercise their leadership responsibilities, but also about leaders of the past throughout the world. Some of their behaviour have been captured on film so that we can compare our perception of what we see on the screen with what historians and psychologists, and others, say about them; and often with what they say about themselves. Not surprisingly there are many inconsistencies — some would say that no leader's apologia can be trusted. Leadership is difficult to define but easy to recognize: its absence is rapidly apparent.

According to Hodgetts (1980), "Leadership is the process of influencing people to direct their efforts toward the achievement of some particular goal[s]." Koontz et al. (1980) say, "Leadership is the art or process of influencing people so that they will strive willingly toward the achievement of group goals." The main difference here is the use of the word "willingly" which may be taken to symbolize the differences between good and bad leadership. The essence of leadership is "following", i.e., it is the willingness of people to follow that makes a person a leader; or perhaps a "good leader". If you were told to stop reading now and to get up out of your comfortable seat you would be most reluctant to do so. However, if you were told, "MOVE OUT of your seat quickly because there's a poisonous snake underneath", you'd be less reluctant to remain seated, provided that you believed what you were told. Such a situation demonstrates the importance of communication, motivation, trust and integrity in the exercise of leadership.

However, returning to the question of the differences between good and bad leadership. These differences may lie in the absence or presence of "leadership characteristics" i.e., the ability to inspire others; drive; initiative; persistence in maintaining the aim; willingness to accept the consequences of action etc. A conflicting argument is that "personal characteristics" (i.e., high intelligence, emotional maturity, the need for power, problem-solving skills, etc.) are at least as important as the more nebulous leadership characteristics. It is worth noting that all managers are leaders but not all leaders are managers (since managers are appointed); and that almost all leaders are also followers — they need support from their superiors as well as from those they lead. It is sometimes said that one cannot be a good leader unless one is also a good follower. The contrary view is presented by Peter and Hull (1970), "How can the ability to lead depend on the ability to follow? You might as well say that the ability to float depends on the ability to sink." But such comments are less valuable than the studies that have been made of leadership.

Leadership Studies

Three major leadership studies conducted in the United States shed considerable light on leadership. The first, at the University of Iowa, concentrated on comparing authoritarian, democratic and laissez-faire styles of leadership (Lewin et al., 1939). The second study was carried out at Ohio State University and analyzed leadership in numerous types of groups and situations (Stogdill and Coons, 1957). At about the same time a research group at the University of Michigan tried to determine the "principles which contribute both to the productivity of the group and to the satisfaction that the group members derive from their participation" (Katz et al., 1950). These studies have been followed up by hundreds of similar studies in a wide variety of private and public enterprises. The results of years of research have been presented by Likert (1961). This research leads to the same general conclusions.:

1. people prefer democratic leaders who are considerate, friendly, trusting, and concerned for individual needs (i.e., are people-oriented rather than production-oriented); and
2. people prefer leaders who define relationships and goals, and achieve those goals, i.e., those who present a structured situation and are successful.

The remarkable change, for instance, in the apparent popularity of Mrs Thatcher in 1982 was probably linked to her success (as perceived by the British electorate) in the Falklands War. The continued popularity of PAP leaders in Singapore is certainly a reason for their continuing success. The theories of leadership may cast further light.

Theories of Leadership

Trait Theories: The trait approach depends on the theory that good leaders have common traits or distinguishing features. Numerous physical, mental and personality traits were researched from about 1930 to 1950. These attempts to identify a common list of leadership characteristics desirable in all circumstances failed. This is because a leader cannot be considered apart from the situation in which he leads. However, the research does demonstrate that leaders have higher intelligence than the average intelligence of their followers (not surprisingly), that they tend to be emotionally stable and mature, that they have a high need for achievement, and that successful leaders recognize the worth and dignity of their followers and are able to empathize with them.

Situational Theories (also known as contingency theories) say "How you lead depends on the situation". Such a view is based on impressive research findings, especially those produced by Fiedler and his associates. Fiedler (1967) developed a "contingency model of leadership effectiveness" containing the relationship between leadership style and "situation favourableness" defined in terms of:

1. the leader-led relationship (the most critical variable);
2. the degree of task structure (the second most critical variable); and
3. the leader's "position power", obtained through formal authority (the third most critical variable).

Situations are favourable to the leader if all three of the above are high, and vice versa. Fiedler discovered that under very favourable and very unfavourable conditions the task-directed leader was most effective. However, when the situation was in the intermediate range of favourableness the human relations or lenient type of leader was most effective. A more general conclusion was that a leader's personal traits must be compatible with the expectations and needs of his followers, the structure of the group and the problems it faces, and the environment in which the group operates. Fiedler's contingency-leadership model has recently been restated (Fiedler et al., 1976). Another contingency view of leadership is the "life cycle theory" (see Hersey and Blanchard, 1977). This theory also recognizes that different leadership styles are appropriate in different situations. Unlike Fiedler, however, the life cycle theory puts considerable emphasis on the leader's style flexibility and stresses the importance of the leader's ability to accurately analyze a situation and select the most appropriate leadership style.

Path-goal Theory: This theory is based on the concept that leadership is closely related to work motivation on the one hand and power on the other. The path-goal theory attempts to explain the impact that leader behaviour has on subordinate motivation, satisfaction, and performance. The House and Mitchell (1974) version identifies four major types of leadership:

1. Directive leadership — this is authoritarian, subordinates know exactly what is expected of them;
2. Supportive leadership — the leader is friendly and approachable with a genuine concern for followers;
3. Participative leadership — the leader invites and uses suggestions from subordinates but still makes the decisions;
4. Achievement-oriented leadership — this leader sets challenging goals for followers and shows confidence in them to attain these goals.

The path-goal theory, in contrast to Fiedler's model, suggests that these various styles can be and actually are used by the same leader in different situations. Using one of the four styles contingent upon the situational factors (especially the personal characteristics of subordinates and the pressures and demands facing them), the leader attempts to influence the perceptions of his subordinates and to motivate them by linking desired personal rewards or outcomes to organization goals. Thus the leader attempts to make the path to subordinates' goals as clear and as smooth as possible by using the appropriate style contingent on the situational variables present. Figure 1 summarizes the path-goal approach.

Figure 1

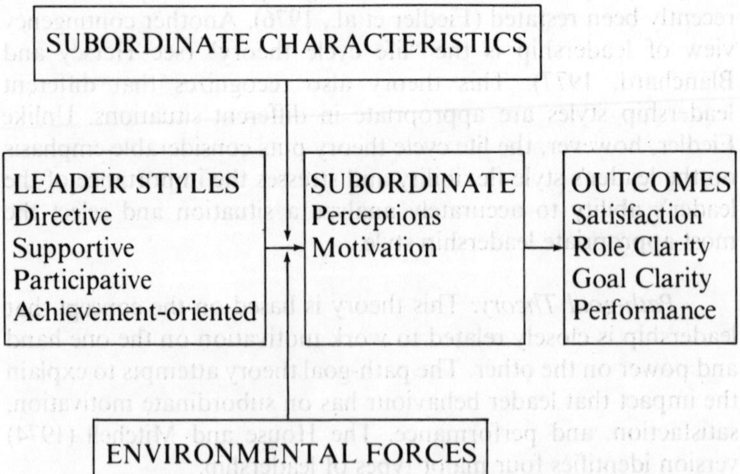

```
           ┌──────────────────────────────────┐
           │   SUBORDINATE CHARACTERISTICS    │
           └──────────────────────────────────┘
                          │
┌──────────────────┐  ┌──────────────┐  ┌──────────────┐
│ LEADER STYLES    │  │ SUBORDINATE  │  │ OUTCOMES     │
│ Directive        │  │ Perceptions  │  │ Satisfaction │
│ Supportive       │→ │ Motivation   │→ │ Role Clarity │
│ Participative    │  │              │  │ Goal Clarity │
│ Achievement-     │  │              │  │ Performance  │
│ oriented         │  │              │  │              │
└──────────────────┘  └──────────────┘  └──────────────┘
                          │
           ┌──────────────────────────────────┐
           │      ENVIRONMENTAL FORCES        │
           └──────────────────────────────────┘
```

As the path-goal theory has been developed only recently more research is needed for greater clarification. Despite inconclusive research findings, this theory offers a potentially valuable way of analyzing effective leadership.

Leadership Styles

The Managerial Grid proposed by Blake and Mouton (1966) is based on the traditional dichotomy of concern for people and concern for production (or results). The two form the axes on a grid in which the horizontal scale shows concern for production (from 1 to 9) and the vertical scale shows concern for people (from 1 to 9) thus giving 81 possible combinations of the two variables, (see Figure 2).

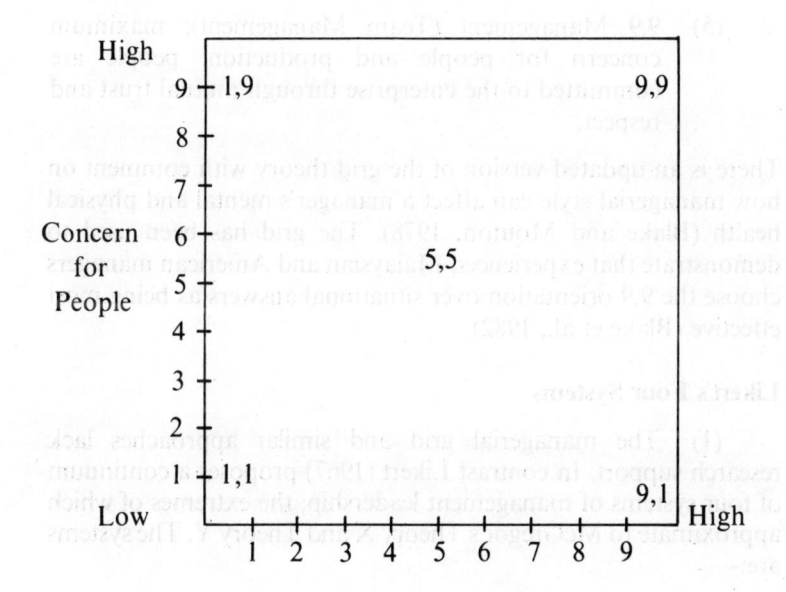

Figure 2

```
High
   9 ┬ 1,9                    9,9
   8 ┤
   7 ┤
Concern 6 ┤
  for         5,5
People 5 ┤
   4 ┤
   3 ┤
   2 ┤
   1 ┼ 1,1
                              9,1
Low                              High
     1  2  3  4  5  6  7  8  9
```

Concern for Production

Five basic styles shown on the grid are:-

(1) 9,1 Management (Scientific Management): Efficiency in operations results from arranging conditions of work in such a way that human elements interfere to a minimum degree;

(2) 1,9 Management (Country Club Management): thoughtful attention to needs of people for satisfying relationships leads to a comfortable, friendly organization atmosphere and work tempo;

(3) 1,1 Management (Impoverished): minimum concern for both work and people;

(4) 5,5 Management (Middle of the Road): adequate organization performance is possible through balancing the necessity to get out work and maintaining morale at a satisfactory level;

(5) 9,9 Management (Team Management): maximum concern for people and production, people are committed to the enterprise through mutual trust and respect.

There is an updated version of the grid theory with comment on how managerial style can affect a manager's mental and physical health (Blake and Mouton, 1978). The grid has been used to demonstrate that experienced Malaysian and American managers choose the 9,9 orientation over situational answers as being most effective (Blake et al., 1982).

Likert's Four Systems

(1) The managerial grid and similar approaches lack research support. In contrast Likert (1967) proposes a continuum of four systems of management leadership, the extremes of which approximate to McGregor's Theory X and Theory Y. The systems are:-

System 1 : exploitive authoritative,
System 2 : benevolent authoritative,
System 3 : consultative,
System 4 : participative group.

Significant research supports this approach, as well as the hypothesis that System 4 leadership is positively co-related with high productivity. Results in several countries (e.g., the United States, Japan, Yugoslavia and Singapore) suggest that this relationship is almost universal. The most important precept for a leader committed to System 4 is the Principle of Supportive Relationships. Simply stated, this says: Leadership must be such as to maximize the probability that each member will regard all interactions with the organization as supportive and enhancing his sense of personal worth and importance. This principle embodies two important concepts about human behaviour: i.e., (i) all persons have a strong desire to achieve and maintain a sense of personal worth and importance; and (ii) all individuals respond to an experience on the basis of its relation to their own values, goals, traditions, expectations, and skills.

(2) It is not enough for leaders to believe that they are supportive. Leaders, often, are wrong in their perceptions of their behaviour. The principle of supportive relationships depends upon the followers seeing the leader's behaviour as contributing to their sense of personal worth. This dimension of the principle emphasizes the necessity of the leader being correctly informed of other people's perceptions and reaction and of behaving so as to respect them.

(3) Since the particular way of applying the principle of supportive relationships must fit the immediate situation, appropriate leadership behaviour varies widely from one situation to another. But leaders should not try suddenly to change their approach to people otherwise they will be seen as "acting", rather than being true to themselves. Fiedler and others believing in the contingency approach (see page 167) might select in each situation a leader whose style fitted the followers, although in practice this is often not possible. A dynamic view is probably better. Leaders and followers can learn to change their behaviour such that a steady shift towards System 4 results. But this is not easy or quick, especially for leaders (who must be sufficiently sensitive to be able to gain an accurate perception of the needs behind the motivation which prompts the behaviour of their followers). At the same time leaders should see themselves as the instruments of change in raising the aspirations and values of their followers, and in increasing productivity by changing attitudes and behaviour.

The Role of the Leader

This section concentrates on what leaders do, and examines some of the ways in which they could improve their leadership. It should be remembered that all managers are leaders (of varying degrees of efficiency). It is also true that every leader is part of a group yet distinct from it too, for example, the captain of a sports team. Now consider some of a leader's important duties.

Representation and Support of Subordinates

All appointed leaders (i.e., managers) represent their subordinates *ex officio*, well or badly, and they can no more abdicate this than they can their responsibility for everything their subordinates do in the work situation. One approach, made famous by Likert (1961, pp. 113-115) is to look at leaders as "linking pins" that connect their group in the hierarchy to the one directly above it. The leader represents his group in all situations but his linking pin function (up and down) indicates his most important representational role. Poor representation means that the group or groups under a leader will not be linked into the enterprise effectively and hence not perform as well as they could. Closely allied is the need for supportive behaviour — if the leader doesn't support his subordinates he can hardly expect them to support him. His supportive behaviour should be based on a knowledge of his subordinates' needs — only thus can he effectively support and motivate them. The fundamental is to know your people, otherwise you won't know their needs. However, getting to know your people may be more difficult than it sounds especially when an atmosphere of mistrust or suspicion exists.

Developing Teamwork

The members of a working group need to know each other's functions and capabilities. Mutual understanding of each other's job and common understanding of the common task are essential, as are building and maintaining effective interpersonal relationships based on understanding the group's norms, processes and culture. The leader alone cannot develop teamwork. The three major factors are:

1. The leader, who must create the right climate by encouraging trust, cooperation and compatibility —this is a

function of his perceived integrity; delegation not only demonstrates trust but also saves time.
2. The subordinates, who expect the leader to satisfy their needs but may resist change, may feel insecure because of bad experiences, may have built up strong group goals in opposition to those of the larger group, or may be in conflict with one another (not necessarily for work reasons).
3. The environment, particularly the way in which the work is organized, especially if the work of one depends directly on the work of others, e.g., on a production line when slowness of one operator may slow down others.

The leader must analyze causes and seek remedies, with maximum participation by the group.

Counselling

A leader needs to counsel the led in order to reduce their frustration, conflicts or stress. The higher their motivation the higher will be their frustration if the goal is not reached. Leaders need to give advice and reassurance, and to resolve problems of conflict. Counselling can provide an important release of emotional tension.

Conclusions

No one theory of leadership has been clearly demonstrated as correct, but the contingency theories seem promising. What is clear is that a leader should choose a style to suit the situation based on a knowledge of those who are led. Knowledge of the research concerning leadership and the various theories should help leaders improve the quality of their leadership. If you have any doubts about your leadership ability, take comfort from Dixon (1979) who says, ". . . in times of stress even the poorest leaders like drunken fathers . . . are clung to with pathetic, if misplaced, dependancy".

QUESTIONS

1. Some leaders are called "charismatic", other "pragmatic". Relate this to the trait approach to leadership and explain the essential differences between these two styles.

2. How should a military leader differ from an industrial manager? How, and to what extent, is the answer to that question culturally determined?
3. "The effectiveness of leadership is determined by the interdependence of leader, followers, and the situation." Discuss.

REFERENCES

Blake, R. R., and Mouton, Jane S. "Managerial Facades," *Advanced Management Journal*, July 1966, p. 31.
_____. *The New Managerial Grid.* Houston: Gulf, 1978.
Blake, R. R., Mouton, Jane. S., and Mohamad Din Abu Samah. "The Situationalism vs One Best Style Controversy in Malaysia and the USA", *Singapore Management Review* 4, 1 (1982): 45-57.
Dixon, F. N. *On the Psychology of Military Incompetence.* London: Futura McDonald, 1979.
Fielder, F. E. *A Theory of Leadership Effectiveness.* New York: McGraw-Hill, 1967.
Fiedler, F. E., Chemers, M. M., and Mahar, Linda. *Improving Leadership Effectiveness: The Leader Match Concept.* New York: Wiley, 1976.
Hersey, P., and Blanchard, K. H. *Management of Organizational Behavior.* 3rd ed., Engleword Cliffs: Prentice-Hall, 1977.
Hodgetts, R. M. *Modern Human Relations.* The Dryden Press, 1980.
House, R. J., and Mitchell, T. R. "Path-Goal Theory of Leadership", *Journal of Contemporary Business,* Autumn 1974, pp. 81-97.
Katz, D., MacCoby, N., and Morse, Nancy. C. *Productivity, Supervision & Morale in an Office Situation.* University of Michigan, 1950.
Koontz, H., O'Donnell, C., and Weihrich, H. *Management.* 7th ed., McGraw-Hill, 1980.
Lewin, K., Lippitt, R., and White, R.K. "Patterns of Aggressive Behaviour in Experimentally Created 'Social Climes' ", *Journal of Social Psychology,* May 1939, pp. 271-276.
Likert, R., *New Patterns of Management.* McGraw-Hill, 1961.
_____. *The Human Organization.* McGraw-Hill, 1967.
Likert, R., and Likert, Jane. C. *New Ways of Managing Conflict.* New York, McGraw-Hill, 1976.
Peter, L. J., and Hull, R. *The Peter Principle.* London: Pan Books, 1970.
Stogdill, R. M., and Coons, A. E. (eds.) *Leader Behavior: Its Description & Measurement.* Ohio State University, 1957.

15
Leadership Effectiveness

V. ANANTARAMAN

SUMMARY

This paper contains two sections. The first section considers the impact of Management by Objectives (MBO) on job attitudes and the performance of individual managers within the framework of the expectancy Model of Motivation postulated by Lyman Porter and Edward Lawler. It explains how the properties of MBO have the potential to make the relationship between key variables of the expectancy model direct.

The second section deals with the Grid Styles of management advocated by Robert Blake and Jane Mouton. The discussion centres round the impact of the various styles of management in dealing with conflict in work groups; evoking commitment from subordinates; achieving goal congruence; stimulating creativity; and encouraging critique learning in the work situation in order to advocate team management as the ideal managerial style, since this shows optimum consideration for both production and people.

MBO and the Porter and Lawler Model of Motivation

Management by Objectives

Management by Objectives or MBO as it is popularly known is a powerful management tool to bring about an integration of the goals of the organization and the individual. As a management technique, it is thoroughly consistent with the Y Theory assumptions about human nature as advocated by Douglas Mcgregor. MBO operates in the realm of satisfying the higher order ego/esteem and self-actualization needs as propounded by Abraham Maslow. MBO provides opportunities for making the manager's job challenging, responsible and meaningful. It is a powerful medium to uncover many hidden problems blocking the realization of the objectives of the organization. It may lead to restructuring of a job or the organization itself. Part of its value lies in opening up communications in the organization and in encouraging man to question existing policies, practices and sacred cows.

Assuming that the top management understands the concepts, methodology and implications of MBO and given their total commitment to its implementation, the process begins with the clear enunciation of the corporate objectives which will be further split into divisional or departmental objectives and point to the identification of the individual manager's objectives. All these follow the set procedures spelt out in any MBO literature. To understand the analysis, it is sufficient if the reader confines himself to what MBO means at the level of the individual manager. After all, we are primarily concerned with the individual manager's job attitudes and job performance.

MBO at this level believes in the manager's job analysis, not with a view to indicate his duties and responsibilities, but to indicate what he has to achieve in the key areas of his job. Hence job analysis is undertaken to identify the key areas in which the manager has to produce results. Once these key result areas are identified, it is left to the individual manager to set up objectives, targets or performance standards in these areas. These performance standards are measurable standards. Simultaneously, the necessary control information is also set up or identified with which the progress of the manager is to be monitored. The requirements regarding the timing, frequency and adequacy of control information are then determined.

Management Guide or Management Job Description is nothing but a document in a pocket book form containing information on key result areas; performance standards with deadlines; and control information. While the manager performs his tasks as per the Management Guide, he submits himself to a periodic performance review when his performance is appraised by the manager against the targets he has set out to achieve in the key result areas. Self-appraisal of performance is a hallmark of MBO. The performance review session is not to criticize or condemn the manager but to understand and help him to improve his performance. Failure to reach targets might be due to ambitious standards, inadequacy of the control information or inadequate skills or abilities of the manager. The performance review identifies the manager's training needs, improves control information and results in a Job Improvement Plan. The manager is allowed to implement the improved plan and this will be reviewed during the next performance review and so forth. This is MBO at the level of an individual manager.

Success of MBO depends entirely on the interpersonal skills of the boss and attitude in understanding his subordinate, from the subordinate's point of view. The job analysis; the identification of the key result areas; the setting up of performance standards and control information; performance reviews; and the rest, are the result of the boss-subordinate interaction in an atmosphere of mutual confidence and trust. Since a conducive interpersonal climate cannot be wished into existence over night, many organizations have created the institution of MBO advisers. MBO advisers at the rate of at least one for every twenty managers, are recommended to be chosen from among managers with a reputation of being respected for their honesty, openness and integrity. The MBO advisers are present during these interactions in the initial stages to minimize the distrust and suspicion between the superior and subordinate managers, but as MBO gains ground and becomes a way of life, the MBO advisers wither away. The centrality of superior-subordinate relationship in predicting the success of MBO in an organization has been emphasized by R.J. Chesser (see References on p. 193).

MBO and Managerial Attitude and Performance

The contributions of Lyman W. Porter and Edward E. Lawler have been significant in analyzing the relationship between job attitudes and job performance. Their theoretical model, reproduced on p. 178 (see Figure 1), provides a way of thinking about the relationship among a large number of variables, nine in all, that have not previously been combined in a meaningful manner.

Essentially the authors elaborate on three sets of basic relationship in their model:

(1) the relationship between job performance and job satisfaction;
(2) the relationship between effort and job performance; and
(3) the relationship between two of the job attitudes and effort.

Figure 1
The Porter-Lawler Motivation Model

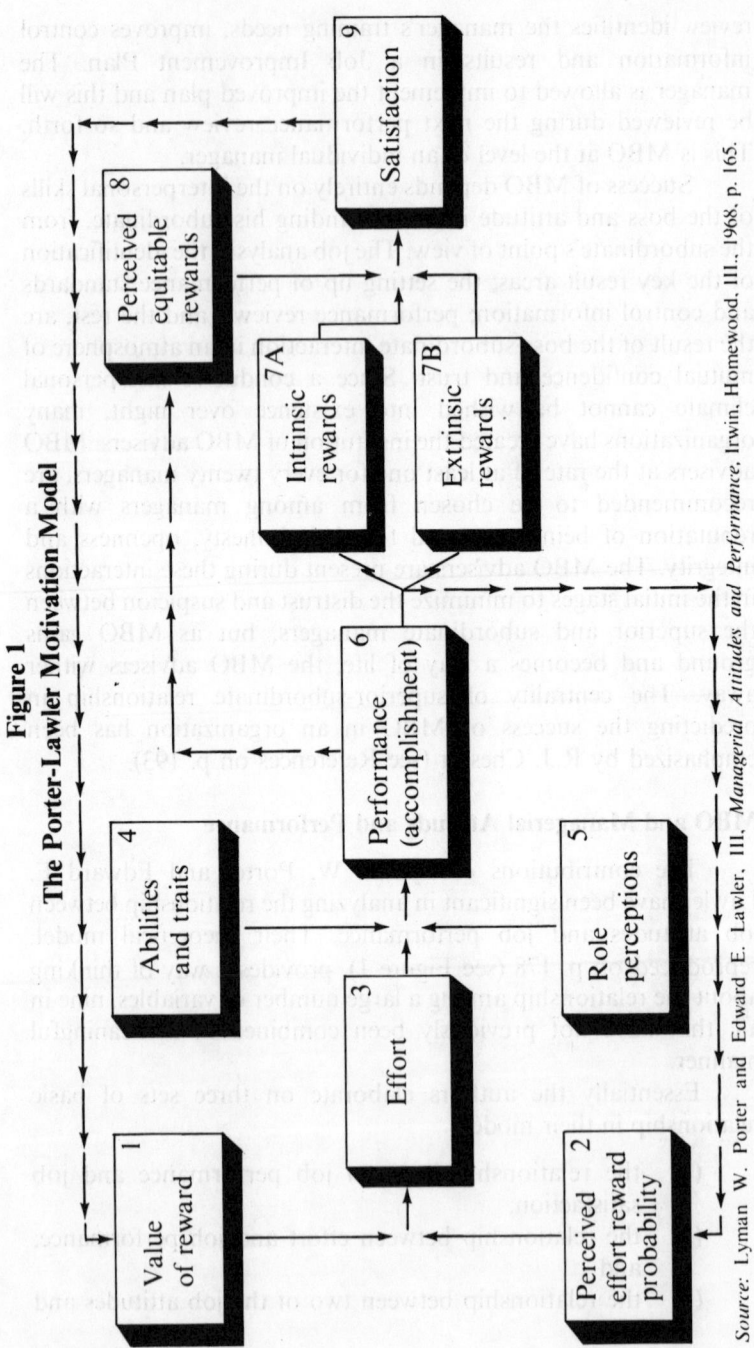

Source: Lyman W. Porter and Edward E. Lawler, III, *Managerial Attitudes and Performance*, Irwin, Homewood, Ill., 1968, p. 165.

Besides these three basic relationships they throw some light on two feedback relationships:

(1) the relationship between job satisfaction and the value the individual attaches to potential reward; and
(2) the relationship between reward and the effort-reward probability as perceived by the individual.

The purpose of this chapter is not to question the direction of the relationships postulated between the variables but to elaborate on the feasibility of strengthening the relationship between the three crucial variables, namely, effort, performance and satisfaction. This chapter also discusses reducing the negative impact of the mediating variables through Management by Objectives. We would, in our approach, like to keep the discussion at a theoretical level in the sense that we are not concerned with what actually happens to these mediating variables in organizations implementing the MBO but with what ways MBO, in its theoretical formulation, is expected to influence these mediating variables. It is our contention that MBO is likely to strengthen the relationship between effort, performance and satisfaction through overcoming the possible negative impact of the mediating variables on them.

Basic Relationship

Relationship between Performance and Satisfaction

According to Figure 1 "satisfaction" is connected to "performance" through a third variable, "rewards". Let us assume, for the sake of simplicity, that "rewards" are directly related to "performance", in other words, the organization ensures that differential rewards are given for differential performance. In this situation, satisfaction may directly be a function of the amount of rewards. In actual practice, the relationship between rewards and satisfaction is not that simple. Satisfaction is a derivative variable, and it is derived not only (1) from the actual amount of rewards, but also (2) from the "perceived equitable reward". "Perceived equitable reward" is defined as the amount of reward that a person feels is fair for the performance of his organizational task. Satisfaction is therefore defined as the extent to which the rewards actually received, meet or exceed the perceived equitable reward. A person is dissatisfied to the degree that perceived equitable reward exceeds actual reward. There is great satisfaction when there is small or little difference; and greater satisfaction when there is a large difference.

MBO theoretically helps to establish a link between "performance" and "perceived equitable reward". In fact Porter and Lawler themselves established this link to depict the fact that self-rating of performance seems to act rather directly upon this variable. When performance is assessed or rated by the superior there may not be any close connection between performance so assessed and perceived equitable reward. But performance assessed by self-rating demonstrates a connection. This comes about because self-rating of performance is a major influence on an individual's feelings, about what levels of rewards he should receive as a result of his performance. The performance review sessions under MBO centre around self-assessment of performance against the performance standards the individual himself has set in the key result areas. In other words, self-rating plays a dominant role in assessing performance under MBO. Porter and Lawler have further demonstrated that the relationship between rewards and performance can at best be depicted by a wavy line, the line connecting "performance" and "intrinsic rewards" being less wavy than the one connecting "performance" and "extrinsic rewards".

By and large, extrinsic rewards are organizationally controlled rewards such as pay, fringes, and promotions. More generally they are rewards external to the individual, given to the individual by others. In spite of the claims of many organizations that they are following a differential extrinsic reward policy in rewarding the performance of their managers, it has been found that there is a low correlation between performance and extrinsic rewards. This is because performance is difficult to measure and in dispensing rewards like pay many other factors are frequently taken into consideration. So long as differential rewards are not strictly based on differential performance, the relationship between performance and extrinsic rewards will be imperfect.

MBO cannot claim that its appraisal system establishes such a direct link between extrinsic rewards and performance. On the other hand, we are warned that if extrinsic rewards like pay and promotions are directly linked to performance standards in the key result areas, MBO is doomed to failure. The reasons for this warning are well-known. While the recommendation of the MBO advocates is to keep the "salary review" entirely separate from MBO, it cannot be denied that the boss, given the task of appraising the performance of subordinate managers even at a separate salary review, has a much better basis for doing the review if MBO is in force. The boss can take into account not only the achievement of the targets set, but also the way in which they have been set, the difficulties to be overcome and the job improvement plans that can be accomplished. This is the same as saying that under MBO, the relationship between extrinsic rewards and performance is likely to be more direct than under "no MBO".

On the other hand, the relationship between performance and intrinsic rewards can definitely be made more direct under MBO. Intrinsic rewards are given to the individual by himself for good performance. Even in the absence of MBO, since intrinsic rewards are internally mediated rewards they are more likely to be directly related to good performance. Porter and Lawler indicate the relationship by a less wavy line (compared to the wavy line linking extrinsic rewards to performance) because the extent to which such intrinsic rewards are obtainable in the work situation will depend primarily upon the way in which the job and tasks are structured by the organization. If the design of the job provides sufficient variety and challenge there will be a direct connection between performance and intrinsic rewards because when a person feels he has performed well he can reward himself. If the design of the job does not involve these characteristics, then there would be no direct connection between good performance and intrinsic rewards. Thus the degree of connection between performance and intrinsic rewards is dependent upon the make-up of the job duties, i.e., whether the job provides opportunities for autonomy, challenge and growth. It is needless to say that MBO based essentially on the principle of self-actualization is expected to provide such opportunities; in fact MBO permits not only restructuring of jobs but also changes in organizational structure, if need be.

To sum up, considering the relationship between performance and satisfaction in the theoretical model, we can postulate that MBO would, to a large extent, either directly or indirectly, mitigate the impact of the mediating variables on the relationship between performance and satisfaction, and make the relationship more direct.

Relationship between Effort and Performance

In considering the relationship between effort and performance, Porter and Lawler have postulated that the relationship of higher effort leading to higher performance has to be qualified to include the effects of two other variables: (1) abilities and traits; and (2) role perception. These two variables interact multiplicatively with effort to determine performance.

Abilities and traits (personality traits like intelligence) are defined as the currently developed power to perform. This definition implies that abilities and traits put a current upper limit on the performance resulting from the application of effort. If additional training results in improved abilities and traits, then a new upper limit would be placed on the performance possibilities of the individual.

The strength of MBO lies not only in not taking these abilities and traits as unalterable but also in not allowing the training needs to be determined by the whims and fancies of the boss. The continuation of the MBO adviser even after the introduction of MBO in an organization is partly to facilitate the training needs of the manager to be assessed and followed up. The MBO adviser sits in on performance reviews on a periodic basis to assess the training needs of managers, coordinates formal training needs and, draws up management training programmes. The continuing importance given to training during periodic performance reviews is sufficient evidence supportive of MBO's concern with increasing the managers "currently developed power to perform". Training in the interpersonal area is aimed at improving the personality traits of individual managers through interpersonal techniques such as non-directive counselling, T-group training, transactional analysis, managerial-grid training or even using the psycho-analytical approach to personality problems. These are totally consistent with MBO's basic assumptions and purposes. In sum, the entire area of "currently developed power to perform" is an area of great interest for MBO, continually interested in raising the ceiling set for individual abilities and traits through properly timed effective training.

The area of role perception is the one which is directly influenced by MBO. Under the conventional management job description there is room for misdirected effort due to role misconceptions. The conventional job description is usually a list of duties and responsibilities, necessary perhaps to outline the job during the recruiting stage but hardly helpful to the manager once he is in the saddle. The fundamental difference between the conventional job description and the MBO job description (MJD) is that the former describes what the manager has to do; the latter, what he has to achieve. There is a world of difference between the two. The management job description under MBO not only mentions the key result areas in which results have to be achieved but also insists on performance standards being set in these key result areas. This helps the manager, through control information, to monitor the progress achieved in the key result areas. There is no room for role misconception under MBO.

Role perception enters into the relationship between effort and performance by determining the direction of the application of effort. High effort, if misdirected, will not result in high task-relevant performance. The scope for proper role perception is infinitely greater under MBO job description than under the conventional job description of the manager.

The model postulates that because both role perception and abilities (including traits) are assumed to intervene between effort and performance, effort will not be perfectly related to performance. Since the model hypothesizes that abilities (including traits) and role perception interact multiplicatively with effort to produce performance, MBO theoretically can ensure that the value of these variables can be kept positive through continual determination of training needs and dynamic management job description. As a result the relationship between effort and performance is greatly strengthened.

Relationship between Job Attitudes and Effort

Traditionally the organizations as well as the researchers have given importance only to one job-attitude variable, namely, job satisfaction, in understanding and modifying employee motivation. Porter and Lawler are of the view that two other job attitude variables, namely, (1) "value of reward" (attractiveness of a possible reward); and (2) "perceived effort-reward probability" are equally important in influencing effort. They hypothesize that the greater the value of a set of rewards and the higher the probability that receiving such rewards depends upon effort, the greater the effort that will be put forth by an employee in a given situation.

People want to obtain various rewards from their jobs — a certain level of pay and bonus, fringe benefits, security, status, rewarding interpersonal relations, personal growth, and the like. Furthermore, each person attaches different degrees of importance or value to these various potential rewards. It follows, therefore, that unless effort is expected to lead to the reward that is valued by the recipient, the employee will not be motivated to expend this effort onto his organizational task.

Organizations very often ignore the fact that regardless of the value the "giver" places on a reward, its motivational influence comes about only as a result of the value the "receiver" places on it. The reward system and practices in organizations have not taken into consideration this motivational aspect of reward, namely, the value the individual attaches to potential rewards. The question is whether MBO can overcome this lacuna in the organizational reward system. In other words, would it be possible to claim that under MBO the performance standards set and achieved in the key result areas lead to rewards which are valued by the recipient? The contention here would be that under MBO the probability of this variable (value of reward) acquiring positive value is very much higher than otherwise.

Porter and Lawler's classification of rewards into extrinsic and intrinsic rewards is meaningful provided we understand that while intrinsic rewards are intangible, not all extrinsic rewards are tangible. Among extrinsic rewards, pay, fringe benefits and promotion are examples of tangible rewards, but rewarding interpersonal relations, pretige, praise, recognition, are intangible extrinsic rewards. Whatever may be the degree of relationship between performance and tangible rewards, it can be postulated that under MBO the relationship between performance and intangible rewards will be very close. Given the skills of the boss to understand the subordinate from the subordinate's point of view (this skill can be built in through training) and the helping relationship between them — a *since qua non* of MBO — the MBO system offers enormous scope for the boss to reward the subordinate (and also the subordinate to reward himself) for his performance in terms of the rewards he values most in the intangible rewards area.

We assume that the periodic performance review sessions under MBO are a dynamic on-going activity — not to criticize, admonish or condemn the subordinate — but to help, and to evolve rewarding interpersonal relationships; to facilitate personal growth through rewards in the realm of self-esteem and other's esteem; and to promote, through suitable job-design changes, opportunities for self-actualization. It is in this context, it is claimed, that MBO, through its built-in flexibility to reward the individual with rewards he values, has a greater probability to ensure that this variable will acquire a positive value and hence becomes a positive influence on motivation and to increasing effort.

The other job attitude, "effort-reward probability" refers to an individual's perception of whether differential rewards are based on differential amounts of effort on his part in the work situation. Effort-reward probability depends on two other probabilities or expectations:

(1) the probability that "reward" depends upon "performance";
(2) the probability that "performance" depends upon "effort". This point need not be laboured on because we have shown already that these two probabilities are likely to be higher because MBO has potential to mitigate the negative impact of the variables; mediating between effort and performance on the one hand, and performance and rewards on the other. To sum up, the two job attitude variables, (value of reward and effort-reward probability) are likely to acquire positive values under MBO, and as a result will encourage increased effort.

Feedback Relationships

Relationship between "Satisfaction" and "Value of Reward"

The model says that each person attaches different values to different potential rewards; it does not specify in detail how various rewards acquire differential value. However, the model does contain a feedback loop from "satisfaction" to "value of reward". The reason for the feedback loop is to indicate that both Porter and Lawler assume that one of the ways that potential rewards acquire value is through their ability to satisfy various needs on the Maslovian scale. This is the assumed impact of satisfaction on "value of reward". The model posits that for any individual at a particular point in time there are a variety of potential rewards to which he attaches differential values. Since

MBO is expected to be highly effective in satisfying higher order growth needs which are not easily satiable, the impact of satisfaction on the "value of reward" is not likely to be negative. MBO in a sense ensures reinforcement of the positive effect of job satisfaction on the "value of reward" by operating more at the level of higher than lower order needs.

Relationship between "Effort-Reward Probability" and "Rewards"

The second feedback relationship relates to the relationship between effort-reward probability and the "connection perceived by the individual between performance and rewards. This relationship implies that the individual's expectations that "effort leads to rewards" will be influenced by the "connection he perceives between reward and performance". Since the perceived connection between performance and rewards is likely to be closer under MBO, this feedback relationship will be stronger under MBO. Furthermore, under MBO, the relationship between self-rated performance and perceived equitable reward is likely to be closer, and the connection between performance and quantum of actual reward becomes less vitiated by the postulated possibility of the equity-reality gap (gap between perceived equitable rewards and actual rewards). In other words, under MBO, the loop can be drawn from the reward boxes with greater confidence.

In short, it may be stated that Porter and Lawler's magnificient effort to combine all the nine variables in a meaningful way reveals that the relationship between effort, performance and satisfaction (even the circular relationship) is subject to severe constraints imposed by mediating variables. It has been explained that MBO has a direct bearing on these mediating variables. MBO's impact on (1) rewards; (2) equity-reality gap; (3) abilities and traits (4) role perception; (5) value of reward; and (6) effort-reward probability is such that it overcomes the negative influence of mediating variables on effort, performance, and satisfaction, and as a result strengthens the relationship between them very effectively. A study of the correlations between these basic variables before and after introduction of MBO in an organization will help test the validity of this postulation.

Robert R. Blake and Jane S. Mouton developed a Managerial Grid as shown in Figure 2.

Figure 2   The Managerial Grid

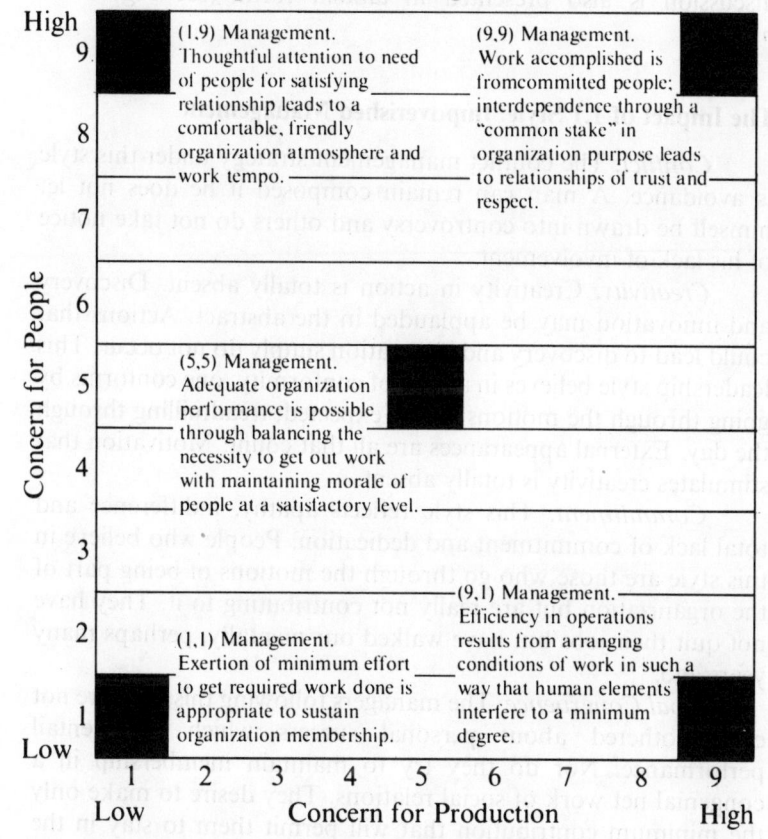

Concern for People		
High 9	(1,9) Management. Thoughtful attention to need of people for satisfying relationship leads to a comfortable, friendly organization atmosphere and work tempo.	(9,9) Management. Work accomplished is from committed people; interdependence through a "common stake" in organization purpose leads to relationships of trust and respect.
5	(5,5) Management. Adequate organization performance is possible through balancing the necessity to get out work with maintaining morale of people at a satisfactory level.	
Low 1	(1,1) Management. Exertion of minimum effort to get required work done is appropriate to sustain organization membership.	(9,1) Management. Efficiency in operations results from arranging conditions of work in such a way that human elements interfere to a minimum degree.
	Low Concern for Production High	

Source: Robert R. Blake, Jane S. Mouton, Louis B. Barnes, and Larry E. Greiner, "Breakthrough in Organization Development," Harvard Business Review, November-December 1964, p. 136.

The grid does not show results produced but rather the dominating factors in managerial thinking with regard to getting results. Based on the findings from the research Blake and Mouton conducted, they conclude that managers perform best under a 9,9 style as contrasted, for example, with 9,1 or the 1,9 styles. The grid has been given considerable importance in the management development programmes, but it should be noted that there is little evidence to support the conclusion that a 9,9 style is most effective in *all* situations.

The following is a brief account of the impact of these managerial styles on dealing with: conflict, creativity, commitment, goal congruence, and critique learning. The discussion is also presented in tabular form, (see Figure on p. 189).

The Impact of 1.1 Style: Impoverished Management

Conflict: The conflict management strategy under this style is avoidance. A man can remain composed if he does not let himself be drawn into controversy and others do not take notice of his lack of involvement.

Creativity: Creativity in action is totally absent. Discovery and innovation may be applauded in the abstract. Actions that could lead to discovery and innovation simply do not occur. This leadership style believes in a kind of conformity, one conforms by going through the motions that is expected, treadmilling through the day. External appearances are all that count. Motivation that stimulates creativity is totally absent.

Commitment: This style reflects apathy, indifference and total lack of commitment and dedication. People who believe in this style are those who go through the motions of being part of the organization but are really not contributing to it. They have not quit their jobs but have walked our mentally, perhaps many years ago.

Goal Congruence: The managers following this style are not even bothered about personal success which may entail performance. Nor do they try to maintain membership in a congenial net work of social relations. They desire to make only the minimum contribution that will permit them to stay in the organization, to be paid and to enjoy the advantages of welfare and retirement.

Critique: This style is alien to learning. However, a manager might rationalize a laissez faire approach of trial and error by claiming that it permits a subordinate to learn by himself from his own mistakes in the school of hard knocks.

The Impact of 1.9 Style: Country Club Management

Conflict: This style believes not in avoiding conflict but in smoothing it by letting a man know that with a little patience he will find that all is right. Peace, harmony and warmth will result in

Figure 3 : Impact of Grid Managerial Styles on Behavioural Variables

Variables \ Styles	1.1	1.9	9.1	5.5	9.9
Conflict	Avoidance	Smoothing	Suppression	Compromise	Confrontation
Creativity	Applauded in the abstract not displayed in action	Smothered in sweetness and love	Functional creativity stifled, dysfunctional creativity promoted	Pseudo creativity. Marginally different from status quo. Imitation rather than innovation	All resources are utilized with maximal creativity
Commitment	Apathy and indifference — not quit the job but walked out of it mentally	Corporate welfarism: gives much asks for little	Present among leaders: absent among members	Commitment to marginal improvements tried out elsewhere	Total commitment because the team owns decisions
Goal Congruence	Minimum acceptable performance	Whatever comes out of gratitude	Leaders drive for results; but unlikely to achieve them	Settles for half-a-loaf not for the whole	Striving for integration of goals
Critique	Alien to all learning. Rationalizing abdication through laissez faire pretense	Dispenses compliments for average performance; and avoids criticism of bad performance. No motivation for self-analysis and self-renewal	Believes in telling not listening; I know complex combined with arrogance and ignorance	Criticism sandwiched between compliments; oblique suggestions	Authority is not the source of truth: looks for facts and evidences through analysis, open and candid.

this style but the problem will persist. Smoothing as a technique of conflict resolution, believes in playing up the similarities and playing down the differences.

Creativity: This style promotes an attitude under which the rule of relationship is "Don't say anything, if you can't say something nice". This attitude smothers creativity in sweetness and love. The kind of disagreement that might provoke resentment is avoided and along with it opportunities of creativity.

Commitment: This style provides a nurturing climate for it gives much and asks little. Merit is muted, incompetence tolerated, and indifference excused. Corporate welfarism is no less debilitating than is custodial treatment of healthy people in other walks of life!

Goal Congruence: Under this style the leader is more concerned about being liked and accepted, not for commitment of members to production. Whatever production results out of gratitude for the congenial social relationships contributes to organizational objectives. While organizational members are warm, friendly and well-related, the organization becomes flabby, sluggish and soft, and neglects all problems and misses all opportunities.

Critique: Dispensing compliments for good or average performance but avoiding criticisms for bad or unacceptable work is the approach in this style. It "teaches" people that their activities are appreciated while discouraging them from thinking differently from what the boss might want or from what they think safe. There is no motivation for self-examination and self-renewal.

The Impact of 9.1 Style: Task Management

Conflict: This style believes that conflict can be controlled by overpowering it or by suppressing one's adversary. "Yours is not to question why" is the attitude of this leadership style, and extracts compliance on the authority-obedience formula.

Creativity: Since this style is based on the authority-obedience model it expects compliance to any decision or direction. The exercise of initiative is equivalent to insubordination. While positive creativity is stifled and smothered, this style provokes creativity of a negative sort. The remarkable creative efforts of informal groups in resisting organizational objectives illustrate this reverse creativity.

Commitment: Under this style some will reveal great commitment to achievement of organizational purposes and others would be negatively committed to defeat the purposes of the organization. The behavioural dynamics under this style is characterized by paradoxes like commitment and resentment.

Goal Congruence: No doubt the leader wants to achieve the organizational goals but he is ineffective in achieving them by working with and through others. He is unable to arouse their commitment or to release their creativity. He may attempt to achieve the organizational goals by dividing people. The goal of success is not absent but the likelihood of achieving it is lessened. The side effects of bottling up resentments reduce the problem-solving capacity of the firm.

Critique: This style believes in telling and not in listening. The communication is always one-way and scope for feedback or disagreement is totally absent. On the other hand, when criticism is stifled, it teaches subordinates to hate their bosses and this hatred prevents them from making any attempt to understand the causes of a problem or the conditions for its correction.

The Impact of 5.5 Style: Middle of the Road Management

Conflict: This style believes in accommodation. The conflict is settled through bargaining, — a compromise solution. The motivation to resorting to compromise is to avoid interpersonal emotion. It is agreeing so as to be agreeable and in this process effectiveness is sacrificed.

Creativity: This style actually believes in blind acceptance of the status quo and produces an imitative type of pseudocreativity. New approaches, even though they constitute only small departures from the outmoded past, are recommended on the basis of their having been tried elsewhere. Imitation rather than innovation is the rule.

Commitment: Morale and commitment look good under this style because members are sure the status quo will not be violently disturbed. Nothing to rock the boat will happen or be allowed to happen. But from the organizational point of view this commitment only amounts to commitment for marginal improvements tried out elsewhere.

Goal Congruence: This style arrives at a compromise between personal and organizational goals for it strives constantly for adjustment, accepting half-loaf, not a full loaf. It avoids problem-solving approaches for fear of disturbing the status quo.

Critique: This style believes in sandwiching criticisms between compliments. Indirect suggestions obliquely exchanged between bosses and subordinates are intended to help one another get the point without direct telling. This approach is equivalent to learning to pass information through crevices without promoting real understanding through openness and candour.

The Impact of 9.9 Style: Team Management:

Conflict: This style believes in a problem-solving approach to conflict situation. This approach does not believe in avoiding conflict but in confronting it. Conflict is not negatively viewed but positively considered. Emotions are confronted through discussion of them directly with the persons involved in disagreement. Insight and resolution are possible but calls for maturity and real human skills. It may be time consuming in the short-run but actually time conserving in the long-run. Understanding is promoted through encouraging disagreement.

Creativity: This style believes conformity is a virtue, provided it is conformity to changing organizational goals. It is conformity in this sense that leads to pursuit of creativity and innovative solutions. This style believes in utilizing the talents and resources of the team members to arrive at better decisions. The leader is not a decision-maker but a decision-leader.

Commitment: Since this style depends on members of the team for decision-making, problem-solving and conflict-resolution, all decisions are group decisions and as such the team owns the decisions. Ownership of decision leads to total commitment and involvement in implementing them. Furthermore, members feel a stake in the outcome of their decisions and therefore this commitment includes spontaneously sought after follow-up measures.

Goal Congruence: The much talked about integration of individual goals and organizational goals becomes a reality under this style. It motivates individuals towards corporate excellence not by driving them towards it but by striving for excellence in a collaborative way, working with and through people. It urges the corporation to enlarge the scope of over-lapping areas continuously so that the scope of merging the individual and organizational interests can be increased. The dysfunctional consequences of informal groups are absent because the informal groups merge with formal groups under this style.

Critique: This style believes in learning through critique. Critique is a learning process that involves comparing something with something else in order to evaluate or assess. This leads to analysis of the organization to see how it is operating and why, and to identifing changes that are essential if it is to be run better. Under this style authority does not become the source of truth but evidences and facts become bases for insight.

QUESTIONS

1. Explain how Management by Objectives as a management technique can improve the relationship between the key variables of the expectancy model of motivation.
2. Discuss Management by Objectives as a technique to satisfy the manager's higher order needs.
3. Consider the impact of the grid styles of management on the behaviourial variables explained in this chapter.

REFERENCES

Anantaraman, V. "Impact of Management by Objectives on the Relationship between Management Attitude and Performance", *The Manpower Journal*, New Delhi, XII, 2, July-September (1976) pp. 92-107.

Blake, R. Robert and Mouton, Jane S. "Managerial Facades", *Advanced Management Journal*, July 1966, p. 31.

Chakraborty, S. K. "Management by Objectives and the Man-in-the Organization", in Joshi, N. C. and Kesary, V. G. *Readings in Management Journal*, July 1966, p. 31.

Chesser, R. J. "The Development of Change Models of MBO Reflecting Moderator Effects of Personality Characteristics", Academy of Management Proceedings, August 1973, p. 391.

Kearney, William J. "Behaviorally Anchored Rating Scales — MBO's Missing Ingredient", *Personnel Journal*, January 1979, p. 20-25.

Lawler III, Edward E. and Porter, Lyman W. "The Effect of Performance on Job Satisfaction", *Industrial Relation*, California, Vol 7, 1967-68.

Porter, Lyman W. and Lawler III, Edward E. *Managerial Attitudes and Performance*. Homewood, Illinois: Irwin, 1968.

Porter, Lyman W. and Lawler III, Edward E., and Hackman, J. Richard, *Behaviour in Organizations*. McGraw-Hill, 1975.

16
Managerial Effectiveness

V. ANANTARAMAN

SUMMARY

This paper contains two sections. The first is exclusively devoted to David McClelland's approach to managerial effectiveness. Postulating his three dimensions of motivation, achievement, affiliation and power. McClelland argues that the qualities of an effective manager must include a right motive combination and a right managerial style and maturity — a rather unusual dimension of managerial effectiveness. He claims that these sets of qualities when present in a manager are likely to lead to high morale and performance among subordinates.

The next section focuses on the pioneering efforts of Fred Fiedler in postulating a contingency approach to managerial effectiveness. Taking into consideration the motivational make-up of the manager, he predicts the leadership situation in which he is most likely to be effective in terms of his group performance.

McClelland: Profile of an Effective Manager

In order to understand McClelland's profile of an effective manager, we should understand his meaning of managerial effectiveness. The index of a manager's effectiveness, according to him, is not performance but the climate he or she creates in his group, reflected in the morale of his subordinates. This does not mean that he ignores performance as unimportant but that the managerial level is characterized by the absence of standard measures of performance. On the other hand, he does not want to consider the superior's judgment of the subordinate's performance as an objective measure since it may be inaccurate.

However, McClelland sought evidence of a connection between morale and performance in the sales area of an organization where objective measures of performance of sales groups are reliable and found that his morale scores were positively correlated with performance in these sales groups — high morale at the beginning is a good index of how well the sales group actually performed in the coming year. It therefore seems very likely, according to him, that the manager who can create high morale among his salesmen can also do the same for employees in other areas, like production, design and so on, thus leading to better performance. In brief, on the basis of his research in the sales area where his morale scores correlate positively with performance, he defines an effective manager as one who can promote high morale among his subordinates.

Morale of the subordinates was measured by him through a questionnaire in which the subordinates answered questions about their work situation that revealed the characteristics of their supervisors along several dimensions, such as, personal responsibility for results; organizational clarity; strong team spirit and perception of appropriate reward. In detail, these dimensions require that the subordinates under an effective manager should perceive that they have a personal responsibility regarding results; that the organizational procedures are clear and they know what they should be doing; that there is strong team spirit; that they display a pride in their work group; and that they would be rewarded promptly and appropriately in the organization. An effective manager, according to McClelland, is one who creates a work climate which makes the morale of his subordinates high on these dimensions.

To quote him, "almost by definition, a good manager is one who, among other things, helps subordinates feel strong and responsible, who rewards them properly for good performance, and who sees that things are organized in such a way that subordinates feel they know what they should be doing. Above all, managers should foster among subordinates a strong sense of team spirit, of pride in working as part of a particular team. If a manager creates and encourages this spirit, his subordinates certainly should perform better."[1]

The Profile: McClelland's profile of an effective manager is based on the analysis and measurement of responses in the

---

[1] David C. McClelland and David H. Burnham. "Power is the Great Motivator", *Harvard Business Review*, March-April 1976, p. 112.

thematic aperception stories written by over five hundred managers who attended his workshops over a period of time. He is well-known for emphasizing the importance of three acquired motives as determinants of managerial behaviour. These are: the affiliation motive; the power motive; and the achievement motive. An individual with a high need for affiliation is likely to show a marked tendency to relate warmly and in a friendly way to others, or to be accepted by others. Power motive reflects an individual's desire to have impact, to feel strong and influential or to control others. Achievement motivation reflects a desire to do something better or more efficiently than it has been done before. An individual with a high need for achievement shows a strong tendency to do everything himself to attain success on his own. McClelland's research on achievement motivation spans over three decades, and in general, an individual with a high need for achievement always sets for himself moderately difficult goals, and takes calculated risks. He is keen on undertaking tasks the outcomes of which are entirely under his control because he would like to own responsibility for them. He would very much like to work in a situation where he can get feedback on how well he is doing at short intervals and in concrete, specific and precise terms. Finally, he is always desirous of reaching his goals through improved ways and innovative methods, and where others see problems and obstacles, he is likely to see opportunities and challenges to excel.

McClelland's description of the motivational profile of an achievement-motivated person, as are his other profiles, is an experimental fact, not the result of conjecture or commonsense. They are derived from analyzing and measuring the Thematic Aperception Test (TAT) stories of people across the world and, as such, his definition of an achievement-motivated person is different from achievement as it is commonly understood.

There is nothing sacrosant about achievement motivation as compared to other motivations. Possession of a high need for achievement is a virtue only insofar as the job a person does demands that he should be achievement oriented, defined in this special sense. It is no wonder, therefore, that McClelland has come to the conclusion that a high need for achievement in an individual may predict his entrepreneurial success or even his success as a salesman, but not necessarily, his effectiveness as a manager or an executive.

Effectiveness

A manager in order to be effective should be higher on his power need than on his need for achievement: A high need for achievement, as psychologists define and measure achievement, leads people to behave in very special ways that do not necessarily lead to good management. For one thing, because they focus on personal improvement, on doing things better by themselves, achievement-motivated people want to do things themselves, they will be highly reluctant to delegate responsibility. For another, they want specific short-term feedback on their performance so that they can tell how well they are doing. Yet a manager, particularly one in a large complex organization, cannot perform all the tasks necessary for success by himself. He must manage others so that they will do things for the organization. Therefore, the manager's job seems to call more for someone who can influence people than for someone who does things better on his own. In motivational terms, the successful manager should have a greater "need" for power than the need to achieve. Whereas a manager with a high need for achievement will try to do most things himself and will be reluctant to delegate responsibility, one with a high power need will delegate with confidence because he is capable of monitoring and controlling the work of his subordinates.

A manager in order to be effective should also be higher on his power need than on his affiliation need: McClelland's research has revealed that the most important factor of higher morale of subordinates was whether the manager's power need was higher than his need to be liked. Sociologists have long argued that for a bureaucracy to function effectively, those who manage it must be universalistic in applying rules. That is, if they make exceptions for the particular needs of individuals, the whole system will break down. The manager with a high need for being liked is precisely the one who wants to stay on good terms with everybody, and therefore is the one most likely to make exceptions in terms of particular needs. A high-affiliation manager creates poor morale because he or she does not understand that other people in his work group will tend to regard exceptions to the rule as unfair to themselves.

Since such managers are overly concerned with people's needs they make so many ad hoc decisions, compelled by this concern, they almost totally abandon orderly procedures. Their disregard for procedure leaves employees feeling weak, irresponsible, and without a sense of what might happen next, or where they stand in relation to their manager or even of what they ought to be doing. In short, the manager who is concerned about being liked by people tends to have subordinates who feel they have very little personal responsibility for results, that organizational procedures are not clear and that they have very little pride in their work group. Order and discipline do not characterize the climate of the work group; subordinates tend to pass the buck on to the boss, and team spirit is conspicuous by its absence.

A manager in order to be effective should not only be high on his power need but more importantly, exercise power or use his influence with restraint and inhibition to build the institution he serves: McClelland in analyzing the power themes in the TAT stories of his subjects scored them for inhibition. A high inhibition score reflected the power orientation of the manager to exercise power with restraint in order to build his institution, one that would not be for personal aggrandisement. In further analyzing the thoughts and actions of these institution builders he found that these managers have four major characteristics:

(1) They are more organization-minded in that they feel responsible for building up the organization they serve. Furthermore, they believe strongly in the importance of centralized authority.

(2) They like to work. In this they are the opposite of managers with a high need for achievement. People who have a high need for achievement like to get out of work by becoming more efficient. They would like to see the same result obtained in less time or with less effort. But managers who have a need for institutional power actually seem to like the discipline of work. It satisfies their need for getting things done in an orderly way.

(3) They are altruistic and seem quite willing to sacrifice some of their own self-interest for the welfare of the organization; they do this in obvious ways that everybody can see.

(4) Finally, they believe in justice above everything else,

that people must have even-handed treatment. It is almost as if they feel that if a person works hard and sacrifices for the good of the organization, he should and will get a just reward for his effort.

To sum up, McClelland and his associates have discovered the motive combination that makes an effective manager. Oddly enough, the good manager in a large company does not have a high need for achievement, although there must be plenty of that motive somewhere in his organization. The top managers should have a high need for power and an interest in influencing others, both greater than their interest in being liked by people. The manager's concern for power should be socialized, that is, controlled so that the institution as a whole, not only the individual, benefits.

The Right Managerial Style

In order to be effective, the manager should have not only the right motive combination but the right managerial style. McClelland's emphasis on a high need for power for managerial effectiveness does not mean that the style of the manager should be coercive or authoritarian. In his earlier work, McClelland distinguished between two types of power, one negative and one positive. The negative use of power is associated with personal power, and it is primitive and does indeed have negative consequences such as personal aggrandizement. In an organizational context it is characterized by the manager's tendency towards fault-finding, destructive criticism and domination. The contrasting social power is characterized by a "concern for group goals, for finding those goals that will move men, for helping the group to formulate them, for taking some initiative in providing the members of the group with the means of achieving such goals, and for giving group members the feeling of strength and competence they need to work hard for such goals".

The managerial style in keeping with this definition of social power is called the coaching style. In fact, in analyzing the responses of effective managers about how they would handle various realistic work situations in office settings, McClelland coded their answers for six different managerial styles or ways of dealing with situations. The styles depicted were: democratic; affiliative; pace-setting; coaching; coercive; and authoritarian. And on the basis of their comments, he came to the conclusion that in order to be an effective manager one should follow the coaching style.

Broadly speaking the coaching style has been found to be a consistent reflection of the institutional power orientation of the manager. It is not difficult to spell out the qualities of an effective coach — he displays both knowledge and skill; he is essentially a supportive leader; he promotes authentic communication with his team members and makes them feel competent and strong by effectively delegating responsibility and authority; he monitors their progress, evaluates objectively and rewards justly.

The case histories of institutional power managers in McClelland's workshops have confirmed that such a manager is not unconcerned about people needs but more concerned about helping their subordinates get things done. Since he is high on his power need, he is lower in his tendency to try to do everything himself. He delegates effectively and is confident of monitoring and controlling his subordinates. He is not authoritarian in the sense that he does not defensively chew them out when they challenge him but tries to figure out what their needs are so that he can influence them. He realizes that his job is more of strengthening and supporting his subordinates than of criticizing them. And he is keenly interested in giving them just rewards for their efforts. As a result his subordinates feel strong rather than weak.

The Maturity Dimension of Managerial Effectiveness

In the foregoing definition of social power, the manager may often be in a precarious position of walking a fine line between an exhibition of personal dominance and the more socialised use of power. More precisely, there is always a danger of the institutional power manager degenerating into a personal power manager in the absence of checks and balances. For individual managers, the regulative function is performed by two characteristics that are part of the profile of the very best managers in McClelland's study. The coaching managerial style provides one of the safeguards against such an eventuality. The other is the emotional maturity of the individuals.

Mature people, according to McClelland can be described as less egotistic; somehow their positive self-image is not at stake in what they are doing. They are less defensive, more willing to seek the advice of experts, and have a longer range view. They are less ostentacious and somehow look older and wiser. It is as if they have been awakened to a need for self-examination leading to self-renewal in the altruistic direction of getting more concerned about the organization than about themselves.

In conclusion, we may say that if a manager is emotionally mature, is higher on his need for social power and follows a coaching managerial style he can be very effective. This may sound like good commonsense. But the improvement over commonsense is that now the characteristics of an effective manager are objectively known. Managers of corporations can select, McClelland claims, those who are likely to be good managers and train those already in managerial positions to be more effective.

Fred Fiedler: Contingency Theory of Leadership

Earlier attempts to explain or predict leadership effectiveness in terms of traits or styles, ignoring the leadership situation have not been successful. This was to be expected because these approaches ignored the most fundamental psychological equation, $B = F(P, E)$, meaning that behaviour is a function of the personality of the leader and his environment (situation) in interaction.

Fiedler's theory represents the first attempt to take both personality and situation into consideration in predicting as well as explaining leadership effectiveness. Fielder was primarily concerned with leadership effectiveness in the face-to-face formal work-group situation in organizations. He therefore defined leadership effectiveness in terms of work-group performance, on how well the leader's group performs its assigned functions. In other words, a leader is effective only when his work group is effective in performance. Fiedler indeed made the bold attempt to predict and explain leadership effectiveness taking into account both the personality of the leader and his leadership situation not withstanding the difficulties of precisely defining personality and comprehensively describing the situation in the context of its many known as well as unknown variables.

He defined the personality of the leader in terms of his basic motivation. In other words one may be a task-oriented or relationship-oriented leader. He was able to identify these two types of leaders on the basis of the scores the leaders obtained by evaluating their least preferred co-workers on his Least Preferred

Co-worker (LPC) instrument (see Figure 1). The least preferred co-worker need not be a person the leader liked least but one with whom he had the most difficulty in getting the work done. Each item on this simple bipolar adjective scale is scored from one to eight with eight as the most favourable point on the scale. The LPC score of the individual is the sum of the items scored. Persons scoring on these scales may produce:

(1) a very negative description or a low LPC score of less than 57;
(2) a middle score between 57 and 64; and
(3) a relatively more positive description or a high LPC score of more than 64.

Situational Variables

Fiedler considered that three variables were relevant to the determination of whether or not a situation is favourable or unfavourable for the leader. Situational favourableness is made up of the following three components:

(1) *Leader-member relations:* This refers to the interpersonal relations between the leader and the members of his work group. Specifically, it refers to the extent to which the leader enjoys the confidence and loyalty of his subordinates in the work group, and is regarded as personally attractive to them. This variable seems to be close in conceptualization to the notion of referent power.
(2) *Task structure:* This refers to the extent to which the work content, the work context, work procedures, work goals and work results are clear, concrete and specific.
(3) *Position power:* This refers to the extent to which the leader can depend on the authority of his position in the organization to reward and punish his subordinates.

According to Fiedler, the extent to which these three variables are present in the leadership situation determines the leader's control and influence over the situation. In fact Fiedler argues that the three variables combine in unequal strength to create situational favourableness. Leader-member relations is twice as important as task structure, which in turn is twice as

Figure 1 Least Preferred Co-worker Questionnaire

Throughout your life you will have worked in many groups with a wide variety of different people — on your job, in church organizations, in volunteer groups, on athletic teams, and in many other situations. Some of your co-workers may have been very easy to work with in attaining the group's goals, while others were less so.

Think of all the people with whom you have ever worked, and then think of the person with whom you could work least well. He or she may be someone with whom you work with now or with whom you have worked with in the past. This does not have to be the person you liked least well, but should be the person with whom you had the most difficulty getting a job done, the one individual with whom you could work least well.

Describe this person on the scale which follows by placing an "X" in the appropriate space.

Look at the words at both ends of the line before you mark your "X". *There are no right or wrong answers.* Work rapidly: your first answer is likely to be the best. Do not omit any items, and mark each item only once.

Now describe the person with whom you can work least well.

										Scoring
Pleasant	8	7	6	5	4	3	2	1	Unpleasant	___
Friendly	8	7	6	5	4	3	2	1	Unfriendly	___
Rejecting	1	2	3	4	5	6	7	8	Accepting	___
Tense	1	2	3	4	5	6	7	8	Relaxed	___
Distant	1	2	3	4	5	6	7	8	Close	___
Cold	1	2	3	4	5	6	7	8	Warm	___
Supportive	8	7	6	5	4	3	2	1	Hostile	___
Boring	1	2	3	4	5	6	7	8	Interesting	___
Quarrelsome	1	2	3	4	5	6	7	8	Harmonious	___
Gloomy	1	2	3	4	5	6	7	8	Cheerful	___
Open	8	7	6	5	4	3	2	1	Guarded	___
Backbiting	1	2	3	4	5	6	7	8	Loyal	___
Untrustworthy	1	2	3	4	5	6	7	8	Trustworthy	___
Considerate	8	7	6	5	4	3	2	1	Inconsiderate	___
Nasty	1	2	3	4	5	6	7	8	Nice	___
Agreeable	8	7	6	5	4	3	2	1	Disagreeable	___
Insincere	1	2	3	4	5	6	7	8	Sincere	___
Kind	8	7	6	5	4	3	2	1	Unkind	___

Total ___

Source: Adapted from Fred E. Fiedler, Martin M. Chemers, and Linda Mahar. *Improving Leadership Effectiveness* New York: John Wiley and Sons, 1976, pp. 70.

important as position power. The combination of variables creates eight octants of decreasing situational favourableness, with a highly favourable situation being characterized by good leader-member relations, a structured task, and high leader-position power. A highly unfavourable situation is characterized by poor leader-member relations, low-task structure, and low-position power for the leader.

On the basis of his own research and subsequent validation studies conducted by his associates and others in the last twenty years and more, Fiedler is able to assert that his contingency model of leadership would predict very well, given the leadership situation, what type of leader would be effective in terms of his work group performance. As may be seen in the diagram, the low LPC leaders will succeed in situations 1,2,3 and 8, and the high LPC leaders will succeed in situations 4,5,6 and 7. To put it differently, while the high LPC or relationship-oriented leader will succeed in moderately favourable situations, the low LPC or task-oriented leader will succeed both in the favourable and very unfavourable situations.

Fiedler's model has remained for long a predictive model rather than an explanatory model. While it could predict leadership effectiveness given the leadership typology and the situation, it was difficult for Fiedler, until recently, to explain why, for example, a low LPC leader was able to succeed both in favourable and very unfavourable situations. As noted earlier, Fiedler is of the opinion that the LPC score measures the basic motivation of the leader, either his task orientation or his relationship orientation in his work group. He comes to this conclusion on the basis of the perceptions of the low and high LPC leaders by the members of their work groups. Generally speaking, the high LPC leader is seen as more considerate, more human relations oriented, more partcipative in his managerial style and more sensitive to the feelings of others. The low LPC leader, on the other hand, is perceived as more directive, more structuring, more goal-oriented and more concerned with efficiency.

This behaviour description may give an impression that these two types of leaders are poles apart in their orientation. This is not so. Actually it refers to their primary orientation, motivation or goals, and once it is achieved they would pursue the other as their secondary goal. In other words, a task-oriented leader may behave in a relation-oriented way and vice versa.

According to Fiedler, whether a leader would pursue his primary or secondary goal is dependent upon the situational favourableness. The situation may be so powerful that it alters behaviour of leaders or swaps their priorities despite their basic orientation or motivation.

It is well accepted in psychology that behaviour consistent with one's basic motivation is more likely to manifest itself in stressful situations; if the situation is not stressful, behaviour different from one's basic motivation could emerge. Making use of this postulation, Fiedler argues that his LPC score is an index of the hierarchy of goals and needs by which each manager orders his priorities between task and relation-oriented goals and, therefore, his behaviour in favourable and unfavourable situations is as tabulated below:

Figure 2

Basic motivation	Unfavourable Situation	Favourable Situation
Low LPC or Task Orientation	Task Oriented Behaviour	Relation Oriented Behaviour
High LPC or Relation Orientation	Relation Oriented Behaviour	Task Oriented Behaviour

To reiterate, the chart emphasizes the point that the basic motivation of the leader can be the same in both the favourable and unfavourable situations but behaviour can be different depending on the situation. With this guideline, it is not difficult to explain why the low LPC leader or task-oriented leader succeeds in both favourable and unfavourable situations.

When the situation is relatively stressful or unfavourable, as in the octane eight, and provides the leader with inadequate control and influence, the low LPC or task-oriented leader will seek to accomplish his primary task goals which to him are most important. In a favourable situation which assures him of task accomplishment, the low LPC or task-oriented leader will seek to pursue his secondary relation oriented goals and succeed. The same logic applies to high LPC leaders in different situations.

Conclusion

To sum up, Fiedler's contingency model of leadership postulates that the performance of the group is contingent upon the motivational system of the leader and the degree to which the leader has control and influence in a particular work group situation or what he calls the degree of situational favourableness. Since a tremendous amount of controversy centres around what actually the LPC score measures, we need not even accept Fiedler's opinion that it measures the basic motivation of the leader.[2] As a result we may even totally reject the edifice of explanation he built on the basis of this basic assumption about what LPC measures. Whatever the LPC may measure, one cannot deny that once we know the favourableness of the leader's situation, the LPC score of the leaders permits us to predict the work group performance in a given situation with a surprising degree of accuracy. This is surprising, even to Fiedler, because according to him there are many other known factors affecting the performance of the work group, such as, leader-member intelligence, task-related abilities, experience, motivation, and the leader's relation with his own superiors. It is in this context that Fiedler is justified in claiming that we are on to some major breakthrough in the contingency approach to leadership.

In conclusion, we may say that even the worst critics of Fiedler are agreed that the LPC is actually a personality variable, though nobody knows for certain what particular personality variable it is. If this is agreed upon, Fiedler should be recognized as a pioneer in relating personality and situation in determining leadership effectiveness, not withstanding the insurmountable difficulties in precisely defining personality and comprehensively describing the complex leadership situation.

However, after extensive research, Rice was able to conclude that "albeit it is still largely unclear as to whether LPC is a measure of social distance, personal need, cognitive complexity, or motivational hierarchy, the most enduring and widely accepted

---

[2]The interaction of LPC and situational favourableness or control is the deciding factor in leadership effectiveness. However, much controversy surrounds the meaning of the LPC measure. Fiedler and Chemers conceded that "for nearly twenty years, we have been attempting to correlate LPC with every conceivable personality trait and every conceivable behavioural observation score. By and large these analyses have been uniformly fruitless. (Fiedler, F.E. and Chemers, M.M. *Leadership and Effective Management*, Glenview, Illinois: Scott & Foresman. 1974.)

interpretation of LPC is as a measure of the relative task versus interpersonal orientation of a group leader".

QUESTIONS

1. Briefly explain the profile of an effective manager according to McCelland's postulations.
2. Distinguish between the criteria of managerial effectiveness as explained by McClelland and Fiedler.
3. Fiedler effectively related personality of the leader with his situation in determining leadership effectiveness. Discuss.

REFERENCES

Fiedler, Fred E. *A Theory of Leadership Effectiveness*, New York: McGraw-Hill, 1967.
────────. "The Contingency Model and the Dynamics of the Leadership Process", in L. Berkowitz ed. *Advances in Experimental Social Psychology*, New York: Academic Press, 1978.
Fiedler, Fred E. and Chemers, M. M. *Leadership and Effective Management*. Glenview, Illinois: Scott and Foresman, 1974.
Fiedler, Fred E., Chemers, M. M., and Mahar, L. *Improving Leadership Effectiveness: The Leader Match Concept*. New York: Wiley, 1976.
Kolb, David A., Rubin Irwin M. and McIntyre, James M. *Organizational Psychology: An Experimental Approach*. New Jersey: Prentice-Hall, Englewood Cliffs, 1971.
McClelland, David C. *Power: The Inner Experience*. New York: Irvington Publishers, 1975.
────────. *The Achieving Society*. New York: Van Nostrand, 1961.
McClelland David C. and Burnhan, David H. "Power is the Great Motivator", *Harvard Business Review*, Vol. 54, No. 2, March-April 1976, pp. 100-110.
McClelland, David C. and Steele, Robert S. *Motivation Workshops*. New York: General Learning Press, 1972.
Rice, R. W. "Construct Validity of the Least Preferred Co-worker Score", *Psychological Bulletin*, 1978, p. 1199-1237.

17
Communication

S. RICHARDSON

SUMMARY

Communication is examined from a human standpoint concentrating on formal communication. Preliminaries to good communication are discussed and the communication process modelled. Various types of communication are described and some common barriers to communication suggested. It is concluded that meanings are not in words or symbols but in the people that use them.

Introduction

People are gregarious, hence communicating is a lifetime activity for most us. Even hermits have to take stringent precautions to escape other people and the media totally. But this chapter is not directly concerned with the communication media, rather it attempts to examine communication from a human standpoint. This is not to underestimate the importance of information technology (IT) either, but merely to say that it is beyond the scope of this paper. Communication is probably best defined as the transmission of information.

One of the commonest causes of inadequate HRM is poor communication. Elsewhere we have discussed informal communication, this chapter will concentrate on formal communication although much of the discussion applies to both forms. It is tempting to think that when A speaks to B and B hears what A has said then good communication has been achieved. In reality life is not that simple: all behaviour conveys some message and even if B can't see A (as on the telephone) the choice of words and the tone of voice and the speed of delivery convey information. Communication could be improved by knowledge of the mechanics of the process.

Improving communication is the responsibility of everyone since poor communication is at the root of most ignorance and prejudice whether it is within a family, between lovers, inside an enterprise, or across generation, cultural or national boundaries. Good communication results in the accurate and speedy movement of meaning with appropriate action if requested or required by the sender. But before communicating there are some necessary preliminaries to help ensure good communication.

Preliminaries to Good Communication

Much communication is rightly spontaneous and instinctive (as between loving parents and their children). However, in a formal context (as in most work situations) there is a need for planning before communication starts. This is discussed below.

Clarification of Ideas is the first necessary preliminary. The more carefully ideas regarding what is to be communicated and why the communication is necessary are clarified the more likely is the desired effect of the message to be achieved. Timings need to be considered too; not only the time that the message will take to reach the recipients but also the mental and physical state of the recipients when the message is received, and the time these people will have to think and act in order to achieve what the sender wants. The time when the message is composed can be important since the mood of the sender can have a great effect on the message.

Defining the Aim of the communication is essential. Is it merely to convey information or is action required? If action is required what is the deadline? Is the information transmitted intended to generate a discussion or not? A sound aim will be precise, realistic, and consistent with the constraints. It is vital to identify the one inescapable result desired — this then becomes the basis of the aim. This identification should (when appropriate) be done with the willing participation of those able to contribute. Such participation will improve the definition of the aim (by the injection of additional ideas and objectivity) and tend to ensure the support of the participants.

A Model of the Communication Process

Communication is a dynamic process since many of the

components (especially the human ones) are constantly changing. Figure 1 attempts to model this process.

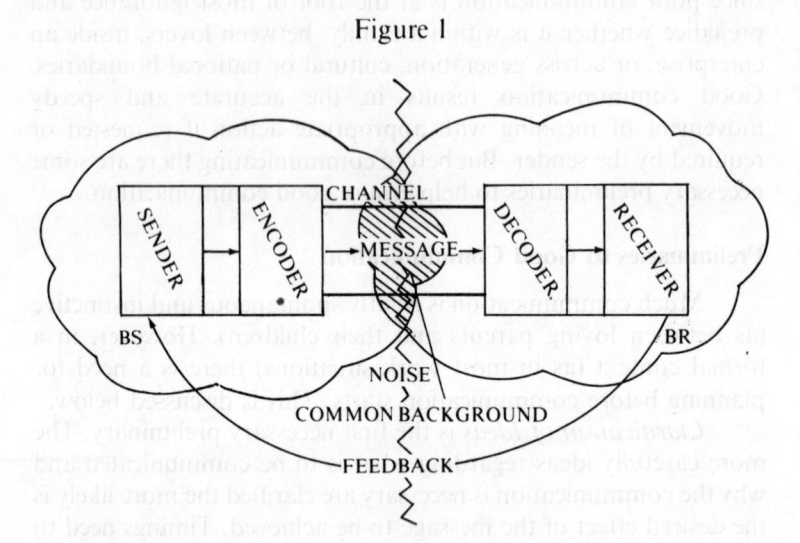

Figure 1

The details are:

(1) *Sender* and receiver may be a person or a group.
(2) *Encoder:* the sender must encode information or ideas to be transmitted (examples of "codes" are words, body language, symbols, morse, smoke signals) and this requires the appropriate skills, especially to ensure that the code and the vocabulary used are intelligible to the receiver.
(3) *Channel* (or Medium) is selected by the sender, e.g., telephone, telegram, TV, letter, picture, public address system, radio, recording (tape/disc), face-to-face conversation (verbal or non-verbal), telex, minutes of meetings, poster, diagram, or chart.
(4) *Noise* is unwanted information, hence this may occur when any of the five senses are used, e.g., redundant writing on a blackboard is "visual noise".
(5) *Decoder:* the receiver interprets the message, i.e., he perceives the message (perception of an identical

message may vary from time to time and from place to place); the ideal is that the sender's meaning and the receiver's perception are congruent.
(6) *Feedback* enables the receiver to confirm that his perception of the message is correct and to so inform the sender; a simple acknowledgement is rarely sufficient feedback — if action is required as the result of the message, then that action usually provides adequate feedback, (although note that feedback is itself a communication, and note also the effects of a time-lag in the system, e.g., on motivation, on time to think or act, etc.).
(7) *BS* means the "background" of the sender which is conditioned by culture, experience, value system, norms, knowledge, etc. This background has a significant effect on encoding, e.g., the larger the common background of the sender and the receiver the less likely is the possibility of false perception or problems in decoding.
(8) *BR* means the "background" of the receiver.

Downward Communication

Superior to subordinate communication not only is needed to convey instructions, and to give information about enterprise procedures, it should also be used to explain the reasons for these, and to give feedback about performance. Research suggests that one-message communication, or reliance upon the written word alone is inadequate. Campaigns (a special form of communication) need to go on until there has been a permanent change in behaviour (e.g., "Don't Come Late", "Keep Singapore Clean").

Upward Communication (the following relies heavily on Luthans, 1981).

This is subordinate initiated. Research has verified the general ineffectiveness of subordinate initiated communication. Upward messages tend to be contracted. This contraction is because bad news is suppressed, especially when superiors don't like bad news from subordinates, or subordinates fear punishment as a result of the information sent upwards in the hierarchy.

Kinds of Upward Communication

(1) Written (sometimes anonymous);
(2) Spoken;
(3) Collective (through trade unions or through informal groups);
(4) Suggestion schemes;
(5) Undesirable behaviour, e.g., increase in the number of accidents, "unjustified" complaints, lateness, absenteeism, sabotage, vandalism, high labour turnover, reluctance to use initiative;
(6) Non-verbal, e.g., facial expressions, body language, avoidance behaviour.

Improving Upward Communication involves:

(1) Having an effective grievance procedure — often provided for in collective agreements with trade unions. There should be a written policy defining the procedure for redress (see Brown 1965, for a detailed example).
(2) Adopting the "open-door" policy, i.e., a situation in which every manager says to subordinates, "My door is always open, you can come in whenever you like." This sounds fine in theory and it can work well with goodwill on both sides, but it can result in popular managers being swamped or the chain of command being short-circuited.
(3) By efficient counselling, attitude questionnaires and exit interviews — these need special skills and mutual trust (e.g., to convince subjects that promises of confidentiality are genuine).
(4) By using participative techniques — examples are joint consultation, quality control circles, efficient suggestion schemes.
(5) By having an "Ombudsman" — originally an official who investigates complaints by individuals against public bodies and government servants, the concept can be applied in any enterprise to promote upward communication and is being used in the United States by the army and some universities and business organizations.

(6) By encouraging a representative system as in trade unions — such a system is well established in Singapore and provides a safety valve as well as a well-practised method of upward communication; but union representatives speak only for their members so non-members have no formal representatives except their managers, and subordinates sometimes are inhibited in commenting to their superiors especially if they feel unsupported by their peers.

Lateral and Diagonal Communication

Lateral communication takes place between people on the same level of a hierarchy, i.e., between nominal peers, e.g., M_1 communicating with M_2 & M_3. (In Figure 2 CE is the Chief Executive; M_1 etc. are the top managers, m_1 etc. the first-line managers, and nm_1 etc. the non-managers).

Figure 2

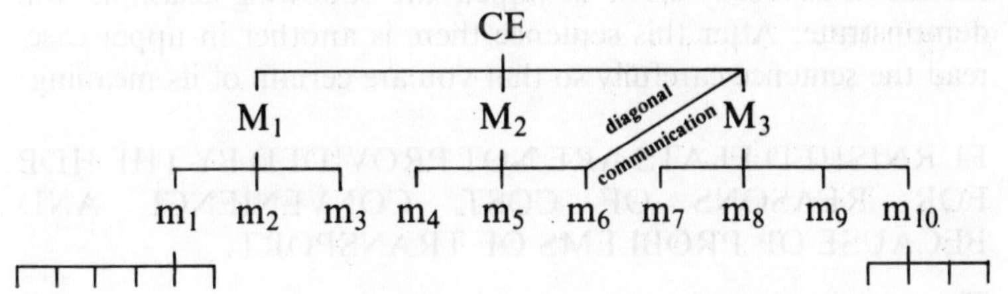

$$
\begin{array}{c}
CE \\
M_1 \quad M_2 \quad \text{diagonal communication} \quad M_3 \\
m_1 \; m_2 \; m_3 \; m_4 \; m_5 \; m_6 \; m_7 \; m_8 \; m_9 \; m_{10} \\
nm_1 \quad\quad\quad\quad\quad\quad\quad\quad\quad\quad mn_n
\end{array}
$$

Lateral communication is always to be encouraged, although an insecure superior (e.g., CE) may not do so for fear that this immediate subordinates M_1, M_2 & M_3) may "gang-up" on him. Conversely the immediate superior should be informed of any significant results of lateral communication.

Diagonal communication occurs between people who are at different levels and not in the same department, e.g., M_3 talks to m_6 or vice-versa — often referred to as Fayol's bridge or gang-plank theory since it was first formally advocated by the French writer in 1916. He says the "gang-plank" allows the two employees "to deal at one sitting, and in a few hours, with some question or other which via the scalar chain would pass through twenty transmissions, inconvenience many people, involve masses of paper, lose weeks or months to get to a conclusion less satisfactory generally than the one which could have been obtained via direct contacts. . . ." (Fayol, 1949). Diagonal communication can be excellent, provided, m_6's superior has no objection, M_3 doesn't attempt to give her/him orders (but genuine requests are permissible) and m_6's immediate superior (i.e., M_2) is told of any significant results of the communication without delay.

Common Barriers to Communication

Perception: one's view of reality based on information intake plus information stored (i.e., in the memory) is one's perception of experience, (it may or may not be accurate). People perceive what they want to perceive or what they expect to perceive. "None so blind as those who do not want to see". "Perceptual difficulty" becomes an increasing barrier to efficient communication the greater the lack of correspondence between sender's perception and receiver's perception, i.e., the smaller the common background (see Figure 1). But even when the message is completely clear and unambiguous this is no guarantee that the receiver will decode it correctly as it is hoped the following example will demonstrate: After this sentence there is another in upper case, read the sentence carefully so that you are certain of its meaning.

FURNISHED FLATS ARE NOT PROVIDED BY THE HDB FOR REASONS OF COST, CONVENIENCE AND BECAUSE OF PROBLEMS OF TRANSPORT.

This sentence has nineteen words and these words contain eleven Es, six As, etc. In a moment count the number of times another letter appears in the same sentence. You may not touch the sentence in any way, and you must read the sentences as quickly as possible. Now, count the number of times the letter F appears, and record the total you have observed. Persuade two or three other people to try the same exercise under the same conditions recording the total each gives. Go back and carefully and slowly count the number of Fs. The probability is that most who have counted will be wrong. The correct answer is at the end of this chapter. The mistakes were made because some words (typically redundant ones like "of") are filtered out, i.e., not perceived, because they are not essential to understanding the meaning of the message. In other words, even when there is no noise, mistakes in decoding are made because of faulty perception. These concepts are discussed in detail in the chapter on perception.

Inference is an assumption made by the receiver; these assumptions are common if the receiver's listening skills are poor, vigilance is low, or the message is long and/or complex — the probability of inference is much reduced by efficient feedback (e.g., in face-to-face conversations). But, it is false assumptions which must be avoided since correct ones promote good communication.

Language, used poorly, gives rise to semantic differences between receiver and sender and hence creates problems. These can be reduced by emphasis on definitions and avoidance of non "common-user" abbreviations (e.g., "econs", "sec.", "aircon", "frus"). It is especially important to be aware of cross-generation and cross-cultural differences (particularly between native and non-native speakers of English). Hence it is better to use simple language as much as possible, with repetition of the message if necessary. Visitors to Singapore are often mystified by some questions directed at them. Witness the following conversations:

"Are you going back?"
"No, I'm going home."
"Are you going to send your daughter to school?"
"No, I'm going to take her."

For a detailed discussion of the use of English in Singapore see Tongue (1974). The book is descriptive not prescriptive.

Noise, since it is unwanted information, can be received by any of the senses or by a combination of them. Excessive unwanted sound is familiar to everyone in Singapore, rightly referred to as noise pollution creating physical and psychological health hazards. What is less obvious is noise which although not likely to affect one's health will impede good communication by reducing attention or causing annoyance. Examples of such noise are distracting mannerisms used by the sender or pain caused by uncomfortable postures.

Communication Chain Too Long. By reducing the number of links in a communication chain not only is the speed of communication increased but also the tendency for the message to be expanded or contracted or distorted is reduced.

Improving Communication

It is axiomatic that by avoiding the barriers to communication, then communication will be improved. In addition, however, a more positive approach is desirable. The need to capture and retain the attention of one's audience is paramount (whether they are physically present or not), and this is a complex matter. It depends on the degree of understanding and acceptance of the message, which is a function of the perception of the receiver, and perception is affected by motivation (and there is no one best way to motivate all persons). The good communicator will empathize with the receiver, achieving maximum identification with the receiver's needs, perception, limitations, and understanding. But good communication is always a two-way process and everyone needs to learn to receive and give feedback in the best way. Receivers need to improve their listening skills and this is particularly important in a multi-lingual society like Singapore. Finally, senders should try to use all five senses when communicating and never forget that bad communication is the fault of the sender.

Conclusion

A knowledge of the mechanics of the communication process should enhance the efficient transmission of messages. Technology has changed communication radically yet it will always be true that meanings are not in words or symbols but in the people that use them. That is why communication is such an important component of HRM.

QUESTIONS

1. In what ways does feedback affect behaviour, and what are the implications for HRM?
2. What are the relative merits of written and spoken communication in work situations?
3. Describe the techniques for improving subordinate-initiated communication.

REFERENCES

Brown, W. *Exploration in Management*. Harmondsworth: Penguin, 1965.
Fayol, H. *General Industrial Management*. London: Pitman, (translated from the French), 1949.
Luthans, F. *Organizational Behaviour*. 3rd ed, New York: McGraw-Hill, 1981.
Tongue, R. K. *The English of Singapore & Malaysia*. Singapore: Eastern Universities Press, 1974.

Answer to question on page 214: Number of Fs = 6.

18
Team-Building

V. ANANTARAMAN

SUMMARY

Team-building refers to a method under which groups experientially learn to increase their skills for effective team work by examining their structures, purposes, setting, procedures and interpersonal dynamics.

Team-building activities are not narrow in scope, but may actually deal with a wide-range of purposes. Generally speaking, they are aimed at three broad problem areas in organizational work groups. As such one can distinguish three models of team-building — the role model, the goal-setting model and the interpersonal model.

The focus of this chapter is on the interpersonal model which is an offshoot of a earlier group development method — sensitivity training or T-group training. In fact, one can argue that the interpersonal model of team-building is essentially a contract group facilitating interpersonal growth through the instrumentality of the contract, prescribing norms of interaction within the group. The rules of interaction are briefly described and a brief outline of guidelines for giving and receiving feedback is also included because these feedback guidelines are central to any team-building effort.

Need for Team Approach

Many organizations are experiencing environmental forces that are rapidly changing and increasingly unpredictable and it appears as if turbulence is now the stable state. Corporate attempts to cope with this turbulence through a process of adaptation and innovation have proved to be ineffective in the absence of involving the individuals in the organization in the change process.

Individuals are crucial in directing or withholding decisions, services, skills or energy. Traditional ways of harnessing their energies have become inadequate since social forces have weakened authority. People are now better educated and less romantic about the ideal of progress. They are less willing to work diligently and conform to rules. Belief in the sacrosant superiority of hierarchical leaders is questioned. No longer are military leaders the oracles of business management styles.

The team approach has become a distinctive style of working, aimed at harnessing the collective talents and energy of people to achieve useful corporate results and, at the same time, respect the needs of the employees.

An Illustration

Here is a fairly typical example. A supervisor has decided to discipline an employee who persistently takes long break periods. On a day when the employee returns ten minutes later than the time allowed, the supervisor fines him a quarter of an hour's pay. The employee complains to his representative, who takes up his case with the excuse that the lateness was justified because of a delay in the cafeteria and that, argues the respresentative, is the responsibility of the management.

The supervisor, knowing that this employee's lateness is part of a regular pattern does not relent, and the company grievance procedure takes the issue to a higher level. Here the more senior managers, fearing the consequences of industrial action, ask themselves, "Is it worth stopping a twenty-million dollar plant for fifteen minutes pay?" Their answer is negative, the supervisor's decision is reversed, and the employee enjoys his victory. The representative has become a little more powerful, and credible to the employees, the supervisor a little less powerful and credible. It does not take many incidents like this before the supervisor feels unsupported and confused.

Supervisors are questioning what their role should be; they are noting that their role has to be played differently. It is here that it is emphasized that supervisors who use the team-building approach have a clearer, more potent, and practical management philosophy to guide them. As a consequence, they develop skills to increase openness, commitment, and the problem-solving ability of their work team. Issues of discipline are clarified and are less likely to degenerate into an "us" against "them" conflict. As self-regulation increases in the team, fewer problems emerge. The work done to build a positive team spirit bears fruit in the form of good will.

Teams in Organization

In an organization team-building efforts may be directed at:

(1) Top management teams;
(2) Management teams;
(3) Project teams/Task forces; and
(4) Work groups for improving their effectiveness.

Top management teams: Teams of top managers often are the major link between the organization and its external environment. They must assess what is going on outside, predict the effects on the organization as a whole, and make hard decisions about the organization's responses. These functions require a farsighted and imaginative appraisal of complex issues that are beyond the scope of most individuals working alone. Complex managements demand complex team-building at the top management level.

Management Teams: Management teams, usually including a manager and those who report to him, most commonly undertake team-building. Such teams are relatively stable and handle a wide variety of assignments, e.g., running a factory, department, or service facility. The quality of relationship between team members can affect a large number of people who look to the team to provide clear and energetic direction.

Project teams/Task forces: Many organizations use temporary project teams or task forces to solve problems quickly or to develop new processes or products. The project team to develop the Boeing 707 is a case in point. Typically the project manager collects personnel from different departments of the organization to achieve a mix of skills that can technically handle the project. They must also create enough drive and enthusiasm to see the project through. Difficult decisions often have to be made on uncertain data, and a well-developed team can use the varied talents of team members in making effective decisions.

Work groups: The importance of team approach in the workplace has been widely recognized, and the team concept at the level of the work group stresses participation and more workplace democracy, with the overall aim of channelling the more creative energy of its people towards benefiting the organization rather than blocking its progress. The supervisor's role can evolve into that of a team leader, whose function is to facilitate the working of the team rather than to direct it. The Swedish Volvo experiment with autonomous work groups under a team leader is illustrative of this kind of team-building.

Team-building: Models and Methods

Having established team approach as an alternate management philosophy to meet the demands of the times and technology, and the consequent need for team-building at various levels in the organization, we should now define a team and discuss the process of building it.

Dave Francis and Don Young define a team as an "energetic group of people who are committed to achieving common objectives, who work well together and enjoy doing so, and who produce high-quality results". Team-building, according to Johnson and Johnson, refers to a method under which groups learn to increase their skills for effective team work by examining their structures, purposes, setting, procedures and interpersonal dynamics.

To begin a process of team-building, a model of what constitutes the ideal, effective team must be available. The following is a model of an effective team. An effective team would have clear, cooperative goals to which every member is committed; accurate and effective communication of ideas and feelings; distributed participation and leadership; appropriate and effective decision-making procedures; productive controversies; a high-level of trust, acceptance and support among members; a high level of cohesion; constructive management of power and conflict; and adequate problem-solving procedures. Once this model of group effectiveness is established, the team needs to structure a self-renewing process. It should gather data about its current functioning and analyze the data in order to find ways and means to raise the team to higher levels of effectiveness.

In this sense, team-building involves the deliberate working through of all blockages to progress until a working group becomes an effective team. These blockages may exist in the domain of leadership, goal-setting, role clarification, interpersonal relations or intergroup relations. The idea of clearing blockages is central to team-building because if a blockage is worked through successfully, then the team becomes stronger; if the blockage is not cleared, then the team regresses. More importantly, "clearing blockages" is the tool team-building consultants use as a means to build teams.

Team-building is usually undertaken initially with the help of a consultant. The first step in the team-building effort is to identify the blockages so that they may be cleared. The effort to build a team that would be able to identify blockages and clear them calls for voluntary acceptance and commitment from the formal leader, members of the work group, and a top management that would be committed to the philosophy of Team Approach. This is essential because team-building efforts should not be undertaken unless the value orientation of the business organization is congruent with that of team-building. Here we refer to the value orientation of openness, trust, understanding and participation as the basic tenet of management, otherwise the question of personal risks involved for members in practising openness in the context of organizational politics and the consequent fear of retribution will loom large in the minds of the participants and make the team-building effort worthless and futile.

Team Review

There are many instruments available for the purpose of identifying the blockages existing in a working group. The classification of blockages and the methods of clearing them are all based on well-known concepts of behavioural scientists as will be seen presently. Those who are interested in the mechanics of team-building, an instrument employed and in a particular classification of blockages and method of clearing can refer to the practical manual for team-building by Francis and Young. Their team review questionnaire containing 108 questions helps a consultant gather data from the working group and identifies blockages under twelve categories. These are, inappropriate leadership; unqualified membership; insufficient group commitment; unconstructive climate; low achievement orientation; undeveloped corporate role; ineffective work methods; inadequate team organization; soft critiquing; stunted individual development; lack of creative capacity; and negative intergroup relations.

This classification, incidentally, emphasizes that team-building activities are not narrow in scope, but may actually deal with a wide range of purposes which affect the individuals involved, the group's operation and behaviour, and the group's relationship with the rest of the organization.

Team-building Models

Generally speaking, team-building efforts are aimed at three broad problem areas in organizational work groups: role clarity; interpersonal relations; and goal setting. Ken Barker goes to the extent of describing three models of team-building: the role model; the interpersonal model; and the goalsetting model.

The Role Model: Its purpose is to examine and clarify the roles of each team member. Under this model, numerous issues such as leadership, power and intergroup relationships may be explored. The most frequently employed behavioural science techniques are: the Role Analysis Technique of Ishwar Dayal and John M. Thomas which clarify the roles of the top management of a new organization in India; and the Role Negotiation Technique developed by Roger Harrison in Europe. In the domain of intergroup relationships, the intergroup team-building intervention developed by Blake, Shepard and Mouton, besides the Organization Mirror Intervention developed by the Organization Development practioners of the TRW Systems, are frequently employed. In the leadership area the Managerial Grid training developed by Blake and Mouton is well-known.

The Interpersonal Model: The major thrust of this model is to improve the climate of the group. Enhancing the level of trust and openness within the group often leads to conflict resolution and problem solving. This interpersonal team-building model has actually evolved from the earlier techniques of T-groups or sensitivity training laboratories. Naturally its focus is on improving interpersonal skills, getting and giving feedback; cultivating better awareness and expression of feelings; and encouraging self-disclosure relevant to the individual's interaction in the work group. Sometimes, certain aspects of transactional analysis are used in this model, for example, to analyze ulterior transactions between the members of the group or to improve the trust level in the group by bringing to surface the games people play in groups. The Third Partly Peace Making Technique is usually built into any team-building effort though Organization Development literature extols the virtues of this technique in its own right.

The Goalsetting Model: This model relies on techniques like participation in setting goals incorporating the principles of Management By Objectives and Locke's postulation on goals, goalsetting and feedback. Sometimes the procedure for setting goals and a plan of action for achieving goals can be based on the basis of the motivational make-up of the individual member along the theoretical postulations of David McClelland.

A great wealth of literature on all these techniques is available in books on Organizational Development. In them you will also find comprehensive techniques to achieve all the separate goals of these three models of team-building. The Confrontation Meeting, Survey Feedback and Grid Organization Development belong to this category. This brief review is intended mainly to impress on you the rich variety of models and methods of team-building available for building teams in organizations.

The Interpersonal Model and T-group Foundation

The focus of this discussion is on the interpersonal model of team-building which is essentially an off-shoot of the well-known T-group or sensitivity training. It is common knowledge that T-group proved to be a remarkable success in groups of strangers in promoting greater self-awareness and interpersonal sensitivity (see Appendices, pp. 230 and 231).

The potential benefits of the T-group experience for the individual lie in behavioural changes which an individual brings back into the organization. This indeed is a problem area and has been termed the transfer dilemma. John P. Campbell and Marvin D. Dunnette, after an extensive review of research studies concluded that there is limited but reasonably convincing evidence that T-groups do result in behavioural changes that can be observed back on the job. However, experience reveals that this problem of transfer dilemma can be greatly minimized through organizing T-group training for in-tact work groups within an organization. The team-building efforts under the interpersonal model differ from those of T-groups in that members of the work group, are now helped in the development of interpersonal skills while engaged in solving their work-group or organizational problems. This is the celebrated process of learning interpersonal skills while solving problems in the group. After all, interpersonal skills are basic to decision-making, problem-solving and conflict-resolution within a group.

Be that as it may, the principles underlying T-group or team-building are based on extensive as well as intensive experiments and research on group process and group development triggered by the seminal contributions of Kurt Lewin. These efforts have culminated in theories of group process and group development, and the theories of Schuts, Bion, Walten, Bennis and Shepard. Furthermore, the postulations of Chris Argyris have provided the basis for a laboratory for human behaviour to improve interpersonal communication.

A Contract Group

It is necessary to emphasize that these efforts at team-building are premised on the value orientations of openness and trust in interpersonal relations. In fact the theorists in group process and group development assert that if you observe an unstructured and goal-less group over a period of a week or two, you will find to your surprise that the members of the group will end up evolving a contract of norms to govern their interactions within the group, which would, in effect, support this value orientation.

This has an important implication for team-building efforts in terms of time. In other words, we need not put the work group through the time consuming process of group development till they reach the stage of grinding out a contract on norms governing their interaction. On the other hand, we can save considerable time in promoting interpersonal growth in the work-group by immediately handing them a standard contract and facilitating its growth through the trainer, provided the members agree to abide by the contract voluntarily. The Interpersonal model of team-building is, in T-group terminology, essentially a contract group.

Objectives

The aim of the interpersonal model of team-building is to promote interpersonal growth in the work group. This, in effect, means the development of the ability of its members to "arrive at a consensus and verify it" on any issue, be it problem-solving, decision-making or conflict-resolution. In other words, the interpersonal model aims at developing an adequately functioning internal communication system within the group through facilitating the members of the work group to interact according to the norms or rules of interaction spelt out in the contract.

Rules of Interaction

These involve:

(1) Frank expressions of feelings coupled with a desire to work one's feelings through. For example, if I feel angry with you, I should say, "John, I am really angry with what you said, but I would like to tell you why, and get some responses from you. If possible, I want to work this out with you here."

(2) In times of heightened emotions we should cry a halt and institute this rule: restate the ideas and feelings of John accurately and to John's satisfaction. This will help one achieve John's frame of reference. This process involves three steps — summarizing, perception checking and negotiating for meaning.

(3) The third rule relates to revealing something of your past which is relevant to the nature of your present interaction in the group. Self-disclosure must be authentic and is in fact a real translation of one-self to others in a group. An authentic self-disclosure will be perceived by others as an invitation to disclose or reveal something about themselves in the same area.

(4) Accepting this invitation is the reciprocal obligation of support to the individual who is either frankly expressing his feelings or authentically disclosing himself.

(5) A most important rule is the requirement of empathic listening. This will not be possible unless one is congruent, this means that the person is aware of the feelings you are experiencing and capable of expressing what you are aware of. As a result, you have no need to be defensive or false or hypocritical. You are free to listen to others since your attention is not on yourself. Empathic listening by definition will be non-evaluative listening.

(6) When an individual member of the group is withdrawing, dominating, manipulating, intellectualizing, rationalizing or otherwise violating the rules of interaction, he may be confronted by someone else. Responsible confrontation, however, is not pointing a finger of a accusation at him or cornering him but is motivated by the desire not to lose but to have him as a fully contributing member of the group. Responsible confrontation should be with love and acceptance and more importantly, it

should be so perceived by the confrontee. In confrontation, the motivation is more important than the manner of confrontation.

(7) If it is so perceived, confrontation will be seen by the confrontee as an invitation to self-examine his behaviour. This attitude of self-examination or non-defensive response to responsible confrontation is possible only when one can respond to the content of the confrontation, and not to the feeling the confrontation evokes.

(8) The final rule of immediacy tries to reduce the distance between members in their interactions. First of all, it requires that the individual should transform his "then" and "there" concerns into "now" and "here" propositions. This is the technique of collapsing time and space to make the past relevant to the present.

(9) Further, it prohibits conversations in the group filled with generalities and vagueness. When one has to use generalities or talk about something abstract as when he talks about a principle, he should illustrate it with an example to make it concrete. Such illustrations should preferably be from personal experiences, not the experiences of any hypothetical person. When he has to illustrate with the experiences of others, out of necessity, he should mention the impact the experience had on him.

(10) Generally this rule requires that every member reveal his feelings by the use of the personal "I" and avoid substitutes like "we", "you", "they", "someone" etc. Again it frowns upon vague questions like a general "why". The "why" should be followed by a very specific reference to a concrete demand.

These rules of interaction in a group situation when observed by members are likely to promote an interpersonal climate characterized by openness and trust and effectively pave the way for the group to arrive at a consensus.

Giving and Receiving Feedback

As some team-building efforts concentrate more on feedback than on self-disclosure, it is relevant to consider the guidelines to give and receive feedback in a group situation. These guidelines are important because giving and receiving feedback are skills that one can learn and practice.

The National Training Laboratory in the United States has recommended the following guidelines for giving feedback. Effective feedback should satisfy the following three conditions:

1. The other person should understand what you are saying.
2. He must be willing and be able to accept it.
3. He must be able to do something about it.

Getting understanding is possible if the following guidelines are observed:

1. Feedback should be specific rather than be general. "You are a warm person" is not an effective feedback because it is general.
2. Feedback should be descriptive in order to be specific. It should describe the behaviour of the person, not the person himself nor should it question his motivation.
3. Feedback should be immediate rather than delayed. Both the confrontee and the group will have only vague recollections as the event has not been significant to them, whereas it was for the confronter.

Acceptability of feedback, particularly negative feedback is possible under certain conditions:

1. The feedback should be responsible. This refers to your motivation of caring and concern for the other.
2. Negative feedback should not be evaluative or prescriptive but be descriptive in order to be accepted.
3. Negative feedback should be appropriately timed. In other words it should be given when the person is mentally ready to receive it or voluntarily solicits it.
4. Negative feedback should be valid. The problem may be with you and you may be projecting it on to the other person. Here the group can help to validate the feedback.

Feedback can be useful only when the recipient can do something about it:

1. Feedback should be directed at some modifiable behaviour, not habitual, hardcore behaviour.
2. Feedback should not be complete and comprehensive and delivered with a vengence. Confine yourself to a few key areas instead of unloading a big list on him.

In sum, we may stress that if you genuinely care for the other person and he perceives you as such, any clumsiness in giving feedback could be ignored. This will not derail the effectiveness of the process. In receiving feedback one should be less defensive. This is possible when a person cultivates the habit of paying attention to the content of feedback, not the feeling it evokes. Sometimes misunderstanding feedback may provoke negative feelings. It is better to adopt the technique of summarizing, perception checking and negotiating for meaning to arrive at the other's frame of reference. Finally, when one does not get specific feedback, nothing prevents one from taking the initiative and saying, "Remember the time we met last Friday, and I did .... Is that the kind of behaviour you are talking about?"

Giving and receiving feedback are central to team-building efforts. However, one can be overly concerned about the risks involved in being open and trusting. It should always be remembered that team-building aims at creating a secure and loving social environment where norms of interaction are meant to ensure that differing perceptions of others of the same phenomenon are not viewed as attacks on the individual. In fact participation in the team-building effort is a rich and rewarding experience, provided prudent risks are initially taken by few uninhibited and non-conflicting members in the group.

APPENDIX 1

T-group and T-group Experience

The objective of sensitivity training is to promote in participants greater self-awareness and interpersonal sensitivity, i.e., to help them become more sensitive to the ways in which they relate to others.

T-group attempts to achieve these objectives through its experience-based educational strategy. T-group owes its origin to Kurt Lewin's advocacy of re-educative groups with their own unique norms of interaction between members, to bring about a change in an individual's normative structure of values, beliefs and attitudes.

T-groups

Essentially a T-group situation is a small group situation and is confined to ten or twelve strangers who agree to undergo this training over a period of two weeks in a setting far removed from the place of work. The group is leaderless, and to begin with, goal-less and unstructured. No agenda is given, nor are guidelines provided. The ways the participants interact in this unstructured situation become the educational material for the facilitator to use as illustrations of participants' behaviour at a later stage; to illustrate how their habitual ways of interaction inhibit openness; and how the new ways would promote this openness.

At the second stage, the T-group really becomes highly structured in the sense that a contract is entered into by the participants to observe the norms or rules of interaction incorporated in the contract. These norms of interaction are in fact alternative ways of interacting, alternatives to our habitual ways.

Thus the T-group becomes a laboratory for the participants to try out these alternative ways of behaving in a supportive, non-threatening atmosphere and to find out whether the new ways of interaction are rewarding or not. The participants discover that they are not only personally rewarded but they also generate interpersonal understanding and facilitate consensual decision-making.

The potential benefits of the T-group experience for the individual lie in behaviour changes which he carries back to the organization. This is not easily forthcoming, and the transfer dilemma has to be resolved. T-groups, therefore, progress from stranger-groups to cousin-groups comprising members from various sister-departments in the organization, to family-groups including only members from a single department, to finally intact work-groups including the boss and subordinate members who report to him at any level in the organization. This has to a great extent made the T-group experience organizationally relevant. Currently team-building efforts based on T-group type of interactions have proven effective in avoiding this transfer dilemma.

It should be noted, however, that even team-building efforts will be of no avail if the values of the organization do not support those of the T-group and, questions relating to personal risks involved in practicing openness in the context of organizational politics remain unanswered.

APPENDIX 2

Reproduced with permission from the Straits Times, January 1984

They were 12 complete strangers, more than a little suspicious of each other.

Seated in a circle, in Room D, a small function room in a resort inn along the San Diego hotel belt, they had no known common interest, nor did they care to find any.

Yet, six days of thrice-daily discussions later, they were a close-knit team, caring about each other's needs, accepting individual idiosyncracies and differences, and were proud to belong to the Room D group.

And when they met the people in the other three groups in the same conference at the end of each day, they found them equally loyal to their groups.

They had all gained a clearer understanding of and insight into human nature, and what team-building was about.

Organised by NTL (which stands for National Training Laboratories) Institute, a US organisation specialising in human resource development, the "Management Work Conference" is like no other executive course.

NTL runs several of them throughout the year, but no two are the same, depending on the initiative and imagination of the instructor (called facilitators) of each course.

Every team's experiences are different. Some have strong leaders; others, like the Room D group, work by consensus. But almost everyone becomes a dedicated and loyal group member.

How, you may ask, does the conference succeed where many companies fail, despite spending fortunes on courses for supervisors and activities for employees?

Procedure

Simply by encouraging and helping people to talk and listen.

The exact procedure depends on the group's facilitator, usually an academician who is an NTL member.

He or she guides the discussion and, if necessary, takes care of any outbursts.

The facilitator in Room D in San Diego was a young psychologist who told the group to talk about themselves and how they felt "here and now".

Reference to family and work was not allowed.

There was no introduction on how to start, but one black woman took the initiative by introducing herself.

The rest followed suit, but after that, they had difficulty carrying on.

Nothing seemed to be happening and no one understood what was going on.

Those who could not tolerate the silence broke it with a few frank remarks.

One smart aleck, a slick New York lawyer, who tried to take the lead, was quickly shouted down. The black woman, an affirmative action executive from the west coast, was told to get off her high horse.

A sales manager with a film star's good looks couldn't stop handing out advice and saying how marvellous he was in solving problems, while a quiet middle-aged administration executive could hardly get a word in.

The oil-industry man with the macho manner yawned rudely and wondered aloud why his company was wasting its money sending him there.

By the end of the first day, everyone was fed-up and miserable. Several spoke of leaving if things didn't improve.

The second day was no better. The atmosphere was almost hostile and the grumbles threatened to erupt into a revolt.

Embarrassed

The facilitator just sat and watched it all, and seemed to be of little help.

"You have to deal with each other," he kept saying. "You have to do the work yourselves." No one knew what he meant.

By this time, most of them were on the floor, some sitting cross-legged, others lying on the floor.

That evening, during the after-dinner session, the youngest in the group, a newly promoted section supervisor, suddenly started to sob quietly.

The rest didn't seem to notice; they carried on as though nothing happened, but were embarrassed by her tears.

After a few minutes, the facilitator declared, sounding annoyed: "What's wrong with you guys? One of you has been hurt. She is crying and no one even cares?"

The haughty woman got up, hesitantly handed the girl a tissue and sat down again without a word. The others kept their eyes glued to the floor.

The macho man, sitting next to the girl, said in a barely audible voice: "I didn't know what to do. I . . . eh . . . I wanted to put my arms around your shoulders to comfort you, but . . ."

The girl sobbed louder and dashed out of the room, followed by the haughty woman who now didn't seem so haughty.

The others remained seated and silent, but the air was choked with guilt and remorse.

After a few minutes, the two women returned. The younger one, though still red-eyed, had stopped crying. She whispered an apology and was greeted by a gush of consolation.

Worried

"Are you all right?"

"I'm sorry if we were mean to you."

"Is there something we can do to help?"

The first seed of team spirit was planted in Room D that evening.

The next morning, members of the group trickled into the room. At first, the atmosphere was strained, but it quickly gave way to warm greetings and familiar exchanges.

When the discussion started, it was noticed that someone was missing, the French Canadian.

They were worried, feeling at the same time rejected and hurt that he had left without a word, as though the group didn't matter to him.

When he turned up after lunch as if nothing had happened, all eyes fell on him, some accusingly, others with concern.

He explained that he needed to get away from the group after the previous night's incident. He needed to think.

"We were so worried," the smart aleck said accusingly. "You could at least have told us." The others muttered in agreement.

The Canadian looked surprised and half-smiled.

"It's nice of you to worry about me."

He said he felt uneasy when everyone rallied around the girl the previous night. He was moved but confused.

He had grown up supressing and ignoring personal needs for the sake of group interest and survival. Yet, here were 12 individuals who were becoming closer because they cared about individual needs.

For the first time, he said, he saw that not only was the self important but necessary if a team was to become close-knit.

Revelation

This revelation, which contradicted more than 40 years of his life's philosophy, created such turmoil in him that he felt he couldn't come to the meeting that morning.

Even before he finished, tears streamed down his face. He quickly buried it in his hand, but couldn't stop the avalanche of silent sobs.

The smart aleck started to speak, but the facilitator said softly but firmly: "Shut up. Just shut up for a minute."

In the days that followed, group members got to know each other better. Discussions were not always calm, nor relations always warm. There were personality clashes which they learned to diffuse and overcome.

As confidence in fellow members grew, guards were lowered. Other facets of their personalities, which possibly their close friends at home or even they themselves never knew, began to emerge.

The haughty woman turned out to be a sensitive soul who feared being victimised, despite her statuesque good looks.

The smart aleck, who had an over-bearing sense of superiority, desperately wanted to be liked, and had a kind and generous nature under the abrasiveness.

Perfect

The good-looker confessed that he suffered from the Great American Male Syndrome, that is, the need to project the image of the perfect man who needed nobody, had no problems, could do anything and always won.

Here at the course, he was able to admit to himself that he did indeed need people and it was all right to be imperfect.

The quiet one, who feared rejection, began to emerge from behind his broad tie when the others went out of their way to include him in conversation.

As for the macho man, he turned out to be gentle and soft-hearted, but had been afraid of being ridiculed if his friends found out.

Each member in turn found new confidence with the help and understanding of teamates.

In the process, all were exposed to facets of vastly different personalities, and understood better the diversity of people's attitudes.

Before the group broke up, the facilitator offered a few final words.

It was important, he said, for people to "deal" with each other, so that they would become sensitive, not only to the feelings of other people, but also to how their behaviour affected others.

And when "dealing", it was necessary sometimes to risk disclosing one's weaknesses or problems. It was a risk because one became vulnerable to hurt, but it could foster closer human relationships.

Useful

And because they cared about each other and the team as a whole, they could always count on the support of each other, without fear of rejection or ridicule.

Each member would be accepted for what he or she was. Each would feel needed, useful and important.

At the end of the conference the Room D team was loathe to part.

Said one member: "Now I know. But how will my colleagues at home understand?"

article written by Lu-lin Reutens

QUESTIONS

1. Establish the need for team-building and briefly explain the basic process of team-building.
2. What are the three models of team-building and discuss the Organizational Development techniques they employ to remove blockages in the team.
3. Explain the interactional rules or guidelines for feedback to promote interpersonal communication in a group.

REFERENCES

Argyris, Chris. *Interpersonal Competence and Organizational Effectiveness.* Illinois: Richard Irwin, Homewood, 1962.

Berne, Eric. *Games People Play.* New York: Grove Press, 1964.

Campbell John P. and Marvin D. Dunnette. "Effectiveness of T-group Experience in Managerial Training and Development", *Psychology Bulletin,* August 1968, pp. 73-104.

Francis, D. and Don Yong, *Improving Work Groups: A Practical Manual For Team Building:* San Diego, California: University Associates.

Fordyce, Jack K. and Raymond Weil. *Managing With People: A Manager's Handbook of Organization Development Methods.* Massachusettes: Addism-Wesley, 1979.

French, Wendell L. and Cecil H. Bell, Jr. *Organization Development: Behavioural Science Interventions For Organization Improvement.* 2nd ed. New Jersey: Prentice-Hall, Englewood Cliffs, 1978.

Harris, Thomas A. *I Am Ok — You Are Ok.* London: Pan Book, 1974.

Huse, Edgar F. *Organization Development and Change.* 2nd ed. Minnesota: West Publishing Company, 1980.

Johnson, David ,W. *Reaching Out: Interpersonal Effectiveness and Self-actualization.* New Jersey: Prentice-Hall, Englewood Cliffs, 1972.

_____ . *Learning Together and Alone.* New Jersey: Prentice-Hall, Englewood Cliffs, 1975.

"Laboratory Training: A Symposium", *Industrial Relations,* California, Vol. 8, No. 1, October 1968, pp. 1-45.

Lewin, Kurt. "Group Decision and Social Change", in *Readings in Social Psychology,* (ed.) G.E. Swanson, T.M. Newcome and E. L. Hartlye. 2nd Ed. N.Y: Holt, 1952, pp. 459-473.

19
Conflict Management

EDITH C. YUEN

SUMMARY

Conflict is an inevitable part of organizational life and can have both positive and negative consequences. The aim of conflict management is not to eliminate all conflicts but to take advantage of the positive effects which a conflict generates and to minimize the negative effects.

The way modern organizations are structured, with differentiated functions performed by highly specialized units which are task-wise interdependent but at the same time compete for limited resources, creates many antecedent conditions for conflict.

Conflict management is easier said than done. To manage a conflict constructively, a manager has to acquire a proper perspective of the conflict by clearly defining the goals and objectives of the organization and their priorities. He has to be open-minded, be able to see both sides of an issue and to understand the system of causality involved in the development of the conflict. The abilities to draw the critical line between constructive and destructive conflicts, and to prevent a conflict from getting onto a destructive course are important in conflict management. Issue control and the institutionalization of conflict resolution can help solve this problem.

There are various strategies for conflict management. The choice of an appropriate strategy depends on the seriousness of the conflict, the amount and kind of resource available for conflict management and the nature of the antecedent conditions of conflict.

Defining Conflict and Related Terms

Conflict, defined briefly, is incompatible behaviour between parties whose interests differ (Deutsch, 1973; Brown, 1983). There are two elements involved in this definition of conflict: "incompatible behaviour" and "conflicting interests" and both elements have to be present before an interaction can be described as a conflict. In this definition, "interests" refer to recognized and unrecognized stakes that are affected by the interaction of parties and "incompatible behaviour" refers to actions by one party intended to oppose or frustrate the other party.

It is necessary to distinguish between conflict and competition. In a conflict, two or more parties strive for goals which are mutually incompatible and winning for one party necessarily implies loss for its opponents. In this respect, competition is not different from conflict. However, in the course of a competition, the behaviours of the competing parties are strictly governed by a set of rules. The emphasis of each party is on winning the event rather than defeating its opponent and once the result is obvious, competition terminates (Filley, 1975).

Conflict is a dynamic process which can be analyzed as a sequence of *conflict episodes* (Pondy, 1967). As each conflict episode unfolds, five stages of development can be identified:

1. *Latent Conflict:* At first, the conditions for conflict may be present without any party being aware of their existence.
2. *Perceived Conflict:* Conflict is perceived when the parties realize that their goals are different from the goals of other groups and that the goal attainment of one group interferes with those of the others.
3. *Felt Conflict:* By the time conflict brings about feelings of anxiety, hostility, anger, fear or mistrust between one party and the other, conflict is felt.
4. *Manifest Conflict:* Felt conflict is often followed by overt behaviour aimed at advancing one's own interests and frustrating the goal attainment effort of the other party.
5. *Conflict Aftermath:* Finally, depending on the way conflict is handled, the legacy of a conflict episode will affect future organizational life. If conflict is satisfactorily resolved, the episode can become the basis of future cooperation whereas ,if it is merely suppressed, it may form the basis of conflict alignment within the organization. Antagonism between the parties may explode in a more serious form at a later stage.

The five stages of a conflict episode are shown in the diagram below.

Figure 1:

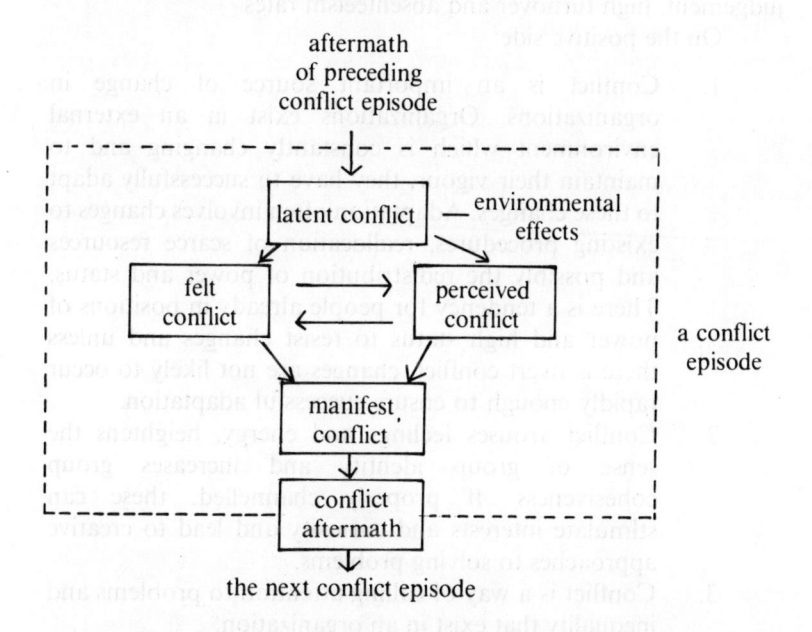

```
            aftermath
           of preceding
          conflict episode
                ↓
    ┌─────────────────────────────────────┐
    │                                     │
    │   latent conflict ── environmental  │
    │        │               effects      │
    │        ↓             ↙              │
    │     felt    ──→   perceived         │
    │    conflict  ←──   conflict         │  a conflict
    │                      ↙              │   episode
    │                   manifest          │
    │                    conflict         │
    │                      ↓              │
    │                   conflict          │
    │                   aftermath         │
    └─────────────────────────────────────┘
                        ↓
             the next conflict episode
```

Within an organization, conflict can occur between colleagues in a work unit, between a subordinate and his boss (*interpersonal conflict*); between two or more units/departments or between a labour union and management (*intergroup conflict*).

Conflict: The Functional/Dysfunctional Controversy

Under the structural/functional perspective, popular in the forties and the fifties, conflict is considered to be "bad" — an abnormal state which signifies the breakdown of normal and "healthy" interaction among individuals and groups. More recent approaches (pluralist and interactionist) not only accept conflict as an inevitable part of organizational life, but come to view conflict as having potentially positive effects.

The negative effects of conflict arise mainly from disruptions in communication, cohesiveness and cooperation. The achievement of the goals of an organization requires the cooperative effort of its members and lack of cooperation often results in sub-optimal performance. Conflict also takes its toll on individuals which in turn affects organizational performance. The experience of stress, frustration and anxiety can lead to reduced job satisfaction, inability to concentrate on the job, impaired judgement, high turnover and absenteeism rates.

On the positive side:

1. Conflict is an important source of change in organizations. Organizations exist in an external environment which is constantly changing and to maintain their vigour, they have to successfully adapt to these changes. Adaptation often involves changes to existing procedures, reallocation of scarce resources and possibly the redistribution of power and status. There is a tendency for people already in positions of power and high status to resist changes and unless there is overt conflict, changes are not likely to occur rapidly enough to ensure successful adaptation.
2. Conflict arouses feelings and energy, heightens the sense of group identity and increases group cohesiveness. If properly channelled, these can stimulate interests and curiosity and lead to creative approaches to solving problems.
3. Conflict is a way of calling attention to problems and inequality that exist in an organization.
4. Constructive competition among groups and individuals can lead to higher productivity.
5. In a conflict situation, dominant values and ideas tend to be questioned. This provides an opportunity for alternative views and ideas to be considered.

While conflict can have both positive and negative effects, whether a particular conflict is functional or dysfunctional depends on the values and objectives one assesses it with. The same conflict can be functional to an organization because it facilitates adaptation but dysfunctional to the individuals concerned in terms of the frustration, anxiety and hostility it generates. The value of conflict to an organization also varies depending on the stage of organizational evolution it is in. For example, after rapid expansion, the objective of an organization is likely to be consolidation. A period of relative stability is important and any extended conflict can be disruptive. Hence it is necessary to define objectives clearly if one is to acquire a proper perspective of a conflict situation.

Destructive Conflict and "Conflict Trap"

There is, however, one type of conflict which is always dysfunctional — destructive conflict. Human beings complicate organizational conflict because they depart from rational, reality-based behaviour in their struggle against one another. As a result of this aspect of human behaviour, there is often a tendency for conflict to escalate. Escalation may occur along the following dimensions (Deutsch, 1973):

1. the size and number of immediate issues involved;
2. the number of motives each party implicates on the other;
3. the number of people drawn into the conflict;
4. the size and number of the principles and precedents that are perceived to be at stake;
5. the costs that the participants are willing to bear in relation to the conflict;
6. the number of norms of moral conduct from which behaviour toward the other side is exempted;
7. the intensity of negative attitudes towards the other side.

Destructive conflict is most likely to occur when participants have a win-lose orientation. That is, each side believes that only one group can win and is determined to be the winner. The course of development of a destructive conflict is fairly predictable. It starts with an issue which both sides regard as important. After a number of confrontations, each group begins to see the other group as an "enemy". Members of the opposing group are perceived in terms of a negative stereotype and evil intentions are attributed to whatever actions they take. Communication between the conflicting parties is unreliable. Under this atmosphere of suspicion and hostility, the groups are more sensitive to threats and less aware of similarities and common interests. Within the opposing groups, group cohesiveness, emotion and pressure to conform increase. These, in turn, lead to the magnification of the conflict.

By this time, the organization falls into a "conflict trap" (Boulding, 1964). The alignment established in the unresolved conflict emerges over and over again on all new issues regardless of their relevance to the old conflict. Under this situation, the ability of the organization to solve problems rationally is critically impaired. In extreme situations, the organization becomes immobilized, unable to take unified action.

The Purpose of Conflict Management

1. The purpose of conflict management is not to weed out all conflicts in an organization. Constructive competition and a certain amount of conflict are, for the most part, useful elements in organizational life. They make an organization creative, adaptive and vigorous.

2. Managers should be aware of both positive and negative effects which a conflict can have on the attainment of organizational goals and on the individuals concerned. Robbins, (1974, p. 25) suggests that the attainment of organizational objectives should be given priority above individual perceptions and sentiments. "In terms of functional or dysfunctional value, it is irrelevant how the participants perceive the conflict . . . (a conflict) would be functional if it furthers the objectives of the organization". However, in view of the link between the two variables and the potential scar which a destructive conflict can leave, such a one-sided approach can be dangerous in the long run.

3. The goal of conflict management is to make the best use of the positive effects which a conflict generates and minimize the negative effects.

4. Competition has to be carefully "managed" so that it does not get out of control.

5. The ability to draw the *critical line between constructive and destructive conflicts* is an important skill in conflict management. The manager's job is to prevent groups from slipping into the course of a destructive conflict. The ideal state to strive for is "conflict without hostility" (Kahn, 1964).

Sources of Organizational Conflict

In most organizations, conditions which tend to create conflict exist. These conditions are called *antecedent conditions*. Six common antecedent conditions are described below although these, by no means, exhaust the list.

1. *Competition for Scarce Resource:* This occurs when there is

a discrepancy between aggregated demands of the competing parties and the available resources such as budget funds, space, supplies, personnel and supporting services.

2. *Divergence of Subunit Goals:* As organizations grow, they not only get bigger, but develop more and more specialized units and subunits. Units performing differentiated functions (e.g., maintenance and production departments) are likely to have divergent goals. Conflict arises when subunits pursuing differentiated goals have to depend on one another in the performance of their tasks.

3. *Drive for Autonomy:* When a subordinate demands more power, more influence in decision-making and/or less interference from his superior in task performance, the superior may find this a threat to his position. The emerging culture among the young people stresses the self and self actualization. This, together with the feeling shared by many young employees that in terms of formal education they are better qualified than their superiors, make the drive for autonomy an important source of conflict in modern organizations.

4. *Jurisdictional Ambiguity:* Conflict is likely when jurisdictional boundaries are unclear (overlapping responsibility or gaps in the allocation of responsibility), and one party attempts to assume more control over desirable activities or relinquishes its part in the performance of undesirable activities.

5. *Status Problems:* The drive for higher status by one party (a department or an individual) is often regarded by other parties as a threat to their position in the status hierarchy. The things which the parties strive for can be the floor on which a unit is located, the use of company cars, the order departments appear in company literature.

6. *Communication Barrier:* It is not uncommon that conflict is perceived even though the positions of the conflicting parties are essentially compatible. Ineffective communication, noises and perceptual problems often account for such "pseudo-conflicts".

Methods to Deal with Conflict and their Application

There are various techniques for handling conflict and they produce different outcomes. One way of classifying these techniques is by the extent antecedent conditions are dealt with.

1. Methods which leave antecedent conditions untouched:

— *Avoidance.* The conflicting parties (or at least one of them) evade each other to avoid overt confrontation.
— *Smoothing.* A technique which plays down differences between the conflicting parties while emphasizing their common interests.
— *Forcing.* A method in which the more powerful party imposes its will on the weaker one.
— *Suppression.* This method involves the use of authority by superiors in reducing the level of conflict.

None of the above techniques deals with the root of the problem. Although conflict cannot be resolved by these methods, they help reduce the level of conflict and can be successful short-term alternatives. Use these methods when:

— the conflict is trivial and does not seriously affect organizational performance.
— the antecedent condition of conflict is only temporary.
— the organization is preoccupied with more important matters and cannot spare the resource, for the time being, to deal with the conflict.
— a change in the external environment is expected which will change the situation.

2. Methods which deal with antecedent conditions through changing either organizational or human variables:

(a) Changing organizational variables:

Increasing size and specialization create problems of integration and coordination and are constant sources of organization conflict. Excessive specialization may make the purpose of the organization obscure and lead to rivalry between units each pursuing its own goals and competing for scarce resources. Techniques to resolve conflict by restructuring organizational variables include:

— making salient the larger structure and its goals.
— modifying the reward system to encourage cooperation between individuals, groups and units.
— establishing "buffers" between conflicting units which are interdependent in task performance.

— redesigning jobs or reorganizing departments to reduce task interdependency if buffers do not solve the problem.
— establishing standard decision-making criteria and procedures when disagreement in decision-making is the cause of conflict.

(b) Changing the human variables:

The aim is to change behaviour patterns through changing values and attitudes or through improving the human relations skills of those involved in a conflict. Sensitivity training, human relations training and educating organizational members to accept the organization's goals and rules, etc., are popular methods to achieve this. Another way of changing the human variable is by the reshuffling of personnel. It has, however, been suggested that the most common and unproductive conflict management trap of all is trying to change the other person.

3. Methods which do not try to remove antecedent conditions, but resolve the conflict, at least temporarily, by having the conflicting groups *compromise* on their *needs and demands*. Usually the conflicting parties will engage in a process of exchanging concessions (bargaining) until a compromise is reached. This kind of strategy is used (i) when making structural changes to remove the antecedent condition of conflict is too costly; (ii) when the conflict is of a recurrent nature and involves fundamental and deep-rooted difference in interests between the conflicting parties. An example of this is labour-management conflict.

Techniques included in this category range from unstructured negotiation between conflicting groups in an organization to formal bargaining and third-party intervention through arbitration or judicial settlement.

4. In addition to the three types of methods mentioned, a fourth method for conflict management is *problem solving*. As a method of conflict resolution, problem solving involves the conflicting parties working together to find a solution that either achieves the goals of both parties, or one which is acceptable to both. Problem solving takes two basic forms: consensus and integrative decision-making methods (Filley, 1975).

In a consensus decision, the parties concerned came to an agreement about means and ends of solving the problem at hand.

Better decisions are usually achieved when certain group process rules are enforced (Hall, 1972):

(a) Participants must focus upon defeating the problem rather than each other;
(b) Voting, trading, or averaging should be avoided;
(c) Participants have to seek facts to solve the problem;
(d) Conflict should be considered as helpful and potentially constructive;
(e) Members should avoid self-oriented behaviour.

Integrated decision-making emphasizes more on innovative ideas which change the conflict from a zero-sum, win-lose situation to a win-win one. To achieve this, the conflicting parties must examine their goals and motivations closely, be honest about facts, opinions and feelings, and sincerely work towards the attainment of high quality decisions that will permit both sides to achieve their goals and satisfy their needs.

Effective Conflict Management

1. It is clear from the above that in order to manage conflict effectively, a manager has to analyze and understand the conflict situation well. Several competencies seem to be associated with a manager's ability to understand a conflict (Boyatzis, 1983).

— Perceptual objectivity: the ability to perceive multiple views or sides of an issue.
— Self control: the ability to inhibit personal needs, desires or impulses when their expression would not serve organizational purposes.
— Diagnostic use of concepts: the ability to interpret events through the application of concepts, principles, etc. to events.
— Logical thought: the ability to perceive the "system" of causality among numerous events and people.
— Conceptualization: the ability to identify themes, patterns of relationships, etc. With reference to conflict management, competence in conceptualization helps in the identification of common objectives and values which the conflicting parties may have in common.

2. Understanding alone is not enough. In all areas of management, decision-making is a key part of the manager's job

and the same applies to conflict management. A manager has to define the goals of the organization and their priorities. He uses these objectives to decide whether a conflict is functional or dysfunctional, whether a conflict should be allowed to continue or not, how serious the problem is and how urgent is the need for conflict resolution. Deciding on the amount of resource allocated to conflict management is another part of the manager's job.

3. In the case of a destructive conflict, it is possible that even if the antecedent conditions are removed, residues of hostility between the opposing camps remain to plague the organization. For this reason, the successful management of conflict may require the use of several techniques concurrently. Antecedent conditions have to be dealt with and at the same time, emotions have to be "cooled out".

A confrontation meeting followed by a series of sessions aimed at establishing a collaborative relationship between the two groups is often useful. The purpose of confrontation meetings is to make a conflict visible in a direct confrontation between the hostile parties. The premise is that the conflict has to be brought out to the open and hostile emotions vented before the parties can deal with the conflict constructively. Once the issue and conflict areas are clearly identified, the parties can proceed to more collaborative and integrative activities such as integrative problem solving.

4. In general, it is better to manage a conflict before it gets on a destructive course.

An effective method of preventing the escalation of conflict is *issue control* (Fisher, 1964). Conflicts are often defined by the conflicting parties in a way that either magnifies or minimizes the size of the disputed issues. Issue control is an attempt to control the importance of what is perceived to be at stake in a conflict.

In issue control, an outsider (usually the manager) tries to help the conflicting parties acquire a proper perspective of the conflict. This is done by localizing the conflict in terms of a given time and place, specifying the particulars and delimiting actions and their consequences. By doing so, the common tendency to define conflicts in terms of principles, precedents, rights, etc. is avoided. The logic behind issue control is quite simple: when a quarrel starts to center on personalities or group membership rather than specific actions, it usually takes a non-productive run.

Similarly, when a discussion focuses on rights or principles rather than on what is specifically taking place at a given time and place, it is not likely to be fruitful.

5. Another way to limit and control conflict is through the establishment of conflict regulators (a process often referred to as the institutionalization of conflict resolution). Institutionalised conflict resolution involves one of the following (Deutsch, 1973):

— the establishment of institutional forms to deal with conflicts, e.g., collective bargaining.
— the establishment of positions and personnel responsible for conflict resolution such as mediators, conciliators and referees.
— the establishment of norms of behaviour which set out clearly the "acceptable" and "unacceptable" behaviour for all parties concerned.
— the establishment of rules for conducting negotiations.
— the establishment of procedures for conducting negotiations.

For conflict regulation to develop and function, several preconditions must exist:

— Each party must be sufficiently coherent and stable as a group to act as an organized unit so that the actions of its members are controlled and unified in relation to the conflict.
— Each party must recognize the legitimate existence of the other party and be committed to accepting the outcome of the regulated conflict, even if it is unfavourable to the group's interest.
— The organization must ensure the strict adherence to rules, established procedures and behaviour norms.

QUESTIONS

1. In what ways can conflict be functional to an organization? Would you subscribe to the view that sometimes it is desirable to promote conflict within an organization?
2. Select a conflict in which you have recently been involved. Identify the reasons for this conflict. How could problem solving have been used to resolve the conflict?

3. What do you think is the most common method of conflict resolution used in Singapore? Are there differences between different ethnic groups in relation to conflict management?

REFERENCES

Boulding, E. "Furthering Reflections on Conflict Management", in R. Kahn and E Boulding (eds.), *power and Conflict in Organizations*. London: Tavistock Publications, 1964.

Boyatzis, R. E. "Managerial Competence and Interpersonal Conflict", in D Tjosvold and D Johnson (eds.), *Productive Conflict Management*. New York: Irvington Publishers Inc., 1983.

Brown, L. D. *Managing Conflict at Organizational Interfaces*. Addison-Wesley, 1983.

Deutsch, M. *The Resolution of Conflict*. New Haven and London: Yale University Press, 1973.

Filley, A. C. *Interpersonal Conflict Resolution*. Illinois: Scott, Foresman and Company, 1975.

Fisher, R. "Fractionating Conflict", in R. Fisher (ed.), *International Conflict and Behavioral Science*. New York: Basic Books, 1964.

Hall, R. M. *Organizations: Structure and Process*. Prentice Hall, 1972.

Kahn, R. and Boulding, E. (eds.) *Power and Conflict in Organizations*. London : Tavistock Publications, 1964.

Katz, D. "Approaches to Managing Conflict", in Kahn and Boulding, *Power and Conflict in Organizations*. London: Tavistock Publications, 1964.

Nadler, D., Hackman, J. R. and Lawler, E. E. *Managing Organizational Behaviour*. Boston: Little Brown & Co., 1979.

Pondy, L. R. "Organizational Conflict: Concepts and Models", *Administrative Science Quarterly,* 1967, Vol. 12, p. 296-320.

Robbins, S. P. *Managing Organizational Conflict*. Englewood Cliffs: Prentice-Hall, 1974.

Schmidt, S. M. and Kochan, T. A. "Conflict: Toward Conceptual Clarity", *Administrative Science Quarterly,* 1972, Vol. 17, p. 359-370.

Wexley, K. and Yukl. *Organizational Behavior and Personnel Psychology*. 1977.

20
The Management of Change: Overcoming Resistance

CHONG LI CHOY

SUMMARY

This paper identifies the factors which enabled rapid change to take place in Singapore. It discusses why people resist change, and how one can overcome such resistances. Illustrations are drawn from the attempts to modernize traditional small businesses in Singapore.

INTRODUCTION

In the last twenty-five years, since 1959, Singapore has undergone rapid social change and has been transformed from a basically entrepot trading centre and colony with high unemployment to a modern financial and industrial centre and nation with full-employment. The country continues with her very rapid economic growth and industrial restructuring. The setting up of high technology industries, the computerization of businesses and industries, and the upgrading of informational and other technologies are all part and parcel of this very rapid social change in Singapore. With these technical advancements is a renewed interest in the individual's well-being. The importance of good human resource management is publicly emphasized by the leaders of Singapore.

Although the people of Singapore easily adapt to change and may even be said to desire change, resistance to change does exist. This chapter attempts to identify some of the factors which enable rapid change to take place in Singapore and focuses on the management of resistance to change. Two issues are crucial to this management — the fact that people resist change, and an analysis of how one can overcome resistance.

Factors Enabling Rapid Change

All societies are constantly changing. Social change is both continuous and irresistible and normally refers to changes in the social structure (including economic, demographic, political and normative structures) and relationships in society (such as decline of neighbourliness and changes in interpersonal relationships in families, companies and other institutions). Whether directly or indirectly, social change normally involves cultural changes.

Why is Singapore so ready and able to change so rapidly?

(1) Singaporeans perceive the need for change. Continual economic development is the goal of the nation. Continual upgrading of the individual's well-being is seen to be necessary by most Singaporeans. Modernization, in terms of technological and scientific advancements and innovations is seen as necessary. Education and training are also considered to be desirable and useful.

This perception is the result of many factors: a modern western-type education; the traditional Chinese reverence for education and learning; and the fruits of economic development (a type of social change) that prevailed in the last two decades.

(2) Singaporeans in general, do hold attitudes and values that are favourable to change. (This is both a cause and effect of change). They are aware of social change and the desired direction of change (modernization and economic development). Given the fact that their traditional cultures (and hence values) are based on agriculture (i.e., cultures evolved in basically agricultural societies where change is slow), and the fact that much of this culture is not appropriate to a rapidly changing urban society, Singaporeans are not surprisingly, somewhat skeptical and critical of some elements in their traditional cultures. Furthermore, as immigrants, the early generations had to adapt to a foreign (British) administration and to foreign ways. This trait of adaptability to, and tolerance of foreign ways, has remained with present day Singaporeans. Hence, Singaporeans are generally willing to consider and experiment with innovations.

(3) Contact with foreign cultures began with the early immigrants. Living in close proximity to other racial, social and cultural groups under a foreign (British) administration, led further to considerable cultural diffusion. For instance the inclusion of the Malay word "sayang" and the English words in the corrupted form of "go-stun" illustrates the cultural diffusion that has taken place. Furthermore, contact with foreigners and foreign cultures (including the influence of the mass media and education), as well as past cultural diffusion, have made Singaporeans very amenable to change.

(4) Change is further made easier by the fact that the traditional cultures of Singaporeans which are nascent to their traditional homelands, were never fully transferred to Singapore. This means that there is considerable vagueness when it comes to the structure of society and culture. For example, how much authority should a Chinese mother-in-law have over her Chinese daughter-in-law in Singapore today? What exactly should be done in a traditional Chinese marriage ceremony and what kinds of adaptive changes are acceptable? These are questions which even the "expert aunties" who are normally consulted, would not agree on. Further, the fact that Singapore is a small country with a highly centralized and modern bureaucracy certainly makes it favourable to change. Changes can often be decided on and be easily monitored by the government.

(5) There exists a relatively wide cultural base in Singapore. This is because of such factors as the high level of literacy and education; the varied cultural origins of Singaporeans; the exposure to life and conditions of many other countries through such means as the mass-media, books, travel, and foreign films; and the presence of foreign businesses and industries in Singapore. Such a wide cultural base presents greater opportunities for innovation.

(6) Finally, the physical environment in Singapore is such that Singapore must continually rely on other countries for trade and investments. Being an island with limited natural resources has resulted in an open economy and society. Thus constant contact with foreign societies and cultures is inevitable.

The fact that Singapore is undergoing rapid change also means that the social institutions and organizations (including business firms) must continually adapt to, and be part of these societal changes. It is inevitable that a manager in Singapore must therefore not only be aware of the necessity and reality of change, but also be ready to implement changes in his own organization. For example, a manager may need to restructure his organization to adapt to changes in society and to keep up with new technology. He may want to change the work habits of some workers. All these require changes in his organization. However, change is often met with resistance. Inspite of the tolerance to change, resistance to change does exist.

Why People Resist Change

The reasons for resistance to change are varied and many.[1] We may classify resistance to change into two broad categories according to their nature, namely, the cultural and emotional resistances, and the rational and information-based resistances. However, it should be pointed out that resistance to change may be both rational and emotional.

Cultural and Emotional Resistances[2]

This kind of resistance is common in all societies. People are emotional and sentimental creatures. They may value certain things which have obviously outlived their usefulness, so much so that they go out of their way to spend useful resources in order to retain them. They may be guided in their behaviour by irrational fears and anxieties. Such emotions, fears and sentiments are often manifested in the form of resistance to change. These feelings may be influenced by past individual and group experiences; by culture; or by people or group(s) influence (these could be primary or in-groups). In all these cases, sentiments and other emotions play a part. These cultural and emotional resistances can be categorized under two broad headings:

(1) Compatibility with the existing culture; and
(2) Specific attitudes and values.

---

[1] Some of these reasons are given by Edward H. Spicey (ed.), *Human Problems in Technological Change*, New York: Russel Sage Foundation, 1952.
[2] The problems of incompatible culture and values have been emphasized in much of the literature on change. For example, see collection of papers in the *International Social Science Journal* 13:3, 1981.

Compatibility with Existing Culture

Traditional Chinese businesses in Singapore are generally organized in the pattern of the traditional Chinese family system. The head of the business is the patriarch and the workers are normally family members. Workers who do not belong to the family are either treated like members of the "family" or as "slaves" in the the traditional Chinese family setting. Modern laws have made the latter (such slavery) rare (if not extinct). Hence, traditional Chinese businesses (normally small businesses) in Singapore are generally family businesses involving family members and relatives, and possibly some close friends (or their children). Inspite of the modifications that have taken place in this kind of business organization, the business culture of these traditional small businessmen, which is based on the traditional Chinese family system, and the culture of modern Singapore are still somewhat incompatible. As pointed out earlier, the traditional Chinese family system which has its roots in traditional China has not been entrenched in Singapore, and Singaporeans are therefore generally skeptical and critical with regard to its application. The older generation would therefore be normally reluctant to modernize their businesses which would involve changes in their business organization and operations. Such changes are however, generally favoured by their children. This is found to be true in the experiences of the coffee shops and the provision shops in Singapore,[3] which are currently attempting industry-wide modernization.

Specific Attitudes and Values

The problem also has its perceptual and emotional aspects. To many of these traditional businessmen, the "old ways" are much better and therefore should not be changed. This could be due to their past experiences which have formed certain values

---

Chong Li choy and Kau Ah Keng, "Modernising Traditional Small Business in Singapore: The Small Businessman's Resistance to Change", paper presented at the conference, *International Perspective on Small Businesses*, 29th Annual World Conference of *the International Council for Small Business*, Chicago, Illinois, June 11-13, 1984.

Also, cf. G.V. Busby, "Modernisation of Provision Shops in Singapore, in *Proceedings of the 10th International Small Business Congress*, September 12-15, 1983, Singapore, Singapore: Applied Research Corporation, 1983, pp. 289-291.

and habits, or to their in-group and primary group affiliation.

For instance, many coffee-shop owners used to think that coffee brewed by machines is inferior in taste compared to coffee prepared manually by using the "traditional method". This perception is untrue[4] but it did give rise to resistance against the use of coffee-brewing machines in coffee-shops. Primary group[5] influence can be seen in the fact that some coffee-shop owners resist change because they are fearful of criticism from their peers (neighbourhood friends, normally of the same generation, who are also their customers) if they introduce certain changes into their businesses; changes such as self-service or the use of coffee-brewing machines. We can also say that such behaviour is the result of specific values in their culture, such as loyalty to friends.

Rational and Information-based Resistances

Resistance to change is not just a matter of emotions and culture although such resistence is real. Resistance can be highly rational and be based on specific information (whether true or false). This latter type of resistance can be due to perceptual difficulties because of the inability to demonstrate the viability of the proposed innovation or change. It can also be due to technical difficulties and costs. Vested interests or the lack of it can also lead to resistances. All these resistances are rational in nature and are based on information provided and/or perceived by the person(s) concerned.

Inability to Demonstrate Viability Innovation

The inability to demonstrate the viability of the proposed changes or innovation is certainly a major problem in the initial stages of introducing new ideas and methods. For example, in both the modernization of the provision-shops and the coffee-shops in Singapore, the lack of evidence concerning the work ability of such proposals made it difficult for many traditional small businessmen to commit themselves, in practice, to

---

[4] A taste test was carried out by Chong Li Choy, Kau Ah Keng and Tan Thiam Soon, who were the consultants to the project on *The Modernization of Coffee Shops*, (ARC Project No. 77/82/33, August 1983).

[5] A primary group is normally a small group in which relationships are intimate and informal (non-contractual), whose existence is an end in itself. This is opposed to the contractual and utilitarian nature of the secondary groups.

modernization. The same problem also exists for other traditional industries seeking change. Here, we see perceptual difficulties in terms of envisaging the proposed modernization possibilities, and appreciating the workability of the proposals. Such resistance is information-based since there is indeed lack of information (demonstration of workability of innovation), although there may also be a lack of confidence in their own abilities as well as in the proposals. It is also rational, since it is perfectly rational for a man to avoid possible failure or expected difficulties. On the other hand, the successful demonstration through a taste-test, mentioned earlier, that coffee brewed by machine is not inferior to that brewed manually in the "traditional way" did cause some coffee-shop owners to install coffee-brewing machines in their shops.

Technical Difficulties and Costs

Percieved technical difficulties (irrespective of their reality), are part and parcel of innovation and change in society. Such difficulties or the fear of such difficulties, are real obstacles to the adoption of new ideas. For example, in the modernization of the coffee-shops, technical difficulties did exist.

Technical difficulties may result from a lack of know-how. For example, coffee-shop assistants may not know how to operate a coffee-brewing machine in the correct manner. As a result, there may be considerable wastage of coffee powder, coffee may turn sour because of "overexposure", or the machine may frequently break down.

The expected dissatisfaction of some customers because of their own inability to accept some of the changes (such as self-service in a coffee-shop) can also lead to the problem of a loss of customers to other shops in the neighbourhood. This type of fear is real and the resistance to change may therefore be a rational one.[6]

The unwillingness of shop assistants and owners to change their old habits is another technical problem, which relates to culture and attitudes (emotional). However, emotional costs are also costs which must be paid for by the individual who accepts change. Other costs involved in change may include the cost of

---

[6] Other considerations, such as, the loss of income through pilferage and the problem of customers leaving without making payments, may render this resistance irrational.

renovations, the cost of new machines, the cost of moving, and other related expenditures.

Vested Interests

People may resist change because of vested interests or the lack of it. Such vested interests may be in terms of monetary gains or losses; gain or loss of personal power, or even emotional attachments and sentiments. It should be pointed out that where vested interests do not exist, there will normally be little motivation to change.

Again in the case of coffee-shop modernization, shops facing urban renewal have little vested interests (in monetary terms) in modernization. In the case of owners who have children who are well-educated and can find better paying or more comfortable jobs, the old traditional businessman normally prefers his business to die a natural death, rather than to modernize. Contentment with existing profits from the business also gives rise to a lack of vested interests in modernization.

There is also considerable vested interests (power, emotional and cultural considerations) in the patriarch's refusal to modernize. The fear of loss of control over business and family is real. The fear that this may lead to the possible disintegration of the family may give rise to a resistance to change. Such vested interests are therefore emotional, sentimental or even cultural in nature.

How to Overcome Resistance

In order to motivate people to change it is important to understand why people resist change. This consists basically of providing additional and relevant information to help bring about change) and also involves appealing to one's reasoning powers. In order to overcome cultural and emotional resistances, appeals may be made to other elements (values) of culture which may lend support to the change (particularly in view of the skepticism some Singaporeans have with traditional culture). Appeals may also be made through people who are close to those who are resisting the change, such as their children and peer group. This may again be applied to the modernization of the coffee-shops and provision-shops in Singapore.

Appeal to Rationality and the Provision of Information

This approach involves the dissemination of knowledge and information to the people who may resist change. They are helped through the so-called "demonstration effect". Through such additional information, these people may be helped to see the reasons for the change and the advantages involved. This will also give them vested interest in the change. In the case of the modernization of coffee-shops, an exhibition was held by the two coffee-shop associations in Singapore to disseminate such information. Brief notes highlighting crucial arguments and information in the consultancy report were also circulated to members. The press also helped by featuring the existing problems of coffee-shops, the need to modernize, and the advantages of modernization.

The use of "demonstrations" to effect modernization has been most effective. In both the provision-shop and coffee-shop modernization, examples of success, however limited, have always proved to be very effective in encouraging others to change. Demonstrations may also be done by the change agent to overcome specific resistance, such as the taste test referred to earlier which proved that coffee brewed by machines is not inferior to that brewed in the traditional way.

Appeal to Values and Emotions

Cultural and emotional barriers to change may be overcome by appealing to other cultural values of the persons involved as well as to their emotions and sentiments. Social pressure to change can also be built up by the dissemination of information through the mass-media. For example, in the modernization of provision-shops, some traditional shopowners who originally resisted modernization, were pressurised by their friends, clients and family members into accepting modernization. Such pressures take the form of questions like: Why are you so backward in your business operation?

Such a question, asked by friendly clients and relatives have caused some traditional shopowners to reverse their original attitude towards modernization.

Appeals through the children of shopowners are also effective. Such appeals are both emotional as well as cultural in nature. The emotional aspect of such appeals is obvious. In the case of the traditional small businesses in Singapore, the assurance that their children are willing to become successors to their businesses if they modernize is indeed very pursuasive. This is because from a cultural point of view, the family is more important than the individual. If modernization helps to keep the family together, it therefore becomes desirable to modernize. It is also the hope of most traditional Chinese businessmen that their sons would inherit their businesses one day.

Conclusion: the Management of Change in Singapore

In the management of change, it is important to understand why the specific proposed changes are being resisted. Although cultural barriers to change in Singapore may not be very strong because of its history and situation, resistance to change does exist. The recent and on-going modernization of the traditional Chinese coffee-shops and provision-shops in Singapore serves to illustrate why people in Singapore resist change and how it is possible to overcome such resistance. Emotional and cultural resistance can be handled by appealing to emotions, sentiments and other supportive cultural values. A rational approach can also be resorted to by providing relevant information.

QUESTIONS

1. Why is Singapore ready and able to change so rapidly?
2. Why do people resist change?
3. How can one overcome resistance to change?

REFERENCES

Busby, G. V. "Modernisation of Provision Shops in Singapore", in *Proceedings of the 10th International Small Business Congress, 1983*. Singapore: Applied Research Corporation, 1983, pp. 289-292.

Chong Li Choy. "How Singapore May Learn From Other Countries", in *Proceedings of the 10th International Small Business Congress, 1983*. Singapore: Applied Research Corporation, 1983.

──────. "Economic Growth and Social Equity in Singapore: A Managerial Perspective", *Contemporary Southeast Asia* 4, 2, (1982): 184-209.

Chong Li Choy and Kau Ah Keng. "Modernising Traditional Small Businesses: The Small Businessman's Resistance to Change". Paper presented at the International Dimensions of Small Business, 29th World Congress on Small Business, International Council on Small Business, Chicago, Illinois, June 11-13, 1984.

Chong Li Choy, Kau Ah Keng and Tan Thiam Soon. "Managerial Adaptation to Environment Change: The Coffee Shop Industry in Singapore", in *Proceedings of the 10th International Small Business Congress, 1983*, Singapore: Applied Research Corporation, 1983, pp. 277-282.

_____. *The Modernization of Coffee Shops*. ARC Project No. 77/82/33, August 1983.

Riaz, Hassan, (ed.) *Singapore: Society in Transition*. Kuala Lumpur: Oxford University Press, 1976.

Kuo, Eddie C. Y. and Wong, Aline K. (ed.) *The Contemporary Family in Singapore: Structure and 'Change*. Singapore: Singapore University Press, 1979.

Yeh, Stephen H. K. and Pang Eng Fong, "Housing, Employment and National Development: The Singapore Experience", Paper presented at the SEADANG seminar on Short-term Employment Creating Projects in Southeast Asia, Baguio, Philippines, 21-24 August, 1973.

21
The Process of Changing Value Orientation

V. ANANTARAMAN

SUMMARY

An individual's value orientation influences both his perception and behaviour. A change in one's value orientation necessarily pressuposes an impact on his perceptions to the extent that it rules his actions. Often, a change in one's value is not complete because it may amount only to a change merely at a verbal level, unless it is the result of the process of internalization.

Values are formed through knowledge inputs from and through experiences with family, friends, schools, religion and work. It is an irony that while knowledge inputs give rise to value and value orientation, attempts to change the value orientation of an individual through knowledge inputs do not always succeed. The re-educative strategy, therefore, puts its faith less in knowledge inputs and more in bringing about a clash of perceptions based on the old and the new values. This is done through the medium of the group which provides a secure, acceptant and loving social environment for personal enquiry, experimentation, acceptance and internalization of the new value. This chapter explains the step-by-step process of bringing about a lasting change in one's value orientation.

Introduction

The literature on planned change has identified three types of strategies to bring about a change in behaviour, practice, or action of an individual or a group of individuals in an organization or a society. These are:

(1) the power-coercive strategies;
(2) the empirical-rational strategies; and
(3) the normative re-educative strategies.

Strategies of Change

The power-coercive strategies generally believe in forcing a change on people with less power by people with more power. Often the power applied to bring about a change in behaviour, in an organizational context, is legitimate, such as, the authority of law or administrative policy behind the change to be effected. It is needless to emphasize that such changes in behaviour take the form of compliance motivated by the fear of punishment or the lure of reward and, as such, are not enduring.

The empirical-rational strategies, on the other hand, are based on the assumption that men are rational and they will follow their rational self-interest once it is revealed to them. In other words, because the person (or group) is assumed to be rational and moved by self-interest, it is assumed that he (or they) will accept the proposed change if it can be rationally justified and if it can be shown that they will gain by the change.

This approach has not always been found adequate to bring about a change, because behaviour at the personal level may be the result of normative structures. These include values, beliefs, attitudes, prejudices, stereotypes, and is also due to the individual's need to conform to his institutionalized roles and role relationships.

Intelligence is social, rather than narrowly individual. If it is individual, it could be guided by reason, but since it is social, it is guided by normative structures like values and beliefs. It is not surprising, therefore, that knowledge inputs, information, and intellectual rationale for new action or practice do not always succeed in bringing about the planned change in behaviour.

This leads us to the third strategy of planned change, the normative re-educative strategy, which seeks to bring about a change through alterations in normative structures, in institutionalized roles and role relationships, as well as in knowledge inputs.

Principles of Re-education

The focus of this chapter is on altering the normative structure of an individual or a group of individuals. Seminal contributions in this area of normative re-educative strategies have been made by three luminaries, John Dewey, Sigmund Freud and Kurt Lewin. That intelligence is social, not narrowly individual was Dewey's contribution and as such a more enduring change in behaviour could be brought about by paying attention to altering the normative structure of the individual. Freud's contributions were: firstly, that these normative structures are largely unconscious in the individual and they have to be brought to the surface, and secondly, a change can be effectively achieved not by forcing it on the client but through a collaborative effort in which he himself participates. Lewin underscored these ideas when he stated that man must participate in his own re-education if he is to be re-educated at all. He added that re-education is a normative as well as a cognitive and perceptual change. These convictions led Lewin to emphasize action research as a strategy of change, and participation in groups as a medium of re-education.

Values, Value System and Value Orientation

In changing the value orientation of an individual, an understanding of the concept of values is necessary. Values are the least flexible among the contituents of an individual's normative structure.

Values are beliefs people have about what they consider to be right or wrong, good or bad, desirable or undesirable. Values are internal to the individual and develop from family, friends, schools, religion and work. Values typically represent ideal modes of behaviour or ideal terminal goals. Some examples of values include, freedom, security, achievement and honesty.

While each individual may have hundreds of beliefs and thousands of attitudes, he may have only a dozen values. Compared to beliefs and attitudes, values are much more deeply held and are more enduring over time. Values tend to be held in a rigid and unchangeable fashion and they contain a moral flavour in that they carry an individual's ideas as to what is right, good, or desirable.

What is the value system of an individual? A value system is merely a rank order of a person's values in terms of importance.

For some people, reason, sincerity, justice and loyalty must be at the top of the list, while for others the order may be reversed. In other words, we all have a set of values that form a value system. This system is identified by the relative importance we assign to such values. We all have values and what we think is important influences our perceptions and behaviour.

How would values influence behaviour? An individual with a value which is relatively more important than the others in his value system develops a value orientation based on that value, and it is this value orientation that influences his perception, and therefore, his behaviour. Perception rules action, and perception is governed by value. A value orientation should have these two influences: it should influence not only an individual's perception of what he should do or should not do, or what he should or should not consider doing, but equally importantly it should influence his perception to the extent that it governs his behaviour in ways consistent with his value.

Value Change: The Aim of Re-education

The normative re-educative strategy aims to bring about a change in an individual's value not at a superficial or the verbal level, but an enduring change which will influence his perceptions and behaviour in ways consistent with the change. Re-education not only means the establishment of a new value which governs his new perceptions but the establishment of a new super-ego or action ideology which guides decisions and actions consistent with the new value.

A value change which does not lead to the establishment of a new super-ego or action ideology only means that the individual has accepted the change in value at the verbal level. An illustration may make this notion clear. A white American soldier who has seen a negro dating a white girl in England and comes to know that there is nothing wrong in it and even goes to the extent of conciously condemning himself for his prejudice, may still hang on to his prejudice and may not bring himself to date a negro girl. This is because, often, re-education only reaches the level of verbal expression and not of conduct. This is merely a change in perception, not in action or in practice. This may heighten the discrepancy between the way the soldier ought to feel and the way he really feels. It leads to high emotional tension, seldom to correct action.

An enduring change in an individual's value can only be brought about through a process of internalization or a voluntary accommodation of a new value in one's value system. Internalization should be distinguished from compliance and identification, both of which can bring about a change in an individual's behaviour, without a change in value in the real sense of the term. Compliance is said to occur when an individual accepts influence from another person or from a group because he hopes to achieve a favourable reaction from the other. He may be interested in attaining certain specific rewards or in avoiding certain specific punishments that the other controls. For example, some individuals may compulsively try to say the expected thing in all situations and please everyone with whom they come into contact with, out of a disproportionate need for favourable responses from others of a direct or immediate kind. In any event, when the individual complies, he does what others want him to do, or what he thinks the others want him to do because he sees this as a way of achieving a desired response from them. He does not adopt the induced behaviour because of any change in his values or beliefs but because it is instrumental in the production of a satisfying social effect. In other words, what the individual learns in this situation is to say the expected things regardless of what his private beliefs may be. Opinions adopted through compliance will be expressed only when the person's behaviour is observable by the influencing agent, an individual or a group.

Identification, on the other hand, is said to occur when an individual adopts behaviour derived from another person or group because this behaviour is associated with a satisfying self-defining relationship to this person or group. Identification can be classical or reciprocal. A good example of classical identification is the adoption of the behaviour of my boss towards his subordinates when I am promoted to his position in the organization. In this case there is no compulsion for compliance. I voluntarily define my role in terms of the role of my boss. So I attempt to be like my boss by saying what he says, by doing what he does, believing what he believes, and maintaining a satisfying relationship with my subordinates, and possibly with him also.

An individual identifies or defines his role in terms of the role of the other when the other person possesses those characteristics that the individual himself lacks, such as, control in a situation in which the individual is helpless, direction in a situation in which he is disoriented or belongingness in a situation in which he is isolated. In classical identification a more or less conscious effort is involved when an individual learns to play a desired occupational role and imitates an appropriate role model.

The self-defining relationship that an individual tries to establish or maintain through identification may also take the form of a reciprocal relationship, as in the case of lovers or friends. In a reciprocal relationship, the roles of the two parties are defined with reference to each other. Thus if an individual finds a particular relationship satisfying, he or she will tend to behave in such a way as to meet the expectations of the other. In other words, he or she will tend to behave in line with the requirements of this particular relationship.

Both in classical and reciprocal identification, the individual will behave like the other and express the other's opinion even when he is not observed by the other because it is important to the individual's self-concept to meet the expectations of his friendship role or those of his occupational role. In classical identification the individual takes over the other's identity. In a reciprocal relationship, the identification is in the sense of empathically relating in terms of the other person's expectations. Most importantly, the change in the individual's values are not integrated with his value system but rather tend to be isolated from the rest of his values — to remain encapsulated.

The Process of Internalization

The internalization of the new behaviour within an individual's value system can be brought about by a step-by-step process of normative re-education. It is interesting to learn that the old value yields to the new only when the individual goes through the following steps: hostility, ambivalence, openness, experimentation, confirmation, friendliness and change in value orientation.

Hostility

Initially, the individual will naturally be hostile to the new value. The intensity of his hostility depends, among others, upon the relative importance of his habitual value in his value system. The greater the loyalty of the individual to the old value, the more pronounced will be the hostility to the new value. Secondly, if the value to be changed is a social value, the hostility to the new value will be great if the individual is more socially inclined than self-centered. He will offer stronger resistance to re-education because these values are socially anchored and not individually held. Thirdly, hostility will be a function of whether the individual has voluntarily accepted his involvement in re-education or has been forced into it. Thus there are different degrees of hostility to new values, and they should be taken into consideration in any re-education effort. Finally, just because the old value of the individual appears to be irrational, one cannot assume that it can easily be changed. It should be emphasized that an individual's value system may be irrational to others, but to him it is rational. Furthermore, congruence with a person's internal value system does not necessarily imply logical consistency either. Behaviour would be congruent, if in some way or other, it fits into the person's value system, if it seems to belong there and be demanded by it. Individual idiosyncracies have no limit!

How can free acceptance of a new value be brought about if an individual to be re-educated is likely to be hostile to the new value and loyal to the old value? Should we attack him for holding old values on some ground so that he would change? We cannot do this because we know that people cannot be taught who feel that they are at the same time being attacked.

Ambivalence

Hostility should be overcome and the individual should move from hostility to ambivalence. This means that hostility to the new value can be reduced only when the person becomes ambivalent about his old values. In other words, he should begin to have doubts about his habitual value orientation and the knowledge and facts underlying this orientation. Herein lies the importance of a group as an effective medium of change. An individual can move from hostility to ambivalence in the context of the clash of perceptions that can result in a group situation. By clash of perception is meant the conflict between self-perception and social perception or conflict between how you view yourself and how others view you.

Habitual perceptions are challenged by open exchange of feedback between members as they share their different perceptions of the same event. In a group situation when the individual is well integrated within the group and attaches positive valence to other members of the group, or to the group as a whole, he can accept the different perceptions as alternatives to his own way of perceiving self and the world. Re-educative groups, in particular, have norms of interaction which are not perceived as attacks on the individual who has a different perception of a phenomenon. The norms of interaction prescribed for a contract group (T-group) are good examples of norms that promote responsible confrontation and non-defensive response from the individual who is confronted.

Values govern perceptions and perception rules action. If one understands this sequence he can readily see that the clash of perceptions in re-educative groups is nothing but a battle between the old values and the new value, bereft of any bitterness, in an atmosphere of love and acceptance. As a result of this exchange of feedback, the individual will begin to have doubts about the knowledge and facts that underlie this value orientation.

Openness

Ambivalence creates in the individual an attitude of openness. In other words, the individual is inclined not to dogmatically hang on to his perceptions but to develop an open mind and be prepared to experiment in order to confirm or disconfirm these alternative perceptions. This ambivalence makes him accept the existence of a problem, that it has to be questioned and solved. Without this ambivalence the individual will see no need to submit his perceptions to an experimental testing. Inclination to experiment becomes potent only when the individual moves from hostility to ambivalence, and a willingness to accept experimentation. The principle of free choice by persons to engage in self and social enquiry is an important element in effective re-education.

Experimentation

In experimentation, the principle of action research is followed. Action research emphasizes that success depends upon the degree to which those whose behaviour is to be changed are made part of the fact-finding on which the action is to be based. An individual will believe in facts he himself has himself discovered. Lacking this personal involvement, no objective fact is likely to reach the status of fact for the individual concerned. His resources are utilized to design the experiment, to provide the criteria for evaluation of data, and to device the methods of collecting and analyzing data.

Confirmation and Friendliness

When the experimentation confirms a person's new perceptions and disconfirms the old perceptions, the individual is ready to embrace the new value, in the sense that he develops a sentiment of friendliness towards it. At this stage, his hostility towards the new value totally disappears. This does not mean that dual perception of the same phenomenon based on both old values and new values will not persist. In reality at this stage one cannot avoid dual perceptions despite the developing faith in the new value. The important point to note is that the new value has been accepted and is in the process of becoming an action ideology.

Change in Value Orientation

This process is reinforced by the continuous support the individual receives from members of his group to perceive phenomena in the light of the newly acquired value. In course of time, he will find his perceptions dominated by the new value he has acquired. At this stage, his old value ceases to influence his perceptions, and since he has developed a strong conviction about his new value, it gradually assumes the form of an action ideology, not only influencing perceptions but also governing his actions. The change in the individual's value orientation is complete. Only then will we be able to say that the new value has been accommodated or internalized within his value system.

QUESTIONS

1. Distinguish between the three main strategies of changing behaviour.
2. Clearly explain the concepts of value, value system and value orientation.
3. Briefly describe the process of changing an individual's value orientation.

REFERENCES

Benne, Kenneth D. "The Processes Of Re-education: An Assessment of

Kurt Lewin's Views", in Warren G. Bennis et. al. *The Planning of Change,* 3rd ed., New York: Holt, Rinehart & Winston, 1976.

Chin, Robert and Benne, Kenneth D. "General Strategies for Effecting Changes in Human Systems", in Warren G. Bennis et. al. *The Planning of Change,* 3rd ed., New York: Holt, Rinehart & Winston, 1976, pp. 22-45.

Klein, Donald. "Some Notes on the Dynamics of Resistence to Change: The Defender's Role", in Warren Bennis et al. 3rd ed., The Planning of Change. New York: Holt, Renehart and Winston, 1961.

Kelman, Herbert C. "Process of Opinion Change", *Public Opinion Quarterly,* Vol. XXVI, 1961, No. 1 pp. 57-78.

Marrow, Alfred J. and French, Jr. John. "Changing a Stereotype in Industry", in Warren G. Bennis et al. *The Planning of Change.* New York: Holt, Renehart and Winston, 1961, pp. 583-586.

Smith, Ewart E. "The Power of Dissonance Technique to Change Attitudes", *Public Opinion Quarterly,* Vol. XXV, 1961, No. 2, pp. 327-339.

22
Training: A Tool For Human Resource Development

ANTHONY T. TSENG

SUMMARY

The main purpose of this paper is to emphasize the importance of having a systematic approach to training efforts. Training is an important tool for developing human potential. However, for training to be effective, training efforts must be engaged in a systematic way.

A systems view of training helps one understand relationships among trainees, the training department, and top-level management. A systems view also provides sufficient rationale for arranging the various components of a training programme.

This chapter recommends that a training programme be designed and implemented according to the following sequence: training needs be identified to provide sound reasons for engaging in training; specific training objectives be spelt clearly to guide the rest of the training efforts; training methods be selected according to the training objectives and strategies chosen; learning and transfer processes be managed when implementing the training programme; and, training outcomes be assessed according to appropriate criteria and valid evaluation procedures.

What is presented represents a "maximizing" approach which is worthwhile striving for whenever possible. However, it should be noted that sometimes modifications of this approach are needed, due to time and other organizational constraints.

Introduction

In recent years, one of the prime concerns of the people and the government of Singapore is how to increase productivity. The concept of productivity can be analyzed at different levels, i.e., individual, organizational, and national, and has been used to refer to different things at each level. At the individual level, for instance, productivity has been equated with individual effort, individual performance, or individual outputs. However, it would be reasonable to state that the bottom line of the productivity concept refers to individual performance and organizational effectiveness.

There are many approaches which may be used to increase individual performance and/or organizational effectiveness, e.g., removing barriers to effective performance; improving personnel selection and appraisal programmes; and enhancing employees' problem-solving abilities. Most of these approaches focus on the human element. Since training is an organizational effort solely concentrating on human components within an organizational setting, training holds the key to productivity. In fact, training is a pre-requisite for the success of many of these approaches. A well-designed performance appraisal programme cannot be effectively implemented without providing the necessary training to supervisory personnel concerning limitations of the instruments, skills of conducting evaluation, and tactics of conveying the results. Furthermore, training is most suitable for developing human potential and for dealing with performance deficiency. Since human resource is Singapore's chief strength, the importance of training can never be overemphasized. Training can be a very powerful human resource development tool, if it is done systematically.

The Need for a Systematic Approach to Training

In order for training to achieve its intended goals, it has to be planned, implemented, and evaluated by a systematic procedure. However, not all training programmes are conducted systematically. In fact, many of them are being done haphazardly, as observed from *The Riddle of Training in Business & Industry* (DePhillips, Berliner, & Cribbin, p. 5-6):

> Few organizations would admit that they can survive without it — yet some act as though they could.

TRAINING: A TOOL FOR HUMAN RESOURCE DEVELOPMENT

Everyone knows what it is — yet management, unions, and workers often interpret it in the light of their own job conditions.

It is going on all the time — yet much of it is done haphazardly.

It is futile to attempt it without the needed time and facilities — yet often those responsible for it lack either or both.

It costs money — yet at times there is not adequate budgetary appropriation for it.

It should take place at all levels — yet sometimes it is limited to the lowest operating levels.

It can help everyone do a better job — yet those selected for it often fear it.

It is foolish to start it without clearly defined objectives —yet this is occasionally done.

It cannot be ignored without costing the company money — yet some managers seem blind to this reality.

It should permeate the entire organization and be derived from the firm's theory and practice of management — yet sometimes it is shunted off to one department that operates more or less in isolation from the rest of the business.

Levels

The systematic approach to training can be analyzed at three different levels:

(1) A *System view* can help one understand the relationships of the three main components of a training system:

  (a) trainee;
  (b) training department; and
  (c) the organization which operates the training department.

The following diagram best illustrates these relationships:

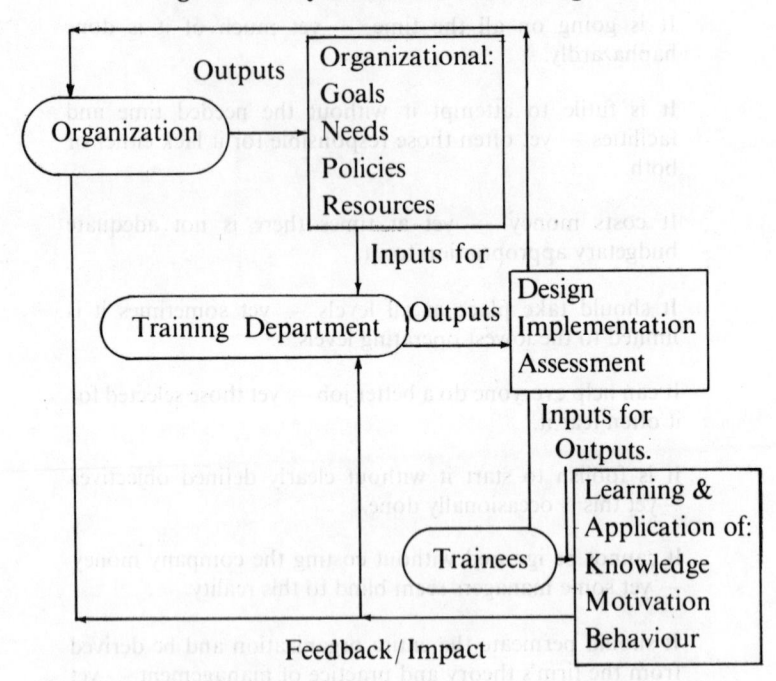

Figure 1: A Systems View of Training

```
                    Outputs      Organizational:
                                 Goals
         Organization            Needs
                                 Policies
                                 Resources

                                 Inputs for
                                              Design
                                      Outputs Implementation
         Training Department             Assessment

                                           Inputs for
                                           Outputs.
                                                    Learning &
                                                    Application of:
                                           Trainees Knowledge
                                                    Motivation
                    Feedback/Impact                 Behaviour
```

This model stresses that:

(a) the training department should take as its inputs not only goals and policies from the organization, but also the feedback of trainees who go through the training programmes.

(b) The effectiveness of a training programme, i.e., the learning and growth of the trainees, is affected not only by the design and implementation of the training programme, but also by characteristics of the trainees, such as ability and motivation.

(c) The success of a training programme will have an impact on trainees, the training department itself, and the organization.

(2) A *System view* also enables us to derive a rational design for a training programme. The following model is useful in achieving this purpose:

Figure 2 A System View of Training Programme

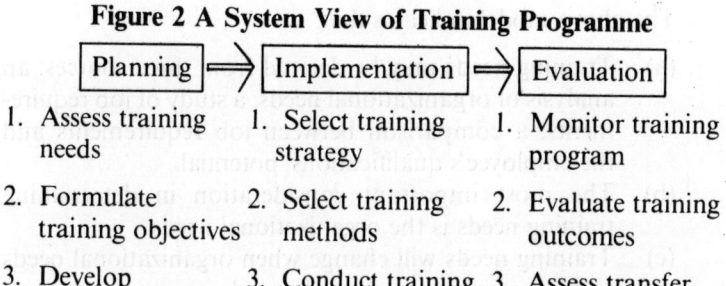

Planning ⇒ Implementation ⇒ Evaluation

Planning	Implementation	Evaluation
1. Assess training needs	1. Select training strategy	1. Monitor training program
2. Formulate training objectives	2. Select training methods	2. Evaluate training outcomes
3. Develop evaluation criteria	3. Conduct training	3. Assess transfer
	4. Manage learning/ transfer processes	

This model for training emphasizes:

(a) The importance of recognizing that there are three distinctive phases in a training programme.
(b) The need to specify training objectives before implementing and evaluating training programmes.
(c) The necessity of controlling learning experiences to achieve training objectives.
(d) The need for an evaluative component in a training programme.
(e) the essential steps of evaluating a training programme systematically.

(3) A *System view* can also be very useful in helping us analyze and identify training needs. The following figure illustrates the need to consider different levels of factors in identifying training needs:

Figure 3 A Model for Identifying Training Needs

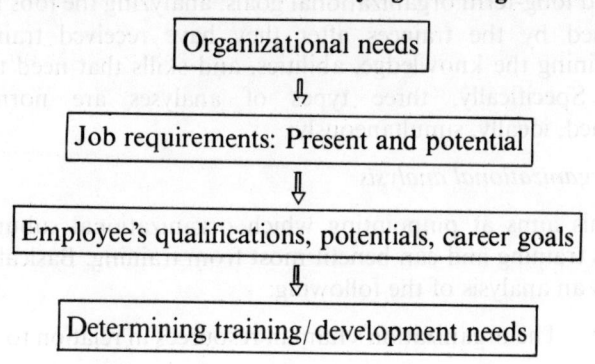

Organizational needs
⇓
Job requirements: Present and potential
⇓
Employee's qualifications, potentials, career goals
⇓
Determining training/development needs

The above model indicates that:

(a) Training needs may be derived from three sources: an analysis of organizational needs, a study of job requirements, a comparison between job requirements and the employee's qualifications/potential.
(b) The most important consideration in determining training needs is the organizational needs.
(c) Training needs will change when organizational needs and job requirements are changed.

To sum up, training must be a planned, systematic effort. A series of steps can be taken in designing, implementing, and evaluating a training programme. By following these steps, training can be an effective, goal-oriented effort for solving performance problems as well as for developing human resources.

A Systems Approach to Training

According to a systems view, it is advisable to follow the steps suggested below to design a training programme:

Step 1   Identify training needs
Step 2   Define training objectives
Step 3   Choose training strategies
Step 4   Select training methods
Step 5   Implement training programme and manage the learning process
Step 6   Monitor and assess training outcomes

Identify Training Needs

Training needs can be identified by delineating both short-term and long-term organizational goals; analyzing the jobs to be performed by the trainees after they have received training; and defining the knowledge, abilities, and skills that need to be taught Specifically, three types of analyses are normally performed, ideally, simultaneously:

(1) *Organizational analysis*

This aims at pinpointing which organizational subunit(s) requires training and can benefit most from training. Basically, it includes an analysis of the following:

(a) The organization's human resources in relation to both

short-term and long-term manpower planning of the organization.
(b) The degree of goal-attainment of the organization and its subunits.
(c) The relationships between the organization and its external environment.

(2) *Task analysis*

The purpose of task analysis is to provide information for prescribing the content of a training programme. It starts with locating or developing a job description. This should include detailed information concerning the duties and conditions under which the job is to be performed. From the job description one may identify the specific task assignments needed to be accomplished by the job incumbent as well as specific knowledge and behaviour that are required in performing the task assignments. Task analysis can be done by using questionnaires, a critical incident technique and through interviews. The result of past incidents are critical in determining the content of a training programme.

Person Analysis

Person Analysis is useful in identifying those who need training and development. A prerequisite for performing person analysis is an effective performance appraisal programme. To begin with, a performance appraisal programme should be conducted to identify employees who are performing below standard. Then, specific nees of sub-standard performers should be analyzed. Information derived from person analysis would be useful in defining the specific objectives of a particular training programme. The same procedure can be followed to identify superior performers and those with great potential so that an effective human resource management programme can be planned.

To sum up, training needs can be identified from three sources, namely, the organization, the task, and the employee. While organization analysis tells us *where* and *when* to conduct the training, task analysis tells us *what* should be included in that training programme, and person analysis identifies *who* needs to be trained.

Defining Training Objectives

Training, like any other organizational activity, must have well-defined objectives. It is not advisable to carry out a training programme because one has just learned a new or popular training method or has a training budget that needs to be spent.

Specific, operational types of objectives are preferred over those which are broad and non-operational. For instance, training objectives can be specific and list performance standards which trainees must meet upon completion of the training programme.

In general, training objectives will fall into one of the following three categories:

(1) *Development of an employee's self-awareness*

   Examples are:

   To help bus drivers understand the impact of their behaviour on passengers.

   To assist managers develop insights about their own leadership styles.

(2) *Improving job skills*

   Examples are:

   To teach individuals how to drive a bus safely.

   To teach first-line supervisors how to conduct a meeting efficiently and effectively.

(3) *Increasing work motivation*

   Examples are:

   To increase the motivation of bus drivers.

   To increase the motivation of factory workers.

Choosing Training Strategies

Training strategies refer to the general approaches adopted to achieve training objectives. Obviously, training strategies should be chosen according to specific training objectives identified. Generally, training strategies can be classified into two types — cognitive versus behavioural:

   (1) The cognitive strategy attempts to increase the

employee's knowledge about self, job, or the organization.
(2) The behavioural strategy attempts to change the trainee's behaviour.

The differences between cognitive and behavioural strategies can be seen from these examples:

(1) A company wants to use training to enable its management to manage organizational conflicts more effectively. When a cognitive strategy is used, the trainer will try to help the managers understand the conflict process by teaching models and theories about the conflict process through lectures or group discussions.
(2) If a behavioural strategy is chosen, the trainer will concentrate training efforts on teaching and practising specific conflict management skills through role playing and behaviour modelling. For instance, conflict prevention skills such as how to expand organizational resources and how to avoid creating a win-lose situation can be taught.

These strategies can be simultaneously used to achieve training objectives. The importance of a training strategy is that it provides a useful guideline for selecting training methods and for putting into operation specific objectives of a training programme.

Select Training Methods

After defining objectives and choosing strategies, training methods should be selected accordingly. Certain methods are more suitable for a particular training strategy and thus will be more effective in achieving a specific training objective. For example, the training method of equipment simulation is appropriate for behavioural strategy and is effective in teaching technical skills.

The following table attempts to identify training methods which are appropriate for a specific type of training objective and training strategy. Note that some training methods are appropriate for more than one type of training objective or strategy.

Table 1 Training Methods: Classified by Objectives and Strategies

		Training Strategy	
		Cognitive	Behavioural
Training Objectives	Self-Awareness	Management Development Seminars Sensitivity Training	Sensitivity Training
	Job Skills	Lecture Case Study Orientation Training Decision-making Training	On-the-Job Training Apprenticeship Programmed Instruction Equipment Simulation Behaviour Modelling
	Motivation	Work Motivation Seminar Need for Achievement Training	Coaching Behaviour Modelling

Note: This table is a modification of the classification scheme introduced by Wexley and Latham, *Developing and Training Human Resource in Organizations.* Glenview, Illinois, Scott, Foresman & Co., 1981, p. 7.

Conduct Training Programmes and Manage Learning Process

Training programmes can be obviously on the job site or away from the physical company. They can also be conducted by line personnel, training specialists, or consultants. Training involves two processes: the learning (acquisition) process and the transfer (application) process. The key to a successful training programme lies in the management of the learning and transfer processes.

(1) The learning process can be facilitated by utilizing learning principles derived from psychological research. The following are some of the more important principles:

The Role of Motivation in Learning

— In the absence of positive motivation, learning is very difficult.
— A moderate level of motivation should be generated

and maintained. Studies from university and college students indicate that high motivation will enhance the learning of very simple tasks but will hinder the learning of complex tasks.
— Intrinsic motivation can be increased by communicating clearly to the trainees the training objectives and the relevance of training materials.
— Extrinsic motivation can be generated by providing positive reinforcement, e.g., verbal praise, recognition, etc. Positive reinforcement should be contingent on a demonstration of desirable performance during the training.

The Importance of Knowledge of Results

The performances of trainees during the learning process should be measured and the results communicated to the trainees. Knowledge gained from the results (feedback) is an important factor in most learning situations since it provides the trainees with a powerful incentive to learn. Without feedback, modification and improvement would be very difficult. There are several guidelines for providing feedback to trainees:

— It should be provided as soon and as frequently as possible, i.e., after desirable performance has been demonstrated.
— Too specific or too general information should be avoided in giving the feedback. If the feedback is too general, it may not be useful. If the feedback is too specific, it may actually confuse the learner and this leads to performance deficits.
— Feedback should include guidelines for corrective action.

The Necessity of Practice

— Whenever possible, trainees should be provided with adequate opportunities to practice what has been learned.
— Practice should be guided by the trainer during the early stages of acquision of a new skill.
— In learning skills, distributed practice sessions with rest periods in between are more effective than continuing practice.

The Power of Modelling

Modelling refers to the process whereby trainees observe and imitate the specific, desirable behaviours being demonstrated by the trainer.

The trainer serves as a "model". His behaviour is closely watched and selectively imitated by the trainees. The trainer and the trainees may or may not be aware of the occurrence of this learning process. However, it can occur in most training situations requiring interactions between the trainer and the trainees. Modelling is a powerful tool for the trainer to instil the desirable behaviour on the trainees without much "preaching". Unfortunately, it is often neglected by the trainer.

- Modelling is most effective when the behaviour model is perceived as competent, friendly, and of high status.
- Modelling tends to occur when trainees perceive similarities between themselves and the model in terms of age, sex, and race.
- Learning by modelling tends to increase when the model is being rewarded for demonstrating the desirable behaviour. The fact that the model is being rewarded for engaging in a particular behaviour will serve as an unmistakable cue for the trainees. It conveys such a message: the behaviour is desirable and if you do likewise you will most likely be rewarded too.

The Transfer Process

Obviously, the utility of a training programme depends on the degree of learning acquired which can be transferred to the job situation. For behaviour to transfer positively, content and methods of training should be as realistic as possible, i.e., they must use real problems and equipment. In addition, there are some principles which may foster a positive transfer of learning:

- Stimuli and responses learned in a training programme should be identical with those required in the job situation.
- Training content should be directly relevant to the job situation. Ideas and skills learned in a training programme must be rewarded appropriately in the job situation.
- General rules and principles for solving problems

should be taught in a training programme to facilitate positive transfer. Detailed facts are applicable only in a very limited number of situations.
— Positive transfer of learning is better if trainers understand the trainee's unique job problems.

In summary, when conducting a training programme, both learning and transfer processes should be controlled to ensure that what has been taught and learned in a training programme will be useful in improving job performance. The management of the learning and training process can be effectively accomplished by using the above-mentioned principles. These principles are based on findings from extensive research efforts in the field of the psychology of learning. If these principles are carefully observed and practiced, the management of learning and transfer process would be the most "scientific" part of the training programme.

Monitor Training Programme and Evaluate Training Outcome

Training usually represents a significant investment of manpower, time and money. However, the effectiveness of such training efforts are seldom known. This is due to the fact that the progress and outcome of training programmes are frequently not measured. Further, among programmes which have evaluative components, the appropriateness of the evaluation procedures adopted are often questionable. Therefore, results generated from such deficient evaluation procedures can only be regarded as weak or serve as insufficient evidence for proving the effectiveness of a training programme.

Monitor the Programme

During the training process, it is important to find out if the programme is progressing towards intended objectives. It is also desirable to find out if the programme has been implemented according to original plans. To achieve these purposes, surveys can be done by using questionnaires or interviews to collect trainers' and trainees' reactions towards the programme. Results from such surveys would be useful to both trainers and trainees:

(a) If the results are positive, trainees can be motivated to learn. Positive feedback from the surveys can also serve as positive reinforcement for the trainer and motivate him to keep up his good performance.

(b) If the results are negative, trainers can begin to identify the causal factors and take necessary action.

Assess Training Outcomes

There are two important considerations involved in assessing the effectiveness of training outcomes. They are, selection of evaluation criteria and the choosing of evaluation procedures.

Evaluation Criteria

Scholars in the field of training generally agree that there are four levels of training criteria:

(1) *Reaction — Trainees' Impressions about the Programme*

When using reaction criteria one intends to know why trainees like the programme (e.g., training settings, schedules, trainers, methods, contents, etc.). Specific reaction criteria should be identified when the training programme is developed. Questionnaires are usually used to measure reactions at the completion of the training programme. Reactions are useful in ensuring organizational support for a programme and in helping training staff in planning for future programmes.

(2) *Learning — Trainees' Achievement from the Programme*

Learning criteria can be used to measure the extent the trainees' knowledge and/or skills have been improved. Contents of a training programme should obviously dictate the selection of measurement instruments for learning; for example, paper-and-pencil type of tests are normally used in measuring knowledge; performance type of tests are typically used in assessing skills.

(3) *Behaviour — Trainees' Job Behaviour after the Completion of the Training Programme*

Behaviour criteria indicate the importance of finding out to what extent the trainee's job behaviour has changed as a result of the training experience. Change can be assessed by questionnaires, rating forms or through interviews. Assessments can be obtained from various sources: from trainees; superiors, peers, or subordinates. Behaviour changes ideally should be assessed after completion of the programme to make sure the trainees have had opportunities to practice what they learned. It should be noted that latent learning ("sleeper effect") is not uncommon. Latent learning refers to the phenomenon that trainees benefit from training experience but it takes longer for them to demonstrate learning on the job.

(4) *Results* — *Impact of the Training Programme on Organization Effectiveness*

Results criteria point to essential questions such as the extent training programmes reduce absenteeism, turnover, accidents, scrap rate, grievances, and production costs and the extent they increase sales, morale, and production quantity/quality, before and after receiving training. A significant difference between before and after measures may not serve as sufficient evidence for proving training impacts. There is always the possibility that factors unrelated to training, such as changes in pay or equipment may have contributed to the differences in the performance noted. When appropriate evaluation procedures are used, this possibility can be controlled. Results criteria are extremely important in proving and evaluating the utility of a training programme.

To sum up, both reaction and learning criteria are essential for assessing the learning phase of a training programme. Behaviour and results criteria are important for evaluating the transfer phase of the training programme. Management, trainers, and trainees may emphasize different kinds of criteria. For instance, management may be more concerned about results criteria. Thus, it is important to keep in mind that the selection of evaluation criteria is largely determined both by training objectives and the parties for whom the evaluative data are intended. Further, to ascertain that changes observed in any of the four criteria are truly due to training effects, evaluation procedures should be chosen carefully.

Evaluation Procedure

DuBrin (1981) recommended a five-step procedure which includes evaluation principles commonly accepted by experts in the field. I have expanded DuBrin's procedure to a six-step model. One hypothetical case illustrates the following: a bus company decides to train bus drivers so that they will provide better service for passengers.

Step 1. *Set Training Objectives*

The management of the bus company and the training consultant may have to decide that the main objective of the training programme is to improve the human relations skills of bus drivers.

Step 2. *Identify Evaluation Criteria*

Decision-makers may have to decide whether behaviour criteria (e.g., the way drivers interact with the passengers) or results criteria (e.g., the number of complaints filed against the drivers during a three-month period), or both should be used in evaluating the outcome.

Step 3. *Take Pre-training Measures on Criteria Variable(s)*

In this case, company records of passengers' complaints against drivers may be used. In addition, the drivers' behaviour while on duty may also be observed and recorded before the training programme starts (behavioural data are needed only if behavioural criteria are chosen).

Step 4. *Conduct The Training Programme and Monitor the Progress*

Lectures, film shows, role-playing, or behaviour modelling methods could be used to teach desirable behaviours to the drivers selected for the programme. Both timing and location factors should be considered carefully to avoid the possibility that training activities may interfere with normal on-going organizational functions, e.g., the bus company's ability to serve the public. In the course of conducting training, any significant or unusual events should be noted and/or recorded.

Step 5. *Establish of Control Group(s)*

Drivers may be randomly assigned to two groups. One group receives training (this is the training group). The other group would either receive no training at all or be trained at a later time.

Step 6. *Take Post-training Measures on Both Training and Control Groups*

In this hypothetical case, the driver's on-the-job behaviour and passenger grievances would be recorded during a period, e.g., three or six months, after the completion of the programme.

The first two steps, i.e., setting the training objectives and the identification of evaluation criteria in an evaluation process are necessary to ensure that whatever is being evaluated is relevant both to intended training goals and the content of the programme. The third step, i.e., taking pre-training measures, provides baseline measures to be compared with post-training measures so that the magnitude of changes can be assessed. The information collected in the fourth step, conducting and monitoring the training programme, may provide alternative explanations to the training outcomes observed. The fifth step is essential to ensure that changes detected are attributable to training effects, and not due to other variables such as a decrease in the number of passengers (which may result in a decline of grievance). In summary, there are four important ingredients in an effective evaluation procedure: clear training objectives; well-specified evaluation criteria; pre-training and post-training measures; and control group(s).

Many training programmes are either not evaluated at all or evaluated with deficient procedures. For example, quite a few training programmes are evaluated by taking post-training measures on training groups only. Some evaluation studies do include both pre- and post-measures on training groups but fail to use a control group. Outcomes derived from evaluation procedures which do not include either a pre-training measure or a control group are not very useful because we can never be sure whether there are some significant changes after training and whether these changes are actually caused by training. Thus, pre- and post-measures with control group(s) are highly recommended by almost every writer in the field. Sometimes it may not be feasible or desirable to have pre-training measures. In this case, evaluation outcomes can be derived from a comparison of the post-training measures between the training and the control group. This post-only control group design can be effective if the characteristics of the members of training and control groups are carefully matched (Wexley and Latham, 1981). While training staff should be encouraged to use appropriate procedures to demonstrate the effectiveness and the utility of their programmes, they should also be reminded that it is often not easy to isolate the effects of their programmes from the effects of other simultaneously occuring organizational programmes or changes.

QUESTIONS

1. What are the advantages of adopting a system view towards training?
2. How would you identify the training needs of a given organization in Singapore?
3. How would you evaluate a specific training programme?

REFERENCES

Bass, B.M. and Vaughan, J.A. *Training in Industry: the Management of Learning.* Monterey: Brooks/Cole, 1966.

DePhillips, F.A., Berliner, W.M., and Cribbin, J.J. *Management of Training Programmes.* Homewood, Ill.: Irwin, 1960.

DuBrin, A.J. *Personnel and Human Resource Management.* N.Y.: D. Van Nostrand, 1981.

Goldstein, I.L. *Training: Program Development and Evaluation.* Monterey, California: Brooks/Cole, 1974.

Laird, D. *Approaches to Training and Development.* Reading, Mass.: Addison-Wesley, 1978.

Siegel, L. & Lane, I.M. *Personnel and Organizational Psychology.* Homewood, Ill.: Irwin, 1982.

Wexley, K.N. and Latham, G.P. *Developing and Training Human Resources in Organizations.* Glenview, Ill.: Scott/Foresman, 1981.

PART FOUR

AN INDIVIDUAL PERSPECTIVE

23
An Individual Perspective

S. RICHARDSON

SUMMARY

This chapter describes the historical background to the study of the individual and then takes a micro-approach to perception, personality, motivation and learning. Team-building is discussed and the problems of HRM examined. The importance of cross-cultural differences is stressed. It is concluded that HRM depends primarily on a knowledge of the individual.

Introduction

The aim of this chapter is to give an overview of the last section of the book with the addition of some material which is intended to be provocative. After an outline of the historical background of human psychology this chapter deals with individual behaviour and then discusses some aspects of interactions between individuals. The chapters in this section takes a micro-approach to perception, personality, and motivation.

The Background

What differentiates human beings from other animals? Why do managers and non-managers behave as they do? How can the behaviour of people be explained scientifically? These, and numerous related questions, have exercised the brains of many people over the centuries. Although much pertinent knowledge has been gained there are still vast areas of ignorance (and hence disagreement) concerning psychology. We are concerned with human psychology which is particularly difficult to study as we are poor observers of ourselves — it is easier to be dispassionate when dealing with other animals. The historical background of psychology is worth examining. On it is based the theory and practice which is part of the foundation of this book. The reader may become impatient with the theories and research described in the literature and be more concerned with finding out why people like each other, or how to get more fun out of a boring job. But answers to these problems are more likely to emerge if the practical application of HRM is based on a knowledge of some of the pioneering thought and work in human psychology. Freudian psychology makes a suitable starting-point.

Freudian Psychology, named after Freud its founder, relies on a psychoanalytic view of human behaviour, i.e., that the major motivating forces are in the unconscious — that realm in each of us containing those fearful facts and ideas which we avoid; they are ever present but not readily available to the conscious. Repression is the process we use to banish frightening and unacceptable impulses and desires to our unconscious. The "id" is the core of the unconscious — primitive, aggressive, pleasure seeking; as individuals mature they learn to control their basic instincts, or to sublimate them. The "ego" is the conscious which keeps the id under control, thus there is constant conflict between the id and the ego because the id demands immediate pleasure or gratification while the ego dictates denial or postponement, or (at least) moderation. The moral perfectionist "superego" supports the ego; it provides (from the unconscious) the norms enabling the ego to decide what is right or wrong; the individual is not aware of the workings of the superego which is a kind of conscience developed by absorption of a society's values, usually through parental influence.

Behaviourist Psychology resulted from reactions against Freudian theory which was regarded as unscientific. Behaviourism is based on the scientific approach — experimentation designed to test hypotheses. In other words, behaviourists (indeed most psychologists today) tend to ignore all except observable and measurable events in their attempts to explain and predict behaviour. This does not mean that Freudian theory has no value, although opinions vary from "Freud's influence has never been extensive in psychology" (Thomson, 1968) to "We are deeply indebted to Freud for his painstaking and pioneering efforts to establish the theoretical foundation upon which we build today" (Harris, 1967).

Individual Behaviour

Perception is an individual's view of reality. It depends on several factors, some inherited, some acquired. Perception is essential to thought and judgement and is therefore vital to an understanding of HRM. The topic is examined to detail in Chapter 24.

Personality has been defined in so many different ways that it might help to look at the word's derivation. According to Luthans (1981) it can be traced to the Latin "per sonare", in English "to speak through". The Latin term was used for the masks worn by actors in ancient Greece and Rome. Contemporary common usage of the word "personality" emphasizes the roles which the person (actor) plays in real life, whereas academic definitions concentrate on the person. Probably the best approach is to include both person and role. One such simple definition is: personality is the totality of all an individual's qualities, as that manifests itself to others. Chapter 25 aims to give an introduction to the concept of personality.

Many attempts have been made to measure personality, none of them completely successful. The paper by Dolores Thomson describes some research using two psychological instruments to investigate some aspects of the thinking of Singaporean managers, and the perceptual differences between them and their Western counterparts. Some personality tests measure the strength of various motives, thus giving an insight into both personality and motivation.

Motivation has been dealt with in several papers which underlines its importance in human resource management. Motivation is a hypothetical construct that cannot be seen (just like personality); only behaviour can be seen. Understanding of motivation lies in understanding the need-drive-goal cycle. Needs may be either primary (instinctive and physiological); general (instinctive but not physiological, e.g., curiosity, activity and affection); or secondary (i.e., learned, e.g., power, achievement, affiliation security and status). Probably the most important facts about motivation are that satisfied needs are no longer motivators, and that effective managers satisfy their subordinates' needs (although the most difficult task is often to discover what these needs are).

Various theoretical models exist which attempt to explain motivation: some assume that satisfied people perform well and others propose that performance leads to satisfaction — this writer can see no conflict here. It is certainly true that motivation will not be fully understood without further considerable research taking into account cross-cultural differences (so far largely ignored), and this is particularly important in Singapore because its population is multi-racial and because of the large shifting population of non-Singaporeans. Some basic ideas on motivation and behavioural modification are discussed in detail in Chong Li Choy's paper.

Learning is perceived by some as a process in which only the teacher takes a truly active part, and the job of the student is to observe and memorize as a necessary preliminary to regurgitating "what has been learned" in examinations. This concept of learning frequently seems irrelevant to the real problems of daily life and work. Yet the ability to learn is one of the most important skills. Someone has learned something if they demonstrate a relatively permanent change in behaviour — this may be the result of experience (often unplanned) or practice (always deliberate), and is necessarily linked to the individual's motivation. Most behaviour (especially perceptions, skills and attitudes) is learned. From a HRM viewpoint the purpose of learning is to enhance problem-solving skills. The most important concept in learning is reinforcement, (i.e., anything that increases the strength of response and that tends to induce repetitions of the behaviour that preceded the reinforcement). The effective administration of reinforcement and reward is one of the most critical challenges facing modern human resource management. This writer's subjective view is that greater use of non-financial rewards in Singapore would have a significant effect on productivity, and this has been demonstrated by companies such as Hewlett-Packard and Shell.

Interactions Between Individuals

Team-Building may be regarded as a necessary

preliminary to increasing productivity. Although developing teamwork is a vital role of a manager, it is also the responsibility of non-managers too. A group only becomes a team when all its members know the roles of the others and accept that these roles will be performed effectively with due regard for the needs of others and the norms of the group. One approach to team-building being increasingly practised in Singapore is the emergence of Quality Control Circles in the private sector and Work Improvement Teams (in the public sector). Other approaches need to be explored. What can we learn from other countries? What should we learn?

Discussion

One of the objects of this book is to relate knowledge of human behaviour at work to the problems of real life in enterprises. Human Resource Management is a new discipline, and its stage of development, compared to the "hard" sciences, might be equated to alchemy, or pre-Newtonian mechanics, or pre-Darwinian biology. Our method has been to borrow freely from various sources (an eclectic approach) although we have depended largely on "management science", psychology and sociology.

Human Resource Management presents several problems. First, as it involves studying people it is more difficult than many other disciplines because man is the most complex living organism; measuring instruments for his many variables are inadequately developed; further, man is not a good observer of complex events, and does not think of himself objectively. Secondly, due to the many areas of ignorance there are numerous questions that cannot be answered yet with precision. This causes frustration to managers and non-managers who require realistic answers to their practical problems, and to many students (especially those studying engineering or science) who have been conditioned to believe that most problems have a unique solution. Human problems are not like that! The situation is compounded by the semantic difficulties met at every turn. We have yet to have a universally accepted definition of "manager". Thirdly, human beings come in assorted sizes, shapes, cultures, ages and varieties. Although we are often forced to cater for the "average person", individual differences (both physical and psychological) make work design and increasing productivity more difficult than otherwise they would be. Fourthly, many problems arise from the increasing rate at which technology changes: man hasn't caught up yet. Man's evolution is much slower than technology's change. The machines we use are more expensive, powerful and dangerous to an extent that was almost unthinkable even two generations ago. Changing technology and increasing densities combine to create various kinds of pollution and accelerate the pace (and hence the strain) of life. All this underlines the importance of the human factor and of good human resource management.

Although the importance of cross-cultural differences should not be underestimated, many lessons can be learned from the successes and failures of other countries. A recent book about excellence in management says: "Good management practice is not resident only in Japan. But, more important, the good news comes from treating people decently and asking them to shine, and from producing things that work" (Peters & Waterman, 1982). We agree.

Cross-cultural differences are an important factor in the "nature versus nurture" debate recently revived in Singapore. The opposing views have been well presented thus: "In support of the idea that the human brain learns everything and inherits nothing, is put the observation that different societies . . . show widely differing behaviour patterns. Since we all belong to the same species . . . men everywhere are learning to behave rather than following some fixed set of genetic instructions. Against this . . . is put the observation that cultures are not as different as they seem. If you look for differences you will find them, but if you look for similarities you will find plenty of those, too" (Morris, 1982). The debate continues.

Conclusion

Human Resource Management depends primarily on a knowledge of the individual. This is not to suggest that materials, machines and money can be ignored in the struggle to enhance productivity. However, concentration on the human factor does highlight the need for greater emphasis on the most important link in work situations — homo sapiens.

REFERENCES

Harris, T. A. *I'm OK — You're OK*. New York: Avon, 1967,
Luthans, F. *Organizational Behaviour*. 3rd ed, New York: McGraw-Hill, 1981,
Morris, D. *The Pocket Guide to Manwatching*. London: Triad/Granada, 1982.
Peters, T. J. & Waterman, R. H. *In Search of Excellence: Lessons from America's Best-Run Companies*. New York: Harper & Row, 1982.
Thomson, R. *The Pelican History of Psychology*. Harmondsworth: Penguin, 1968.

24
Perception

S. RICHARDSON

SUMMARY

The importance of information is discussed. The perceptual processes in an individual are examined. Interpersonal behaviour is discussed from a perceptual viewpoint with emphasis on cross-cultural differences especially in Singapore. A plea to avoid false perception is made and the importance of enhanced self-awareness stressed.

Introduction

The aim of this chapter is to examine perceptual processes largely from the standpoint of the individual, and to discuss the importance of perception in human resource management. The factors that influence our perception of people and things will also be discussed, together with their effect on interpersonal relations especially at work.

Individual Behaviour

Information This can travel or be translated from one form to another. It can be stored (in the memory or records) and it can be measured. Information is the essential ingredient of activity and behaviour. In any activity a person receives and processes information and ideas, makes decisions and then acts upon them; or does nothing. Where activity involves the operation of a piece of equipment the human being usually forms part of a closed loop system having many of the feedback characteristics of such a system (a hand moving from rest to grasp an object is a simple example). But there are limitations to the accuracy and speed of human interpretation of information, however simple that information may be.

The Senses. Everyone is being constantly bombarded by information in the form of stimuli received by the five senses, i.e., seeing, hearing, tasting, smelling, and touching. In use, however, the senses often overlap. Two examples are the increase in hearing efficiency if the listener can see the speaker's face, and the close links between taste and smell.

Sensation and Perception. To help explain this overlapping of the senses it is important to differentiate between sensation and perception.

(1) Sensation: External forces falling on the body will produce definite patterns of stimulation in the sensory parts of the nervous system (i.e., the control system of muscular activity) and the resulting messages will be conveyed to the brain. This is sensation and it is definite and measurable in relation to the external stimuli; sensation is objective.

(2) Perception exists in the brain of a person and is the picture gained (as the result of external stimuli) of an environment. It is a synthesis giving an impression of size, position, distance, colour, shape, texture, etc. This impression may or may not be accurate since it is liable to modification in the brain. Hence perception is subjective — we "see" what we expect to see, or what we want to see, we hear what we want to hear, and so on. The senses transmit information to the brain (as the result of pain, heat, light waves, sound waves, smell and taste) where this information is compared with stored information (memory) and the information is interpreted. An individual does not behave in a certain way because of what the situation actually is but because of what she or he believes or perceives it to be. One's perception of information becomes the motivation on which behaviour is based, or the basis for opinions (true and false). "Beauty is in the eye of the beholder" is a statement about perception. "There are none so blind as those who don't want to see" is another statement about perception but it refers to "perceptual selectivity", i.e., the brain filtering out or suppressing unwanted (often unpleasant) information.

(3) Visual perceptual problems: The difference between sensation and perception is more easily demonstrated with sight than with the other senses (see Gregory, 1977). Consider some

visual illusions. Figure 1 is an impossible object: it cannot be seen. In all such objects the perceptual system has to construct three dimensions from the two given by the image on the retina. Here the information is contradictory and the perceptual system fails.

Figure 1

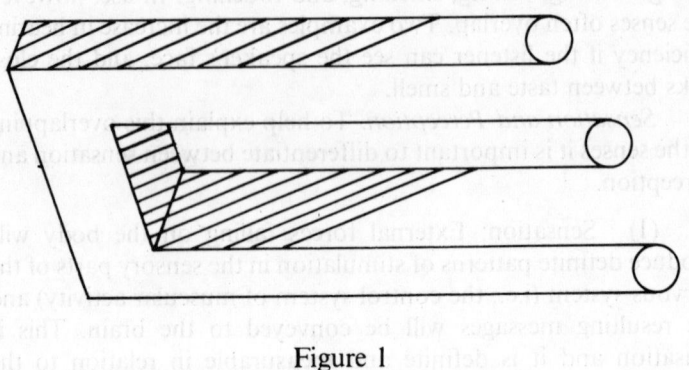

Figure 2

Figures 2 and 3 are both example of misinterpretation of displays because of incompatibility between display structure and human perception. (In Figure 2 the horizontal lines are of the same length and in Figure 3 the four horizontals are all parallel).

Figure 3   Figure 4

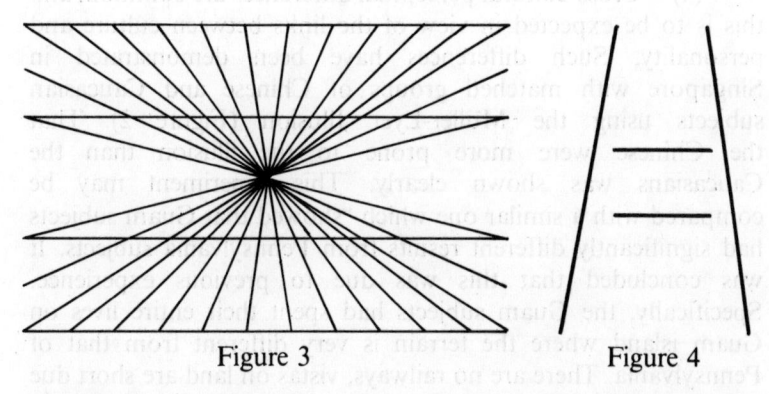

In Figure 4 the upper of the two horizontals appears the longer, in fact they are equal. The Necker cube (Figure 5) is ambiguous in depth and it spontaneously reverses, although with practice the reversal can be controlled. There are insufficient cues for deciding which square represents the nearest face and the perceptual system accepts first one hypothesis, then the other. But the hypothesis that is preferred (i.e., the initial perception) is a function of the observer's experience such that there is an expectation of one view rather than the other (this is due to "perceptual set", i.e., a preference for a particular type of activity or response). Frequently visual perceptual problems arise because of the limited capacity of the human central nervous system; sometimes the perceptual set of an individual results in false perception. Perceptual set occurs because people select stimuli (compatible with their motivation and personality), i.e., "perceptual selectivity".

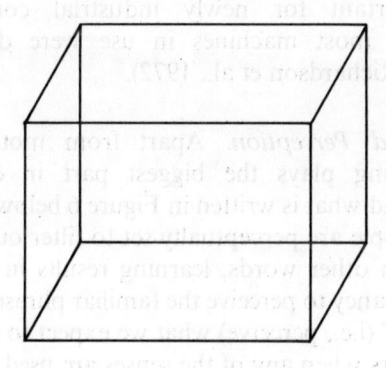

Figure 5

(4) Cross-cultural perceptual differences are common, and this is to be expected in view of the links between culture and personality. Such differences have been demonstrated in Singapore with matched groups of Chinese and Caucasian subjects using the Müller-Lyer Illusion (Figure 2). That the Chinese were more prone to the illusion than the Caucasians was shown clearly. This experiment may be compared with a similar one which "showed that Guam subjects had significantly different results from Pennsylvania subjects. It was concluded that this was due to previous experience. Specifically, the Guam subjects had spent their entire lives on Guam island where the terrain is very different from that of Pennsylvania. There are no railways, vistas on land are short due to the hilly terrain, etc. . . . few of the differences are valid in this case. Singaporeans live in an environment that is virtually indistinguishable from a modern European industrial city with large sea and airport facilities . . . although the Chinese were 'English-educated' . . . it is certain that the Chinese subjects had more experience and knowledge of Chinese characters than the European subjects. This exposure to Chinese characters may have affected the perceptual processes of the Chinese subjects. . . . The results demonstrate the known fact of cross-cultural perceptual differences (whatever their causes). The design implications are clear, namely, that cultural perceptual differences must be accounted for in displays whether dynamic (e.g., pointers moving over scales) or static . . . . Most machine designers take account of the anthropometric differences between populations and have standard data to help them. A similar approach is required to perceptual differences for which no standard data exist. This is particularly important for newly industrial countries like Singapore, where most machines in use were designed for Europeans. . . ." (Richardson et al., 1972).

Learning and Perception. Apart from motivation and personality, learning plays the biggest part in conditioning perceptual set. Read what is written in Figure 6 below. Because of learning, most people are perceptually set to filter out one of the definite articles. In other words, learning results in a set which results in an expectancy to perceive the familiar phrase rather than the truth. We "see" (i.e., perceive) what we expect to see, and this phenomenon occurs when any of the senses are used.

```
      /\
     /  \
    / TURN \
   /        \
  /  OFF THE \
 /            \
/  THE ENGINE  \
-----------------
```

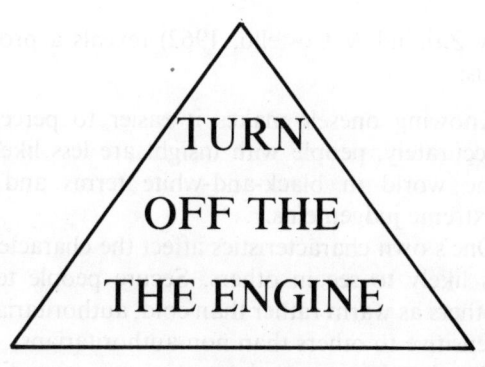

Figure 6

Interpersonal Behaviour

Perceptual Set at Work. The implications for HRM of perceptual set are varied and considerable especially in Singapore and similar countries Cross-cultural differences have been mentioned already and every culture tends to induce different perceptual sets. Figure 5 demonstrates that the same stimulus may be perceived in two different ways depending on the set of the observer. Such situations are common at work. They occur frequently in appraisal and selection procedures — the same individual may be praised by one superior and criticized by another, or opinions about the same candidate for a post may vary widely among the interviewers depending upon their set. Perceptual set can be seen frequently in the way safety hazards are regarded — an operator who has suffered injury in the past is not likely to have the same set towards a potentially dangerous situation as a manager who rarely leaves the office. Industrial disputes, too, are often the result of differing sets by union officials and employers.

Social Perception (i.e., the perception of people rather than of inanimate objects) plays an important role in HRM in that social perception is concerned with all aspects of the details of and the reasons for one individual's perception of others. For instance people vary widely in what they look for first in others. It has been found that women tend to look first for social techniques and personality characteristics in others whereas men are more concerned with status and achievement (although these traits are often perceived differently cross-culturally). Research (it is suggested by Zalkind & Costello, 1962) reveals a profile of the perceiver thus:

(a) Knowing oneself makes it easier to perceive others accurately, people with insight are less likely to view the world in black-and-white terms and to make extreme judgements.

(b) One's own characteristics affect the characteristics one is likely to see in others. Secure people tend to see others as warm rather than cold, authoritarians are less sensitive to others than non-authoritarians.

(c) People who accept themselves are more likely to be able to see favourable aspects of others, we like others who have traits we accept in ourselves.

(d) Accuracy in perceiving others is not a single skill.

Further it has been shown that the status and appearance of the person perceived will greatly influence the perception of him or her, even to the extent of over-emphasizing the role component of the behaviour of the people involved, resulting in the repression of "self" in favour of "role". Activities of managers and non-managers are guided by their role perceptions, just like everyone else. But in the work situation, since managers play many different roles they must be able to switch from one to the other with ease. Within a few hours a manager may have to adopt the roles of planner, leader, counsellor, superior, friend, subordinate, disciplinarian, mother, and many others. Rapid role switching places great strain on some people, it may also lead to the use of certain devices or strategies which may depend on distorted perception.

Distorted Perception is sufficiently common that certain forms of it merit special attention:

(a) "Stereotyping", refers to judgements about people who belong to certain ethnic or other groups; that is, a particular form of behaviour is believed to be followed by every member of the group stereotyped. Thus people develop stereotypes about members of trade unions, army officers, university teachers, men with long hair, and so on, without regard for their individuality (i.e., the facts). Because it is an easy way to generalize about behaviour, stereotyping is very common and insidious because many people using stereotypes do not realize that their perception is thus distorted. It is easy for many of us to believe that members of groups to which we ourselves do not belong are less intelligent, dirtier, lazier, noisier, more dishonest, etc. than the members of our own group or ourselves. Stereotyping cross-culturally is a well-established fact (see Stening, 1979). Evidence from Singapore comes from Leong (1978) who quotes nine profile studies of "the countable nameless faces", i.e., the ordinary national serviceman who never becomes an officer or a delinquent. All nine men exhibited stereotypes concerning other Singaporeans, seven of them racial.

A study of the Japanese manager in Singapore (Everett et al., 1981) reveals that "a well-defined image of the Japanese manager is held by various non-Japanese managers in Singapore". The stereotype held by non-Japanese employed by Japanese companies is significantly different from the stereotype of Japanese held by the low-contact groups studied. As the authors point out, it is in the interests of any multinational organization to have information on the various stereotypes held by each nationality employed in order to improve understanding between intercultural colleagues. The need for such improvement is demonstrated by Stening et al., (1981). Their study examined the perceptions of American, British, Japanese and Singaporean managers in multinational enterprises operating in Singapore. Both the American and Japanese managers see themselves as better performers than they are seen by anyone else, and the British managers regard themselves as more efficient than any of the other groups see them; this view is not held by Singaporean managers in Japanese firms. "The Japanese report a low assessment of the Singaporeans with whom they work, whilst the Americans and British have about the same opinion of their Singaporean colleagues as those Singaporeans have of themselves . . ." and so on.

Stereotyping is a special case of "attribution". The occurrence of an event leads people to try to attribute a cause to that event. Attribution refers to how someone explains the cause of behaviour. It is a common tendency to speculate on the reasons behind someone's action although often this speculation is ill-informed and irrational, (see Aronson, 1980 for a fuller discussion).

(b) "Halo Effect" describes the process in which a general feeling (good or bad) influences the judgement of all a person's qualities. This can be seen often in parents who love their children and see nothing about them that could be improved. An opposite example is of a superior who knows that one of his subordinates is sometimes late for work and hence believes that the subordinate is irresponsible and idle in everything he does, whereas the truth is that his work is above reproach (see Luthans, 1981). The "halo" is such cases may be likened to a blinding brightness preventing the observer from actually perceiving the trait or quality judged.

(c) "Tunnel Vision" takes its name from the phenomenon observed among long distance truck drivers that after some time on a particular route all they perceive is that is happening on the road, other activities and objects (except road signs) are filtered out. Generalizing, this phenomenon can be observed in those who take an insufficiently broad view of a particular situation thus their perception of totality is distorted; the converse can be called "lateral thinking" or "helicopter view" (although these terms are not·synonymous). An illustration of tunnel vision will result if you are unable to complete the following exercise. You are required to join up all the nine dots below with four straight lines. You may not take your pen or pencil off the paper nor retrace a line. Try it Now!

. . .

. . .

. . .

(d) "Projection" (originally a Freudian term) means, for HRM purposes, the attributing unconsciously to other people our own characteristics or perceptions. A common cause of misunderstanding is to assume that one's perception and faults are shared by others when this is not true. Frequently projection is a defence mechanism (of which there are many) in which one reduces one's feelings of failure or guilt by projecting them (in the form of blame) onto others. Thus projection influences the perceptual process. But projection can be used to enhance self-awareness by questioning one's admiration or accusation of others to determine whether or not the trait praised or blamed really originates with the perceiver. Examples are legion but common ones are people who call others stupid to conceal their own stupidity, or those who complain that no one listens to them when in fact they are the ones who never listen. The need for a scapegoat is not far below the surface in many of us, especially when we have not learnt to accept the consequences and hence responsibility and hence (sometimes) blame for our actions. The cry, "its not my fault", often means that it is.

Conclusion

A knowledge of perception is not only likely to improve the efficiency of people and hence enhance productivity, it will also tend to improve psychological well-being at work — there is no conflict here. Perception is an individual's view of reality. Everyone is being contantly bombarded by stimuli received by the five senses. Our cultural experience persuades us to reject information which conflicts with the stereotype view. Most perceptual processes are automatic and unconscious so vigilance is needed to avoid false perception, which is far more common than most of us realize. The difference between sensation and perception, and the possibility of false perception, need to be more widely appreciated. A common cause of misunderstanding is to assume that one's perception is shared by another, when this is not true. Enhanced self-awareness is vital to everyone. How did you feel about the nine dots?

QUESTIONS

1. How can a knowledge of perception increase productivity?
2. "Empathy and self-insight tend to go hand in hand." Discuss.
3. "It is a person's perception of a situation which defines it as stressful: the stress reaction depends on how the person perceives the significance of a harmful, threatening, or challenging event." Discuss.

REFERENCES

Aronson, E. *The Social Animal.* 3rd ed., San Francisco: Freeman & Co., 1980.
Everett, J. E., Stening, B. W. and Longton, P.A. "Stereotypes of the Japanese Manager in Singapore", *International Journal of Intercultural Relations* 5 (1981): 277-289.
Gregory, R. L. *Eye & Brain.* 3rd ed., London: Weidenfeld & Nicolson, 1977.
Leong, C. C. *Youth in the Army.* Singapore: Federal Publications, 1978.

Luthans, F. *Organizational Behavior.* 3rd ed., New York: McGraw-Hill, 1981.
Richardson, S., Chan H. L., Lee, A. and Teo, S. T. "The Muller-Lyer Illusion: A Cross-Cultural Study in Singapore, *Ergonomics* 15, 3 (1972): 293-298.
Stening, B.W., Everett, J. E. and Longton, P.A. "Mutual Perception of Managerial Performance & Style in Multinational Subsidiaries", *Journal of Occupational Psychology* 54, (1981): 255-263.
Stening, B.W. "Problems in Cross-Cultural Contact: A Literature Review", *International Journal of Intercultural Relations* 3 (1979): 269-313.
Zalkind, S. S. and Costello, T. W. "Perception: Implications for Administration", *Administrative Science Quarterly* 7, 2 (1962): 218-35.

25
Personality

S. RICHARDSON

SUMMARY

The term "personality" is described and defined, and reasons for studying the concept advanced. The effects of heredity and environment on the development of personality are discussed with reference to some of the theories and cultural factors. Some attempts to classify individuals by their personality are described. Personality and social perception, and the testing of personality are discussed. Finally the concept of enterprise personality is examined. It is concluded that understanding personality and its determinants should lead to happier and more creative relationships at work and elsewhere.

Introduction

Everyone has at least a general idea of the concept of personality. Most people know others who are perceived as impulsive, or self-seeking, or reflective, or generous; the same individual could have all these traits (though hardly at the same time). These characteristics, and others, are evidence of a person's personality. This paper attempts to define and describe the terms personality and to discuss its importance with special reference to Human Resource Management (HRM). Personality disorders will be ignored.

Why study personality? HRM is divided into processes (like perception, motivation, and learning) for convenience, but this division is also artificial and somewhat unrealistic especially when individual behaviour is considered. Except for a tiny proportion of the mentally ill an individual acts as a whole rather than as an assembly of components. The study of personality is directed at the whole person not the parts. It is necessary to take an integrated view of an individual otherwise false perception of that person is likely, especially when the individual adopts many roles.

Definition

The term personality is used both popularly and psychologically. A comprehensive definition is: "the integrated and dynamic organization of the physical, mental, moral, and social qualities of the individual, as that manifests itself to other people, in the give and take of social life. . . ." (Drever, 1978). Thus is stressed the uniqueness that distinguishes one individual from all others. A simpler form (preferred by this writer) is: personality is the totality of all an individual's qualities, as that manifests itself to others.

Many people assume that personality is something within the individual which is taken from place to place or situation to situation, rather as one's hands are; and in each case the personality touches or even moulds the situation. This assumption implies that an extravert, for instance, always has interests directed towards nature and other people, rather than inwards to the self. This approach is well expressed by Sampson, 1980: "Our task is to search for the particular imprint that people give to the situations they are in. When we follow the same person across all situations, is there a particular style that characterizes his or her behaviour? If we can answer 'Yes', then we have a sense of his or her personality."

In contrast Mischel (1973) has emphasized the need to recognize person-situation interaction, i.e., the social learning aspects of personality. He believes that the more dissimilar the situations the less likely they are to produce similar responses from the same person. There seems little doubt that situation and unique personal style (i.e., personality) interact, the resultant being behaviour. But how does personality develop?

The Development of Personality

Personality is the result of social determinants and heredity, but data on the latter is sparse since human beings cannot be bred under controlled conditions like rats or sweet peas. It is possible that in some relatively homogeneous inbred societies a gene pool has developed favouring a particular personality; there is a large lacuna here. Traditionally the study of personality has been the area of the behaviourist although the Freudian approach came first. This is worth examining.

Freudian Theory: This postulates a series of stages through which a child progresses, i.e., oral, anal, phallic, latent, genital or pubertal. This theory has been criticized on several grounds, not least that the terms used rely on a "body language" and that, for instance, "dependant" should replace "oral", and "compulsive" replace "anal". Freudians might respond by calling such criticisms evidence of repression. There seems to be general agreement that the Freudian approach provides some valuable insights. (For a fuller description of Freudian theory see Thomson, 1968.)

Cognitive Theories: These concentrate on intellectual development based on the conviction that the conscious (rather than the instinctive unconscious) is the critical variable in the development of personality. These theories suggest that for the first two years of life children gain knowledge or cognition through sensorimotor experiences. Later, they begin to use symbols and language until, at about seven years, they enter the concrete stage of cognitive development when they are able to understand simple concepts. The final stage of cognitive development is most interesting to HRM students since it is the stage reached by mature adults — those capable of logical, conceptual and analytical thought.

Other Theories: These theories attempt to break away from the stage approaches described above, arguing that a person progresses along a continuum from birth to death, and that the role of heredity (mentioned earlier) and the role of the brain (itself affected by heredity) need emphasis. Knowledge of the role of the brain is in its infancy, yet it has been known for over a century that damage to the frontal lobes of the brain, for instance, can change personality. Eysenck has suggested that inhibitory brain-cell signals outnumber excitatory signals in introverts, while in extraverts the imbalance is the opposite.

Cultural Factors: It is axiomatic that learning is culturally conditioned and that the development of personality is largely a learning process (although the influence of instinct cannot be ignored). The effect of culture on learning is largely on what is learned rather than how it is learned — on the content, rather than on the process. Every culture teaches its children to behave in ways which are acceptable to the adults of that culture; this is clearly demonstrated in Singapore where behaviour acceptable in one component culture is often not acceptable in another. At work this can be easily observed on the telephone — visitors to Singapore are often incensed when told "you hang on", a phrase which most Singaporeans accept without demur. Documented evidence from Singapore relevant to cultural effects on personality is almost non-existent.

A problem inherent in all such investigations is deciding what are personality traits; for instance, it has been discovered that the number of words used in English to describe personality traits is 17,953 (Sandstrom, 1968). However, aggression is certainly a personality trait, and considerable light is thrown onto aggressive behaviour in Chinese society by Bond & Wang, 1982. They conclude, from a wide selection of sources, that "the fundamental concern of the Chinese has been to maintain the harmony of the in-group . . . authority in these groups is not the rule of law but an individual acting as a leader . . . use of aggressive behaviour to challenge these sources of authority is suppressed from an early age. High density living and low residential mobility contribute their additional inhibiting effects on aggression. . . . The obverse of this picture is the existence of two dramatic and extreme forms of aggression, public reviling and collective violence towards an out-group . . . ."

The continuing effect of culture on personality may be demonstrated clearly, it is claimed by McClelland & Harris, 1971, by examining children's stories. Similar stories can be found in many countries, they say. In one country a textbook had a story about children building a boat; the construction was stressed, it had to be seaworthy — emphasizing successful accomplishment. Another country's textbook told the same story but with the stress on the fun the children had in building and sailing the boat — emphasizing social skills. A third country had the same story but including a boy who persuaded other children to build the boat and how to do it — emphasizing managerial skills, influence and male dominance!

Personality Types

Attempts to classify individuals into personality groups have been attempted for centuries. "Yond Cassius has a lean and hungry look/ He thinks too much. Such men are dangerous", was Shakespeare's contribution reflecting the view held in his time (and now by some) that fat people are not dangerous because they are happy. More recently several attempts have been made to correlate body-build with personality traits. The most rigorous attempt has been that of Sheldon & Stevens (1942) who postulated three body types (or somato-types) and related these to personality. Cassius was an ectomorph, i.e., a thin person with a flat chest and delicate body and therefore (according to the theory) restrained, anxious and intellectual. The other types are endomorphs who are fat and spherical and hence love comfort, relaxation and sociability; they contrast with mesomorphs (those who have the hard rectangular body of the athlete) and who hence love exercise and adventure but are aggressive and insensitive to others' feelings. Attempts to validate these postulated relationships have been inconclusive but it seems clear that body-build does affect personality or that personality affects body-build, or both. Other researchers have developed systems of types of social character each linked to a different historical era and using terms like tradition-directed, receptive, and exploitative. In work situations many researchers hold that attitudes are determined by class and education, as well as personality. For HRM purposes one useful classification is given by Gilmer, (1971) who describes three personality types:

(1) Upward Mobiles — they identify strongly with the enterprise and are rewarded with power, pay and promotion; failure is more likely to result in self-blame than blame of the system;
(2) Indifferents — these are the vast majority of employees, frustrated or bored by their work, reluctant to compete, seeking off-the-job satisfaction;
(3) Ambivalents — such people are both creative and anxious, intellectual, non-conformist, eager to change the status quo when necessary, they are often subjective, withdrawn, or introverted, unable to bargain effectively, unable to accept the compromises people make in status seeking.

Useful though this classification is, it is often difficult to put many individuals into one group rather than another, so some theorists prefer a continuum approach. One such is Kirton (1977) who contends that all individuals can be placed on a continuum ranging from a "do things better" approach to a "do things differently" ability. An objection to this view is that personality is not two-dimensional (as this continuum suggests), but multi-dimensional. We are still waiting for more efficient instruments in order to classify personalities more effectively.

Personality and Social Perception

Social perception is the perception of other people, either as individuals or as groups. The HRM implications are mostly concerned with superior-subordinate and peer relationships. Managers are sometimes accused of being authoritarian, especially if they are perceived as Theory X people. "Authoritarianism is regard as a personality syndrome — a collection of separate traits — including rigid adherence to conventional values, concern for power and toughness in interpersonal relationships, and a tendency to shift responsibility for events with negative consequences away from the self. . . . If there is any validity at all to the hypothesized nature of this personality syndrome, authoritarianism should be an important determinant of social perception, and a number of studies suggest that it is" (Shaver, 1977). It is clear from these studies that a personality disposition, such as authoritarianism, can distort an individual's social perception. Other common personality dispositions that can distort social perception are dogmatism ("I have made my decision: don't confuse me with facts"), and Machiavellianism (perceiving other people merely as objects to be manipulated).

Testing Personality

Measuring personality is a significant contrast to testing abilities, e.g., intelligence or specific skills. There are many reasons for this, the most important being that in testing personality it is difficult (sometimes impossible) to reproduce the social situations in which personality is demonstrated. Nevertheless, the only way to measure personality is by observing and recording behaviour under controlled conditions. This may be done in four ways:

(1) By questionnaires answered by the person tested — responses may be distorted by inadequate self-knowledge or deliberate "faking" (although there can be built-in safeguards against this).
(2) By ratings made by observers on the frequency and intensity of various types of behaviour: the problem here is that the presence or the judgement of the observer may affect the response or its perception.

(3) By objective tests — miniature situations are created to which the subject reacts, their dependability rests largely on the quality of the objective key used for scoring;
(4) By projective tests — the subject is presented with ambiguous stimuli (e.g., inkblots or pictures of human situations) and asked to respond, the subject is said to project into the stimulus his own attitudes and ideas.

The commonest and most reliable method is by questionnaire. Cattell's (1965) sixteen personality factor test is probably the best known of these; designed for ages 16 and over it yields 16 scores in such traits as reserved vs outgoing, humble vs assertive, and shy vs venturesome.

Enterprise Personality

So far this chapter has concentrated on individual personality. From a HRM viewpoint it is also necessary to consider enterprise personality. Enterprise personality is the totality of all the qualities of the enterprise as that manifests itself to the outside world. In other words, enterprise personality is the public image of an enterprise. It is tempting to think that enterprise personality is the summation of the personalities of the individuals who, for the time being, form the enterprise. This is an over-simple view — the whole is greater than the sum of the parts. It is possible to identify passive and aggressive enterprises and those which are paternal, impersonal or Machiavellian. Measuring enterprise personality presents significant problems so subjective judgements are often used. From the individual's viewpoint it is important to work only for those enterprises whose personality is compatible with one's own. Much job-hopping in Singapore may well be due to incompatibility between individual and enterprise personality.

Gellerman (1960) investigated enterprise personality. He described four types of enterprise personality:

(1) Paternal, Passive — an established institution more like a public library or a government hospital than like a profit-oriented company; ably managed with a lifetime employment policy; expansion and promotion are slow; recruitment is easy but many employees leave before completing ten years' service thus tending to

create two camps — the younger and the older, and a resultant clash of interest, tending to enlarge the factors causing labour turnover.

(2) Paternal, Aggressive — an enterprise expanding into new fields with appropriate sales backup; vigorous management expecting a lot of subordinates but rewarding well those who are successful; regular meetings are held at each level in the hierarchy; turnover is low largely due to the sacking of the inefficient.

(3) Impersonal, Aggressive — this firm has a sales policy similar to the paternal, aggressive enterprise but managers keep close control always; although salesmen make much money the personal touch is absent and group morale low: the independant thick-skinned people survive but turnover is high.

(4) Impersonal, Passive — if large and diversified each division acquires a personality of its own, nevertheless there is a common denominator of apathy whatever the enterprise's size; promotion is slow and the chances to demonstrate initiative few; complacency at enterprise level is commonly manifested in unwillingness to respond to market or technological changes.

The four above were in fact given originally as examples of enterprise personalities, I have generalized them to stress the truth that compatibility with the enterprise personality is essential for an employee's success.

Conclusion

Personality is a term used in various senses. For HRM purposes it means the totality of an individual's qualities as that manifests itself to others. It is important to study personality because it is necessary to regard an individual as an integrated whole rather than an assembly of parts, despite the various roles that an individual plays from time to time. Understanding of another's personality (and one's own) and the factors creating them should lead to happier and more creative relationships at work and elsewhere.

QUESTIONS

1. How is personality related to labour turnover?
2. In a group that you know (e.g., your extended family, your tutorial group) classify everyone according to Sheldon & Stevens (1942) and relate this to their personalities. Repeat the exercise using Gilmer's (1971) classification. Explain the results. What do you conclude?
3. "Harmony in our system" is a concept central to many Japanese enterprises. If an impersonal, aggressive Singapore enterprise wanted to achieve such harmony what problems do you foresee? How should such problems be resolved?

REFERENCES

Bond, M. and Wang S. H. "Aggressive Behaviour in Chinese Society: the Problem of Maintaining Order and Harmony", *Hong Kong Psychological Bulletin* 8 (1982): 5-25.

Cattell, R. B. *The Scientific Analysis of Personality.* Harmondsworth: Penguin, 1965.

Drever, J. *The Penguin Dictionary of Psychology.* Harmondsworth: Penguin, 1968.

Gellerman, S. W. *People, Problems, and Profits.* New York: McGraw-Hill, 1960.

Gilmer, B. H. *Industrial and Organizational Psychology.* Tokyo: McGraw-Hill Kogakusha, 1971.

Kirton, M.J. *Manual of the Kirton Adaption-Innovation Inventory.* London: National Foundation for Education Research, 1977.

McClelland, D.C. and Harris T.G. "To Know Why Men Do What They Do", *Psychology Today,* Jan 1971, p. 39.

Mischel, W. "Toward a Cognitive Social Learning Reconceptualization of Personality", *Psychological Review* 80 (1973): 252-283.

Sampson, E. E. *Introducing Social Psychology.* New York: New Viewpoints, 1980.

Sandstrom, C. I. *The Psychology of Childhood and Adolescence,* Harmondsworth: Penguin, 1968.

Shaver, K. G. *Principles of Social Psychology.* Cambridge, Massachusetts: Winthrop, 1977.

Sheldon, W. H. and Stevens, S. S. *The Varieties of Temperament: A Psychology of Constitutional Differences.* New York: Harper, 1942.

Thomson, R. *The Pelican History of Psychology.* Harmondsworth: Penguin, 1968.

26
Singapore Managers: Some Aspects of Personality

DOLORES THOMSON

SUMMARY

Two psychological instruments have been used to measure 125 Singaporean managers with the purpose of delineating similarities and differences from their British counterparts. On the Kirton Adaption-Innovation Inventory, Singaporean managers did not display fundamental differences in inherent disposition. Within the organization, Singaporean managers gravitated to departments on the same basis as their British counterparts. There were fundamental differences between Singaporean and British managers on motivational orientations identified by the Personal Preference Questionnaire. Within the Singaporean sample, Chinese education did not affect basic constructs in thinking. The concept of "achievement" has been further identified.

Scope

This study examines some Singaporean managers with the purpose of ascertaining the extent to which basic cultural and inherent behaviour tendencies affect their thinking. Current thinking favours adapting from societies consistent with the needs of Singapore. Managers represent both the control and reception of influence. Entrepreneurs and managers are the leaders and shapers of an evolving culture of mental programming, which can be the product of eastern socialization and western education.

Modern management activity in Singapore (both in theory and practice) has come from books and training imported from the West. However, local Chinese companies practise a traditional form of management which has some features akin to the paternalistic management approach of the Japanese. Such management approaches may not have been formalized into theories and principles but have been transmitted from previous generations. As many Singaporeans find themselves in the first generation operating in the environment of large organizations, it is not surprising that the role demands and structure within such organizations are new. The aim of this study is to present findings on select areas of thinking which can be shown to apply to both Eastern and Western managers and to local areas where there are distinct differences. The aim is to offer guidelines to a situation identified by Redding (1980) as the indiscriminate transfer of knowledge based on Western assumptions of reality creating problems for the people to whom such Western assumptions are being taught, as they do not question what they are being taught nor do they examine the business systems of their own culture. The study supports Hofstede's (1982) statement that "management is a cultural process: not primarily a matter of techniques, but of finding ways to reach objectives within an existing socio-cultural system. Socio-cultural systems, however, differ between countries".

Method

The Instruments

Two psychological instruments which were complementary in coverage were selected. A battery of tests would have produced more comprehensive data but it was felt that Singaporean subjects would not have consented to rigorous testing. In 1980 when the study commenced, the phenomenon of participating in social science research was relatively new. The Kirton Adaption-Innovation Inventory (KAI) was chosen to measure macro-aspects of thinking whereas the Personal Preference Questionnaire (PPQ) measured micro-aspects of thinking. The KAI evolved from Kirton's theory (1976) of adaptors and innovators which contended that all individuals can be located on a continuum ranging from an ability to "do things better" to an ability to "do things differently". The ends of this continuum are labelled adaption and innovation respectively, and the instrument uses thirty-two items to measure this dimension of personality. Its five-point scale is scored so that innovators are higher than the theoretical mean of ninety-six and adaptors are lower. Managers with the same abilities could have sharp differences in style. The theory stipulates that the adaptor tends to operate within the confines of the appropriate consensually agreed paradigm within which a problem is initially perceived. The adaptor will reinforce the paradigm by refining and modifying it. The innovator solves problems by bringing about a switch of paradigm.

The Personal Preference Questionnaire was developed by the Industrial Training Research Unit, U.K. (M. Belbin and W. Harston, 1974) and claims to define the whole range of mental responses into five basic constructs; namely, talent; achievement; personality; justice; and subjective feeling. Fifty pairs of famous names elicit free responses indicative of what a person admires in others. These responses can be converted into the five basic constructs which summarizes the person's outlook, orientation and motivation. The behaviour measured is affected by culture.

The Subjects

The samples were: (1) a general management sample drawn from local small to medium-sized companies; (2) general management sample from Western-owned companies; (3) middle-ranking civil servants from the public works and the public health departments. (See Table 1). For the total group of 75 persons in small companies, 36 were men, 6 women (for the rest sex was not recorded). Their ages ranged from 25 to 37 years. The 18 general managers from Western-owned companies were 10 men and 8 women, aged 28 to 42 years. Of 32 middle-ranking civil servants in the last sample, 12 were women and 20 men. Their ages were between 21 and 45 years.

Table 1: Characteristics of the Singaporean Respondents

	Total Group	Men	Women	No Response	Age Range
Institute of Management Training	75	36	6	33	25-37
Civil servants	32	20	12	—	21-45
Western-owned companies	18	10	8	—	28-42
Total	125	66	26	33	—

Although Singapore uses English as the main business language, it was felt prudent to conduct interviews with all subjects on items and phraseology to establish whether there were any in the Kirton Adaption-Innovation Inventory which may have been unknown or strange to Singaporean subjects. Similarly, names used in the Personal Preference Questionnaire were checked to ascertain familiarity of Singaporeans with those given. There were some personalities named which were not familiar and local substitutes were put in their place. (See Table 2).

Table 2
Findings for Singaporean Managers on the Kirton Adaption-Innovation Inventory

	Mean	Standard Deviation	Sample Size	Range (KAI)
1. Middle-level managers from the Singapore Institute of Management	95.2	12.6	75	72-125
2. Middle-level managers from the Civil Service Institute	89.1	10.5	32	67-110
3. Middle-level managers from Western multinationals	107.0	11.4	18	85-128
Whole sample	94.3	14.4	125	67-128
Note: The differences between means using a one-tail test are significant for A and C t = 3.93 (p < 0.0005) A and C t = 2.55 (p < 0.01) A and C t = 5.51 (p < 0.0001)				

The results show the Singapore managers are compatible with their Western counterparts on cognitive style; the mean score of 94 is near to that of 96 postulated for Westerners. It has also been postulated that Adaptors and Innovators are equally distributed in any population. The sample from the Singapore Institute of Management is representative of the distribution of this personality dimension for the population. The lower mean of 89 for managers from the Civil Service suggests that Adaptors in Singapore gravitate towards managerial functions concerned with internal processes, referred to as uni-paradigm organizations. However, within such organizations there can be both multi- and uni-paradigm departments. In multi-paradigm oriented departments the manager acts as interface either between parts of the same company or between the company and the outside, e.g., sales. Within the Singaporean group, managers inclined towards the Innovative dimension find themselves in multinationals. In amplification of the original KAI theory it is assumed that managers in such companies are faced with two switches of paradigm, the first of which occurs when they become part of the organization milieu. In the commercial society of their parents there was little acquaintance with Western-type industrial and organizational problem-solving. Learning the rules of the new framework means learning to "do things differently" and this starts on entry into this Western organizational world. The second switch of paradigm occurs in the adjustment of middle managers to top personnel, who are invariably representatives to run the organization as nearly as possible like that of head office. Their subordinate managers have to deal with the Eastern public and their own subordinates and cope with the two different cultures simultaneously. (See Table 3)

Table 3
Singapore Samples and Their Mean Scores on the Kirton Adaption-Innovation Inventory

	Mean	Standard Deviation	Size
1. Essentially uni-paradigm departments, e.g., production, costing, maintenance, etc.	94.9	12.9	36
2. Essentially multi-paradigm departments e.g., sales, personnel, planning, etc.	100.6	12.7	39

Note: For differences between Singapore means (one-tailed) was significant. t = 1.96 (p = 0.05)

They must also cope with the clashes that arise, e.g., differences in attitudes and values. A high level of initiative, foresight and flexibility is needed to succeed. Thus the manager in Western-owned companies in Singapore may have made two switches of paradigm; that from a commercial to an organizational economy, and that from Eastern to Western culture. Significant differences found between groups in Table 1 confirms that the gravitation of Adaptors and Innovators to their respective organizations did not happen by chance.

Table 2 shows Singaporean managers and their identification of jobs according to paradigms. The difference between means scores of managers in uni-paradigm and multi-paradigm oriented departments was significant but not large.

Table 4
Findings for British Managers on the Kirton Adaption-Innovation Inventory

Studies	Mean	Standard Deviation	Number of Subjects
General Management UK, Kirton, 1977	97	16.9	88
Pharmaceutical company UK, Kirton, 1980	96	15.1	71
Research engineering companies USA; by Keller and Holland, 1978	101	14.3	256

Table 4 supports the previous claim that the consistent gravitation of Innovators and Adaptors towards their respective organizations was displayed in similar fashion among British managers which confirms the universality of this personality dimension regardless of ethnic and cultural differences. Other assumptions related to Innovation-Adaption can be safely adopted and incorporated into Singapore managerial practice.

Table 4 also shows that the overall responses of the two national groups are highly significant. However, examining Appendix A discloses the four main factors which distinguish between the two groups of managers. Singaporean managers admire "talent" to the same extent as British managers. The "achievement" factor characterizes Singaporean thinking as importance is placed on the ability to organize success. This way of thinking has been further reiterated by the managers' indication of what success has been identified with (Appendix B). Singaporean managers respond less to "personality"; which refers to flamboyance and physical appearance. The impact of personality in the organizational environment is a phenomenon that has taken impetus in the West. The popularity of training courses similar to Dale Carnegie's on "How to Win Friends and Influence People" has reiterated the faith that Westerners have on the impact and accomplishment by the right personality. Eastern thinking incorporates authority and influence into the role and position defined. Where the British manager feels "justice" is more important, the Singaporean manager responds to his "subjective feeling". This refers to the subjective feeling one develops towards another person. Redding (1980) suggested that in business relations the Chinese place great reliance on trust. "Justice" and morality may be given different importance according to whom one is dealing with — i.e., the ingroup or the outgroup.

Table 5
Comparative Performance of Singaporean and U.K. managers on the Personal Preference Questionnaire

PPQ Factors	U.K.	Singaporean
Talent	24.8%	24.3%
Achievement	24.8%	31.6%
Personality	25.4%	18.8%
Justice	16.6%	10.9%
Subjective feeling	8.0%	14.4%
Number of subjects	210	117
Note: Chi² on differences between groups has been significant Chi² = 423.3 @ 9df, p < 0.01		

Among Singaporean managers the study identified those who were educated in the Chinese media from an early age. In Table 6 their (PPQ) performance is being compared with those of English-educated managers.

Table 6
Comparative Performance of English-educated and Chinese-educated Managers on the Personal Preference Questionnaire

	English-educated Manager	Chinese-educated Manager
Talent	25.7%	29.5%
Achievement	31.6%	28.3%
Personality	18.3%	17.3%
Justice	10.7%	10.2%
Subjective feeling	13.7%	14.8%
Number of respondents	105	35

Note: Chi^2 on differences between groups has not been significant Chi^2 = 4.6 @; 9df, not significant.

In order to pursue the hypothesis of Singapore managers as high "achievement" aspirants, the study included the question: "Who do you consider to be the most successful man/woman you have come across and give reasons for your choice?" Responses were assembled into six categories:

Prime Minister;
Other statesman in and outside Singapore;
Family;
Persons in the organization/industrial/millionaires;
Persons historical, sports, socialites etc.;
Personal — someone known to the respondent.

Appendix B shows choices in descending order of popularity. It supports earlier findings on "achievement". It has become possible to describe what the Singapore manager sees as achievement and its complementary process — success. The Prime Minister was given the highest choice while other statesmen came second. This implies that Singapore managers admire those who have led the country to survival. Contribution to the community has to be related to the people's economic progress. It is not likely that someone who has contributed to culture and the arts would enjoy similar homage. Implied is some suggestion that there is admiration for the power to achieve.

Conclusions

From the findings using the two instruments, the adoption of managerial thinking by Singaporeans must be selected on the basis of nature and nurture. Where principles based on inherent dispositions are adopted little validation seems necessary. On theories and practices based on cultural effects, Singaporeans must exercise discrimination and further validation seems necessary. Responses of Singapore managers to the Personal Preference Questionnaire have indicated that in matters connected with motivational orientation, local adaptation is needed.

The most important recommendation arising from the present study is that of role-playing in management training. Relevant to this approach were the findings of Chin (1972), whose empirial evidence indicated that Chinese managers show preference for a task-oriented style of management whereas Western managers preferred a style which emphasized interpersonal relationships. Similar studies must be encouraged on Singaporean managers in order to contribute towards successful adoption and indigenization of theories and practices.

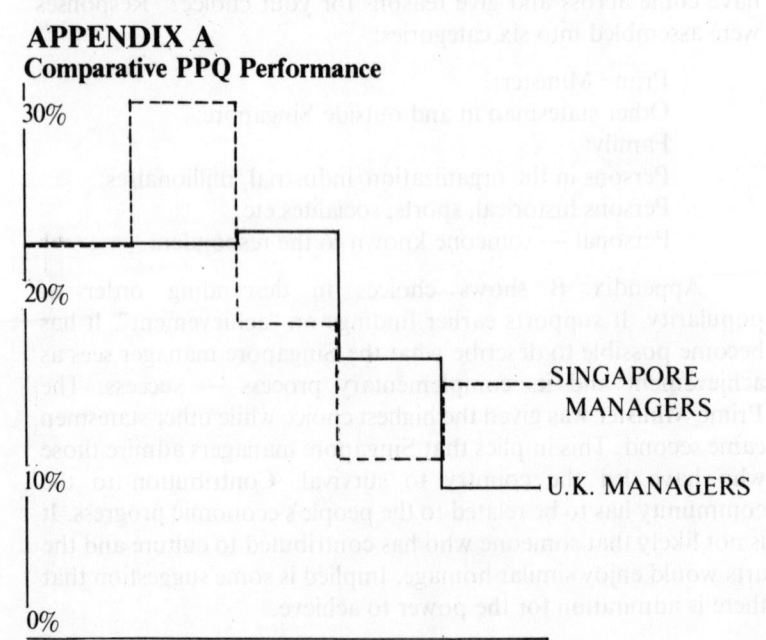

APPENDIX A
Comparative PPQ Performance

------- SINGAPORE MANAGERS

———— U.K. MANAGERS

APPENDIX B

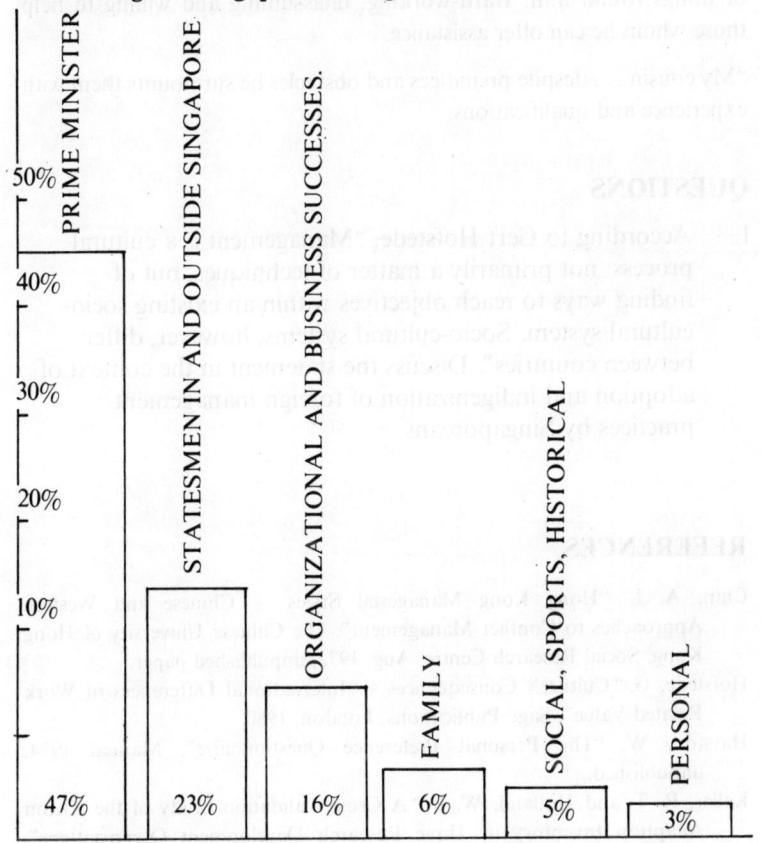

Success Figures Singapore Managers Admire

PRIME MINISTER	STATESMEN IN AND OUTSIDE SINGAPORE	ORGANIZATIONAL AND BUSINESS SUCCESSES	FAMILY	SOCIAL, SPORTS, HISTORICAL	PERSONAL
47%	23%	16%	6%	5%	3%

APPENDIX C

Quotations Illustrating Singaporean Managers' Concept of "Achievement".

"Lee Kuan Yew . . . great political leader, contributed tremendously to Singapore's development."

"Prime Minister of Singapore . . . impresses as a born leader, unbending to corruption. Authoritative, intellectual, well respected, diligent, far-sighted, organized."

"Lee Kuan Yew . . . sets very high standards for himself, able to strive hard to reach his goals."

"My father who has brought us up despite very trying circumstances".

"Personal friend ... always striving to improve himself in his knowledge of things round him. Hard-working, unassuming and willing to help those whom he can offer assistance.

"My cousin ... despite prejudices and obstacles he surmounts them with experience and qualifications.

QUESTIONS

1. According to Gert Hofstede, "Management is a cultural process: not primarily a matter of techniques, but of finding ways to reach objectives within an existing socio-cultural system. Socio-cultural systems, however, differ between countries". Discuss the statement in the context of adoption and indigenization of foreign management practices by Singaporeans.

REFERENCES

Chin, A. L. "Hong Kong Managerial Styles — Chinese and Western Approaches to Conflict Management", The Chinese University of Hong Kong, Social Research Centre, Aug. 1972, unpublished paper.

Hofstede, G. "Culture's Consequences — International Differences in Work Related Value", Sage Publications, London, 1980.

Harston, W. "The Personal Preference Questionnaire", Manual 1974, unpublished.

Keller, R. T. and Holland, W. E. "A Cross Validation Study of the Kirton Adaption Inventory in Three Research Development Organizations", Applied Psy. Measurement 2, 4 (1978): 563-570.

Kirton, M. "Adaptors and Innovators: a Description and Measure," Journal of Applied Psychology 61, 5 (1976): 622.

_____. "Adaptors and Innovators in Organizations", Human Relations 33, 4 (1980): 213-224.

Redding, G. "Management Education for Orientals," in R. Garrat and J. Stoppard (eds.), "Breaking Down Barriers" in International Aspects of Management Education, Gower Press, 1980.

Tadashi, Fujita. "Japanese Personnel Management System and its Relevance and Applicability to Singapore", Productivity Digest, January 1983.

Thomson-Yong, D. "Adaptors and Innovators: A Replication Study on

Managers in Singapore and Malaysia", *Psychological Reports* 47 (1980): 383-387.

Wong, K. C. "Learning from the East and West", *Singapore Monitor*, 26 January 1983.

27
Motivation and Behavioural Change

CHONG LI CHOY

SUMMARY

This chapter examines the two major approaches to changing the individual, namely, motivation and behavioural modification. It discusses various related ideas and theories with particular emphasis being paid to the modification approach.

Introduction

There is little doubt that human resource management must involve changing the behaviour of individuals within the organization. Two basic approaches have generally been adopted for this purpose although they are not necessarily mutually exclusive. The motivation approach is based primarily on human needs and needs satisfaction while the newer behavioural modification approach is based on conditioning the individiual through reinforcements as prescribed by the learning theory.

The expectancy/valence theories emphasize the anticipated value of results; the perceived probability of work effort yielding the required level of task performance; and the perceived probability of task performance yielding the desired results. The equity theories point to inequity and the desire for equity in individuals as the motivating force.

What is Motivation?

In their discussion on the nature of motivation, Steers and Porter identified three primary concerns:

(1) what energizes human behaviour;

(2) what directs or channels such behaviour; and
(3) how this behaviour is maintained or sustained.[1]

The first concern suggests the existence of "inner drives" causing a person to behave in a certain manner which may be triggered off by some external or environmental factors. The second concern suggests the orientation towards a goal or goals. The third concern suggests interaction between the individual and his environment in such ways as to encourage and sustain these goal-directed drives within the individual. We may therefore define the motivation of an individual as the activation or the sustenance of the inner drives within the individual by changing or maintaining certain environmental factors so as to direct his behaviour towards the attainment of desired goals.

Within an organization, the desired goals are given and often clearly defined. In motivation, a manager normally seeks to change or maintain certain environmental factors so as to influence the inner drives which may change or sustain the behaviour of his subordinates. Most commonly, incentives or rewards are given to encourage certain undesirable behaviour while disincentives or punishments are used to extinguish undesirable behaviour. However, the use of such incentives and disincentives have not always been successful. A better understanding of the "inner drives" in individuals is necessary if external factors are to be manipulated to motivate them.

Human Needs in Motivation

At the core of motivation is the idea of human needs satisfaction. The inner drives within an individual are believed to be activated to give rise to appropriate behaviour, where such behaviour could lead to the fulfilment of hitherto unfulfilled needs. The desire to fulfil unfulfilled needs is said to give rise to the inner drive to accomplish (i.e., motivation). However, once fulfilled, needs will cease to motivate and new needs will arise which require fulfilment. These propositions on needs and motivation are generally found in need theories of motivation.

Maslow, in his hierarchy of needs theory postulated that individuals are motivated by their desire to satisfy certain specific needs. Most individuals will pursue the following needs with

---

[1] Richard M. Steers and Lyman W. Porter, *Motivation and Work Behaviour,* Auckland: McGraw-Hill, 1979, p. 6.

differing intensities: physiological needs; safety needs; belongingness needs; esteem needs; and self-actualization needs. These needs are hierarchical in nature, in that the higher needs will not seek satisfaction until the lower needs are fulfilled. The order of need fulfilment is sequential in accordance to the hierarchy. It must be pointed out here that Maslow did deny this "well established" understanding of his "hierarchy of needs". In his attempt to clarify his position, Maslow pointed to what he calls "the false impression that a need must be satisfied 100 per cent before the next need emerges". To him, "A more realistic description of the hierarchy would be in terms of decreasing percentages of satisfaction as we go up the hierarchy of prepotency. As for the concept of emergence of a new need after satisfaction of the prepotent need, this emergence is not a sudden, saltatory phenomenon but rather a gradual emergence by slow degrees from nothingness". In other words, the more a prepotent need is being gradually satisfied, the less powerful it becomes in relation to some other previously unimportant needs which become gradually more important.[2]

Alderfer modified Maslow's hierarchy of needs by collapsing the five need levels into three, namely existence needs, relatedness needs and growth needs.[3] Although Alderfer's model is quite similar to Maslow's there are two important differences. Firstly, Maslow's progression of needs up the hierarchy is based on the satisfaction of lower needs. Alderfer pointed out that in addition to this satisfaction-progression process, there is also a frustration-regression process in that an individual whose attempts at satisfying higher needs are continually frustrated, may the redirect his efforts towards satisfying lower-order needs. Secondly, Alderfer's formulation is less rigid. Unlike Maslow's original formulation, more than one need may be activated at one and the same time point in time.

Yet another popular model of the needs theory is that by Henry A. Murray.[4] Like Maslow and Alderfer, Murray's theory assumed the existence of a set of needs as goals towards which behaviour is directed. However, unlike Maslow and Alderfer,

---

[2] A. H. Maslow, "A Theory of Human Motivation", *Psychological Review* 50, (1943): p. 370-396.

[3] C. P. Alderfer, "A New Theory of Human Needs", *Organizational Behaviour and Human Performance* 4, (1969): p. 142-175.

[4] H. A. Murray, *Explorations in Personality,* New York: Oxford Univ. Press, 1983.

there is no hierarchical relationship between the various needs. For example, an individual may have a high need for achievement, a high need for power, and a low need for affiliation, all at one and the same time. It is therefore a multivariate approach to needs and motivation.[5]

Murray postulated that needs can only be inferred from observed behaviour observed. Needs may be manifest or latent. A latent need may be strong, but it has been inhibited and hence cannot find expression. Such an idea would suggest that should a need, such as the need for achievement (n-ach) be latent, it could be aroused and made manifest by changes in the environment, so that the poor performance of an individual with latent n-ach may become successful performance. Researchers like McClelland and Atkinson linked the need for achievement with high levels of excellence and success in performance. Training and the learning process are said to be able to alter the "need states" as well as the "need strength" in people.

Learning Motivation: Socialization, Conditioning and Personality

In learning motivation, it is often difficult to differentiate between attempts at altering "need states" and "need strengths", and the attempts at behavioural modification. This is particularly so when needs, and hence motives, can only be inferred from observed behaviour. Both attempts involve changes in the environment, particularly the rewards structure that would facilitate changes in the individuals. Both infer success or failure through observed changes in the individual's behaviour. But the two attempts are nevertheless different. The first seeks to change the inner needs and motives of the individual, which are observable only through changes in behaviour. The second seeks to change observable behaviour directly and not necessarily as a result of the changes in "need states" and "need strengths" within the individual. These two processes of change are perhaps similar to the processes of socialization and conditioning.

The "need states" and "need strengths" in a person may seen to be a result of socialization. Socialization is the process whereby a person acquires the beliefs, attitudes, values and customs of his

---

[5] The difference may not be that stark if we compare Murray's position with the modified position of Maslow.

culture. It is also the process which prepares a person to perform his social roles. It equips the person with the right attitudes, feelings and expectations appropriate to his roles and status. It also serves as a means for the development of individual personality and self-awareness. Training may be seen as a form of socialization whereby a person is equipped with the right skills and knowledge as well as the right attitudes, feelings and expectations appropriate to his role. Where role transitions are involved, training may be seen as an attempt at resocialization, giving the individual new self-awareness and even a new personality in his new roles and status.

The identification of the motive acquisition process with socialization is consistent with the work done by researchers like McClelland. McClelland "believed that the motive acquisition process is facilitated by an individual's beliefs concerning the desirability to acquire the motive. That is, the more an individual believes he or she should and can acquire a high need for achievement, for example, the greater his or her willingness to work to develop the motive".[6] He also believed that "the acquisition of the achievement motive is facilitated to the extent that the individual thoroughly understands the nature and underlying processes relating to the motive, as well as how this motive is related to other actions and behaviour. Moreover, motive acquisition is also facilitated when individuals see the new motives as a way to enhance their self-image; when feedback on progress towards acquiring the motive is provided; and when the learning environment for the new motive is a warm and non-threatening one".[7]

"Beliefs" are culturally acquired by individuals through socialization. The ability to understand "the nature and underlying processes relating to the motive" and "how this motive relates to other actions and behaviour" is also acquired through socialization. "Self-image" is also a direct result of socialization. To desire to acquire a new motive and a new self-image is to desire resocialization. Before any resocialization can take place in great measure, the "resistance to change" in the individual must first be overcome. More explicitly, McClelland identified high "n-ach" in societies with high rates of economic growth, and such "n-ach" is

---

[6] Richard M. Steers and Lyman W. Porter, *Motivation and Work Behaviour,* Auckland: McGraw-Hill, 1979, p. 6.
[7] *Ibid.*

culturally transmitted through socialization, since n-ach may be identified through content analysis of literature in these societies.[8]

Behavioural modification through reinforcement follows the processes of conditioning. There are, according to psychologists, two distinct types of conditioning or learning processes — classical conditioning and operant conditioning.

Classical conditioning is the learning process whereby an originally neutral stimulus become a conditioned stimulus such that the subject will respond involuntarily by reflex action to it, as if it were the unconditioned stimulus which elicited the same response.[9] In the classical experiment by Pavlov (1902), the laboratory dog salivated (an unconditioned response) when food (unconditioned stimulus) was presented to it. By repeatedly ringing a bell (a neutral stimulus) each time before presenting food (unconditioned stimulus) to the dog, the dog was later found to salivate (conditioned response) at the ring of the bell alone (conditioned stimulus). This new relationship is called a conditioned reflex, and the process whereby this pairing of conditioned response with conditioned stimulus is attained is known as classical conditioning. It involves the generalization from one setting to another (unconditioned to conditional stimulus) without regard to the validity of such a generalization. This kind of generalization and hence conditioning occurs frequently in our daily life, often without us being conscious of it. It also explains some of our irrational fears and unrealistic expectations which affect motivation.

Unlike classical conditioning, where the subject's behaviour is involuntary and where the sequence of events is independent on his behaviour, the subject's response or failure to respond is fully voluntary in operant conditioning,[10] and the consequences (rewards and punishments) are made to occur as an outcome of the subject's behaviour. Reinforcement is not given each time the stimulus is presented but is given only when the correct response is made. In other words, the subject's behaviour is "instrumental" in determining the consequences (rewards or punishments). In order to elicit such behaviour in the future positive reinforcements

---

[8] D. C. McClelland, *The Achieving Society*, Princeton: Van Nostrand, 1961.
[9] Classical conditioning is also known as respondent conditioning and Pavlovian conditioning.
[10] Operant conditioning is also known as instrumental conditioning and Skinnerian conditioning.

(rewards) are given whenever the subject responds with the desired behaviour. Negative reinforcements (punishments) are given whenever the subject responds with the undesired behaviour.

The use of the reinforcement principle (conditioning) to change the behaviour of others or to motivate them is common in work situations. However, not all such attempts have been successful. Some rewards or punishments fail to elicit the right response or behaviour. This can be due to the fact that such stimuli are not consistent with the felt needs, personalities, or the socialization behaviour of those affected. Differing personalities also mean different valuation of the consequences (rewards or punishments), as well as different expectations.

For example, Myers, in a study of 282 employees of Texas Instruments using Herzberg's Two-factor theory found that what motivates individuals was largely a matter of personality.[11] In Herzberg's theory, which is a modification of Maslow's needs theory, needs are divided into two groups, namely, motivation and hygiene factors. Motivators are factors which relate to job content, such as work that is challenging, achievements, growth in the job, responsibilities, advancement and recognition.

The existence of the above factors can yield satisfaction, and hence motivate. Hygiene or maintenance factors include environmental factors like status; interpersonnal relations; company policy and administration; quality of supervision; working conditions; job security; salary; and personal life. These factors do not motivate, but their presence is essential in organizations because their absence will give rise to dissatisfaction. Myers found that "growth seekers" (persons who seek opportunities for achievement and responsibility), are concerned with motivators, while "maintenance seekers" are greatly concerned with hygiene factors.

Expectancy/Valence and Motivation

An alternative approach was given by the expectancy/valence theories.[12] Vroom in his approach suggested that a person's motivation in certain behaviour is determined by his

---

[11] M.S. Myers, "Who are Your Motivated Workers?", *Harvard Business Review* 42, 1, (1964): p. 73-86.

[12] Other names for this theory include: expectancy theory, instrumentality theory, path-goal theory and valence-instrumentality-expectancy (VIE) theory.

valence or the anticipated values of the outcome on him, and his expectancy that the desired goal would be achieved.[13]

The three basic concepts in this theory are: force or the strength of a person's motivation; expectancy, which is the perceived probability that a particular behaviour will yield the desired outcome; and valence, which is the anticipated value which an individual places on the outcome. Porter and Lawler refined this model by pointing out that the effort, that is the strength of motivation and effort that exists, depends on the perceived value of the reward, the perceived required energy of the effort, and the perceived probability of gaining the reward. The latter two being influenced by past experience.[14] More recent theorists like Campbell, et al.,[15] and Lawler[16] have divided the generalized concept of expectancy into two specific types: namely the "E $\rightarrow$ P expectancy" and the "P $\rightarrow$ O expectancy". The "E $\rightarrow$ P expectancy" refers to the expectation that the effort will lead to the desired performance, and the "P $\rightarrow$ O expectancy", the expectations that the performance will lead to specific outcomes. We may restate the key ideas in the expectancy/valence theory as follows: The force (strength) of motivation in an individual is determined by:

(1) expectancy (E $\rightarrow$ P expectancy) — the perceived probability by the individual that his work effort will give rise to a certain level of task performance;

(2) instrumentality (P $\rightarrow$ O expectancy) — the perceived probability by the individual that a given level of task performance will lead to various desirable and undesirable work outcomes; and

(3) valence — the value given by the individual to various work outcomes. To these, as pointed out earlier, Lawler and Porter have added the influence on motivation by the perceived required energy for the effort and the perceived probability of gaining the reward, both of these being influenced by past

---

[13] Victor H. Vroom, *Work and Motivation*, New York: John Wiley & Sons, 1964.
[14] Porter L. W. and E. E. Lawler, *Managerial Attitudes and Performance*, Homewood, Illinois: Richárd D. Irwin, 1968.
[15] Campbell, J.P., et al., *Managerial Behaviour, Performance and Effectivess*, New York: McGraw-Hill, 1970.
[16] Lawler, E.E., *Motivation in Work Organizations*, Monterey, Calif: Brooks/Cole, 1973.

experience.[17] The influence of individual perception, (itself influenced by past experience) on expectancy and valence should not be overlooked.

Perception of Equity/Inequity

Motivation is without doubt affected by individual perception. Equity theories[18] in general, suggest that individual motivation is largely influenced by a person's perception of his own well-being, particularly the treatment he receives, compared to others around him. Unlike the need theories, which are individual-based, equity theories emphasize group influences and the individual's perceptions of others. Like the expectancy/valence theories, equity theories attempt to understand the processes of energizing and sustaining behaviour (motivation). It can even be argued that the "perceived equity" affects "the valence" and hence the motivation of individuals, thus relating the equity theory with the expectancy/valence theory.

According to Stacey Adams, perceived inequity is a motivating state of mind. People are aroused to remove the discomfort of the felt inequity, and to restore the sense of felt equity. Inequities exist whenever people perceive that the rewards received for their work inputs are unequal to those received by others for their work inputs. The rewards that are especially visible and hence are most likely to give rise to feelings or perception of inequity are salary (including increments and incentive payments) and promotion. Attempts to restore the sense of equity by the individual may result in any of the following behaviour: changing work inputs; changing the rewards received; leaving the work place; changing the standards of comparison; or psychologically distorting the comparisons. However, such behaviour may be postponed if the individual expects a "redress" in the near future. It should be emphasized here that the motivational outcome is not determined by the allocation of rewards but by how an individual perceives this allocation.

---

[17] *Op. cit.* See also Stacey Adams, "Towards an Understanding of Inequity", *Journal of Abnormal and Social Psychology* 67, (1963): p. 422-436. Other names given to these theories include "distributive justice" and "exchange theory" (cf, Homans, G. C., *Social Behaviour: Its Elementary Forms,* New York, Harcourt and Brace, 1961. E. Jaques, *Equitable Payment,* New York: John Wiley, 1961. M. Patchen, *The Choice of Wage Comparisons,* Englewood Cliffs, N. J.: Prentice Hall, 1961.)

[18] I will not discuss group dynamics here as it has been discussed in an earlier section of the book.

Motivation: Some Observations

Motivation, it has been seen, is related to human needs. The desire to fulfil unfulfilled needs by individuals provides the "inner drives" or motivation to behave or act in certain ways. However, the type of needs which is "manifested" in a person is dependent on the physical and social environment in which the individual finds himself, and his personality which relates also to his expectancies and valence with regard to needs, behaviour and outcome. These factors of expectancies and valence are related to individual perception, which is influenced by past experiences and socialization, (including conditioning), as well as social or group affiliation and dynamics. Social affiliation is an important type of human needs. It is the value placed by the individual on needs that enable the group to affect individual behaviour and perception.[19]

Motivation as defined at the beginning of this chapter as "the activation or the maintenance of the inner drives within the individual by changing or maintaining certain environmental factors so as to direct his behaviour towards the attainment of desired goals". By asking the following questions related to this definition, it is hoped that an integrating framework would evolve:

(1) What are the desired goals?
(2) Where did the "inner drives" to achieve these goals come from?
(3) What processes enable changes in environmental factors to activate, maintain or extinguish such "drives"?

It is my opinion that individual perception is the crucial concept in answering these questions.

According to the needs theories, the goal in motivation is the fulfilment of these needs. Yet some needs are perceived by the individual to be more important that others. Murray for instance refers to manifest and latent needs as well as strong and weak needs. The hierarchy and the expectancy/valence theories evidently share the same sentiments regarding the varying importance of different needs. The equity theory makes equalizing inequities the motivating factor. The desire to equalize inequities may be related to the esteem needs or the affiliation needs in

---

[19] This is a well-established contention in psychology.

Maslow's hierarchy; since dissatisfaction may result from a perceived loss of esteem or the feeling of rejection by the organization or group. Perception is crucial in the valuation of needs. The goal in motivation is therefore the fulfilment of needs, perceived to be needed by the individual.

Such perception may or may not be consistent with the extent of actual deprivation, and is affected by such factors as individual personality and value systems; past experiences (including socialization and conditioning); the actual situation; future expectations; and group affiliation. For instance, a man's job may be dull and repetitive, requiring long hours and giving him few opportunities for social interaction. Yet he may not feel wanting in terms of social affliation and self-actualization needs. On the other hand, another man's job may be varied and interesting and may give him opportunities to interact with others and to make friends, yet he may still find his job boring, wanting in affliation and self-actualization needs.

In examining the second question, it is evident that the "inner drives" must come from within the person. In other words, a person is self-motivated rather than motivated by others. Attempts "to motivate an individual" by changing various environmental factors may be likened to attempts to tempt a person to sin. An individual can resist being motivated even as a person can resist sinning. This may explain why some attempts to motivate fail even though the person may actually be wanting in terms of the needs. A person's perception is also an important determinant here, considerations such as what is right or wrong; moral or immoral; and suspicions of hidden motives and pitfalls. One may also argue that personality is important and that personality influences perception. This is obviously true. The theories of socialization and conditioning are appropirate here. In this context, one may argue that motivation can be learnt.

There is probably no satisfactory answer to the third question. Yet, the process theories discussed earlier on partially explained these processes. All these theories seem to suggest that outcomes or the perceived probability of their attainment are crucial. The latter view is, in my opinion, more valid since it is the perception of reality rather than reality itself which influences behaviour. The importance of perceived probability of attainment of desired outcomes is found in the expectancy/valence theory. This is complimented by the ideas of perceived energy required for the effort, and the perceived probability of gaining the reward.

In this light, one can argue that valence, expectancy and instrumentality are all based on individual perceptions of reality. One can also argue that it is the individual's perception of reality (effort or behaviour, and goal attainment or outcomes) which motivates him (or makes him willing) to undergo operant conditioning and other learning processes, so as to achieve the desired behaviour. Perceived inequity of the equity theory, which may affect the "valence", and hence the motivation of individuals, also fits in well with this understanding. One can also argue that perceived inequity gives rise to the perception of reality which sees one's own effort as unrecognized and hence futile in terms of attaining one's goals or fulfilling one's needs. Whereas the continual attainment of goals (that is, the fulfilment of one's perceived and manifest needs) through one's efforts would tend to motivate and maintain the motivation, the continual frustration of one's efforts will cause motivation to be extinguished. This does not seem to be very different from what positive and negative reinforcement can do in behaviour modification.

Conclusion

Although the ideas on motivation are rather simple to grasp, the subject of motivation is nevertheless complex. The fact that there is no satisfactory or complete understanding of the processes of motivation does not mean that managers should abandon all efforts relating to the motivation of employees. It is true that the "inner drive" (motivation) is not part of the external environment in which the individual works and lives, and that the individual is self-motivated, yet the environment provides the factors that can encourage or extinguish such drives (self-motivation) within the individual.

Although a manager may not be able to motivate employees, he may create the environment (including such factors as are inherent in the systems of compensation, supervision and control, employee welfare, etc.) within the firm that gives hope to the employees in terms of fulfilling their perceived and desired but hitherto unfulfilled needs. He can also provide the necessary training to help employees who are willing to learn to be motivated or to have their behaviour modified. It is important to note that the perceived continual fulfilment of a person's perceived needs, the perception that he is being treated more generously than others (possibly in the same society) for similar effort, the hope of having his other needs fulfilled in the future, is likely to lead to satisfaction and motivation. The perceived continual non-fulfilment of his perceived needs, the perception that he is being treated unfairly for his effort, the feeling of helplessness in terms of ever fulfilling his other needs in the future, is likely to lead to frustration and a lack of motivation. A frustrated employee is also the least likely person to want to learn to be motivated unless he is given some hope of change in the future. This hope is perhaps what a manager should give him if the manager ever wants that person motivated.

QUESTIONS

1. What is motivation? How are human needs related to motivation?
2. Can movitation be learned? How would you relate behavioural modification to motivation?
3. What causes people to be motivated or demotivated?

REFERENCES

Adams, J. Stacey. "Towards an Understanding of Inequity", *Journal of Abnormal and Social Psychology* 67 (1963): 422-436.

Alderfer, C.P. "A New Theory of Human Needs", *Organizational Behaviour and Human Performance* 4 (1969): 142-175.

Campbell, J. P. et. al., *Managerial Behavior, Performance and Effectives.* New York: McGraw Hill, 1970.

Lawler, E. E. *Motivation in Work Organizations.* Monterey, Calif: Brooks/Colo, 1973.

Maslow, A. H. "A Theory of Human Motivation", *Psychological Review* 50 (1943): 320-396.

McClelland, D. C. *The Achieving Society,* Princeton: Van Nostrand, 1961.

Murray, H. A. *Explorations in Personality.* New York: Oxford University Press, 1938.

Myers, M. S. "Who are your Motivated Workers?", *Harvard Business Review* 42, 1 (1964): 73-68.

Porter, L. W. and Lawler, E. E. *Managerial Attitudes and Performance.* Homewood, Illinois: Richard D. Irwin, 1968.

Steers, Richard M. and Porter, Lyman. W., *Motivation and Work Behaviour.* 2nd edition, Auckland: McGraw-Hill, 1979.

Vroom, Victor H. *Work and Motivation.* New York: John Wiley & Sons, 1964.

Index

Alderfer, C. P., 124, 330
Argyris, C., 116
Attitudes, 183

BEST programme, 33, 54, 76
Behavioural modelling, 282

Central Provident Fund, 77, 83
Communication, 208
Company welfarism, 83
Conflict management, 237
 purpose of, 242
COWEC, 83

Delbecq, A., 151

Employee-centred leadership, 153
Employment Act, 46, 82
Equity, 336
Expectancy, 334

Feedback, 211, 227
Fiedler, F., 201
Flexi-time, 140
Foreign workers, 75
Freudian psychology, 290

Group cohesion, 149
Group dynamics, 144
Group norms, 146
Group structure, 145

Herzberg, F., 124, 334
High technology, 41, 67
Hodgetts, R. M., 165
Hofstede, G., 317
House unions, 80
Human asset accounting, 159
Human relations theory, 144, 158
Human resource development, 61
Human resource management
 and economic restructuring, 32
 and Singapore society, 21
 individual perspective, 7, 28, 289

organisational perspective, 4
overall perspective, 1
scope of, 26
societal perspective, 2, 21

Industrial Relations Act, 46
Informal organization, 12

Job design, 128, 139
Job enrichment, 126
Job performance, 114, 177
Job reorganization, 129
Job satisfaction, 114, 177

Kirton Adaption-Innovation
 Inventory, 317
Knowledge of results, 281
Koontz, H., 165

Learning, 292, 300
Leadership, 164
 contingency model, 201
Likert, R., 160, 170
Linking pin, 157
Luthans, F., 130

Management attitudes, 151
Management by objectives
 (MBO), 175, 180
Management of change, 250
Managerial grid, 169, 187
Maslow's hierarchy of needs, 121, 329
McClelland, 194, 332
McGregor, D., 114, 119
Miles, R., 156
Motivation, 328, 337

National Productivity Board, 33, 55, 79
National Trades Union Congress, 45
National Wages Council, 54

Organizational conflict, 242
Organizations, 9

Participative Management, 153
People-centred management, 112
Perception, 296
Personal Preference
 Questionnaire, 317
Personality, 291, 307
Porter, L. W., and Lawler, E. E., 177

Productivity, 35, 171
 measure of national
 development, 31

Quality Control Circles, 33, 79, 113, 293
Quality of worklife, 135

Reward, 185
Resistance to change, 253

Scientific management, 115
Singapore managers, 303, 316
Singapore society and human
 resource management, 21

Stereotyping, 302
System Four Model, 143, 170

T-group, 223
Team-building, 217, 292
Thematic Apperception Test
 (TAT), 196
Theory X and Theory Y, 119
Trade Unions Act, 82
Training, 271
Training needs, 276

Union management relationship, 43

Valence, 334
Value change, 264
Value orientation, 261
Volvo experiment, 132

Work Improvement Team
 (WIT), 32, 293